Ecological Debt

Ecological Debt

Global Warming and the Wealth of Nations

Second Edition

Andrew Simms

PLUTO PRESS
www.plutobooks.com

First published 2005.
This edition published 2009 by Pluto Press
345 Archway Road, London N6 5AA and
175 Fifth Avenue, New York, NY 10010

www.plutobooks.com

Distributed in the United States of America exclusively by
Palgrave Macmillan, a division of St. Martin's Press LLC,
175 Fifth Avenue, New York, NY 10010

British Library Cataloguing in Publication Data
A catalogue record for this book is available from the British Library

ISBN   978 0 7453 2728 0 Hardback
ISBN   978 0 7453 2727 3 Paperback

Library of Congress Cataloging in Publication Data applied for

This book is printed on paper suitable for recycling and made from
fully managed and sustained forest sources. Logging, pulping and
manufacturing processes are expected to conform to the environmental
standards of the country of origin. The paper may contain up to
70 per cent post-consumer waste.

10   9   8   7   6   5   4   3   2   1

Designed and produced for Pluto Press by
Chase Publishing Services Ltd, Sidmouth, England
Typeset from disk by Stanford DTP Services, Northampton, England
Printed and bound in the European Union by
Antony Rowe Ltd, Chippenham and Eastbourne

Contents

Acknowledgements

To all the people, in no particular order, who were interested, helpful or encouraging, even if they were unaware of being so at the time – including but not limited to: June Simms, David Simms, David Boyle, Rachel Maybank, Simon Retallack, Andy Strauss, Nick Robins, Jenny Scholfield, Caroline Lucas, Jonathan Walter, Molly Conisbee, Ann Pettifor, Romilly Greenhill, Marion Genevray, Etienne Pataut, Peroline Bousquet, Renwick Rose, Ruth Potts, Hetan Shah, Pat Bailey, Matt Rendell, Angela Burton, John Harriss, Alex Macgillivray, Petra Kjell, Jessica Bridges Palmer, Julian Oram, Alex Evans, Aubrey Meyer, Angela Wood, James Marriott, Wolf Hassdorf, Andrew Dobson, John Broad, Ralph Russell, John Magrath, Ed Mayo, Saleemul Huq, Hannah Reid, Judith Dean, David Woodward, Jane Shepherd, Victoria Johnson, Corrina Cordon, Peter Myers, Benedict Southworth, Stewart Wallis, Kevin Anderson, Joe Smith, Pat Conarty, Sarah Butler Sloss, Liz Cox, Fred Pearce, Sue Mayer, Ros Coward, Martyn Day, Charlie Kronick, Rob Hopkins, Satish Kumar, John Sauven, David Castle, Caroline Stewart, Colin Hines, Robin Maynard, Tim Lang, Bevis Gillett, David Adshead, Andy Fryers, Rosie Boycott, Felicity Lawrence and Ethan and Joe Stein. Some specific 'thank yous' are also in the endnotes.

All photographs have been supplied by the author, unless credited otherwise.

To Scarlett Iona Snow,
on behalf of my generation I apologise,
we didn't do enough.
And to Rachel Maybank, thank you for Scarlett.

Preface to the Second Edition

I discovered a flaw in the model that I perceived is the critical functioning structure that defines how the world works.

Alan Greenspan, former chairman, US Federal Reserve, October 2008

Owing to past neglect, in the face of the plainest warnings, we have now entered upon a period of danger ... The era of procrastination, of half measures, of soothing and baffling expedients, of delays, is coming to its close. In its place, we are entering a period of consequences.

Winston Churchill, 12 November 1936[1]

Oil is the trouble, of course. Detestable stuff!

Gertrude Bell, Baghdad, 1921

RETURNING ...

The elephant is still standing. And still dead. Around its feet glisten hundreds of coins thrown by visitors. They might be wishes asked of the soul of the departed animal. Or, small gestures of recompense in lieu of its fate and the fate of the land that was once its home. Three years since I last visited the Museum of Central Africa in the Belgian city of Brussels, little else has changed. Room after room is full of animals stuffed and perched rigidly against crudely realised backdrops of African forest and grassland.

Had they been painted by your three-year-old daughter, you would brim with pride. As the work of a major museum, they look comic and sad. The joke, too, is a bad one. Passing through to another long room that surveys Africa's global economic contribution, maps on the wall dissect and label each country, tagging them like the worn, stuffed big cats and apes, and fish pickled in jars.

This is Africa as the memory and promise of wild, exhilarating and dangerous nature. Life waiting to be hunted, captured, tamed or killed. Two crocodiles in a glass case encircle each other in freeze-frame, flexing long tails and grins that seem to keep widening. This is Africa seen as a cornucopia of natural wealth to be mined, harvested, picked, squeezed and taken. The wall maps speckled with graphs reduce the continent in general, and the Congo in particular, to a series of carefully plotted locations for the extraction of oil, cotton, coffee, sugar, rice, maize, jute, palm oil, diamonds, cobalt, tin, copper and gold. One term for it is the 'resource curse'.

A partial defence by the museum could be that this is real history – it represents precisely how Europe has viewed and treated Africa for more than a century. But the defence fails because there is too little to rescue it from the charge that seen like this, it merely lays the psychological foundations for the future to repeat the mistakes of the past. Somehow, the reality of civilisations wrecked and of peoples brutalised and killed to support Europe's rising economies becomes dissipated.

When a continent is reduced to economic botany, agronomy and geology, it comes to be seen through a lens of cold accounting, by eyes disinterested in rich history and cultural diversity. But, more recently, a new interest in the murderous story of King Leopold II's activities in Central Africa (told briefly in Chapter 5) forced the museum, and the nation more widely, to reassess its colonial past. Two rooms introducing the history have been carved out from among the cases full of still air, masks, spears and bewildered-looking big cats.

Yet in the museum, when it does address the troubled human past, the tone is often reluctant, equivocal and begrudging. With glorious understatement it tells the visitor that this history was experienced 'differently' by Belgians and Congolese. There is a quiet but repeated emphasis on the involvement of the Congolese in their own exploitation, as if to create a moral equivalence between the corruptor and the corrupted. We are warned that 'passions and emotions' concerning the past continue to the present. The display is less forthcoming about another unbroken link with the past, about how there is a continuing pattern of destructive appropriation of Africa's natural resources, one that involves a similar, if slightly longer, list of more powerful nations.

But even with this nod to excavating the buried history of colonialism, an almost morbid fascination drags you around the museum's unchanging stone corridors. A fabulous crassness clings to the walls. Here is a flagship national museum in a capital city that is home to the political machinery and administration of the modern European Union. Yet sitting proudly still in its central courtyard, with an imperially upturned chin, is a statue of the man who embodies international relations built on murder, theft and deception, carried out on a massive scale. These are displays not of historical revelation, but of masked continuity. In late 2008, the Democratic Republic of Congo again stood on the edge of full-scale conflict and calamity. Even before then, in just a decade from 1998, 5.4 million people were estimated to have died from war-related causes in the Congo.[2]

Tram number 44 takes you from the centre of Brussels to the park at Tervuren where the museum stands. As it trundles back again, through extensive woods and parklands and passed the city's famous, grand art nouveau houses, there is time to dwell on its significance. Although I remain unsure how to interpret the fact, imparted almost with pride, that the uranium ore to fuel the first atomic bombs used on Japan in the Second World War came from Belgian-controlled Congo. After the bombs were dropped, Edgar Sengier, head of the Union Minière du Haut Katanga in Belgian Congo, wrote a letter of congratulation (a copy of which is displayed) to Major General L.R. Groves, head of the US atomic programme. It occurs to me that now the nuclear industry is again resurgent, exploiting climate change to argue for its own interests, pressure to mine uranium in Africa will increase. But in the middle of pondering the impossibly complex over-layering of history, my thoughts get interrupted by a ticket inspector who crept onto the tram unseen as we passed through the woods.

I finally produce a ticket after searching every pocket in my ridiculously over-pocketed khaki shorts. Then I look at him in a way that, to him, must seem very odd, when he gives three Japanese students, who speak no French, no Flemish and only a little English, a really hard time. They appear to have bought the wrong ticket and he forces them to get off the tram while we are still in the middle of empty parkland, a long way from the city centre. From African elephants to atomic bombs, a loosely connected flow of thoughts can easily stumble to an illogical conclusion. But behind the questioning look I gave the ticket inspector, I can't help the unspoken accusation that more than half a century of colonialism and two atomic bombs on Japan is surely enough, without having to intimidate confused student survivors of the next generation?

A BELL TOLLS ... EXPANSION AND DIVERGENCE

I went to the museum for the first time three years previously. My intention was to understand better the 'official' version of events about the central idea of this book.

The global economy has expanded vastly, alongside a massive divergence between rich and poor, and has done so paid for by the creation of a huge ecological debt. As a result, we have a world divided, volatile and living beyond its environmental means.

The preface to the first edition began with this quote from Wilfred Owen, that is worth repeating:

> There was a whispering in my hearth,
> A sigh of the coal,
> Grown wistful of a former earth
> It might recall.
> Wilfred Owen, 'Miners'
> (published posthumously, 1921)

It then proceeded:

This is a book about the health of the planet and the wealth of nations, and how the two are linked. It also talks a lot about ecological debt. What's that? If you take more than your fair share of a finite natural resource you run up an ecological debt. If you have a lifestyle that pushes an ecosystem beyond its ability to renew itself, you run up an ecological debt.

Global warming is probably the clearest example ... Parts of the world like Britain and the United States became very rich by burning a disproportionate amount of our finite inheritance of fossil fuels, an act which has triggered climate change. Other parts of the world like Bangladesh, the South Pacific islands and sub Saharan Africa are set to suffer excessively ... [as a result].

[Well over] 80 per cent of the global economy still depends on coal, oil and gas, and demand keeps rising. But, because we must burn less of these to stop climate change, it means that there is no more fundamental issue than the distribution of wealth in a carbon constrained world economy. This book was a long time brewing. It draws heavily on several, separate pieces of work that looked at obstacles to both poverty reduction and environmental protection. Specifically it grew out of my sense of amazement during the international campaign for debt relief at the end of the last millennium that many poor countries in the majority world had to beg for relief from rich countries that were themselves carrying much bigger and more life threatening, but generally ignored, ecological debts.

There is no reason to change these words. However, producing a second edition enables me to test how well some of the observations and predictions contained in the first have fared. The bulk of the book remains the same, with only minor amendments and the occasional, unintentionally amusing typographical error corrected. This preface to the second edition and four additional chapters at the end of the book are, though, entirely new. They address how awareness of the problems highlighted by the first edition has skyrocketed, and discuss possible solutions in more detail.

In revisiting the original themes, the general conclusion that must be drawn is that they have fared unfortunately well. Going through them one by one, each still resonates as clearly as a bell tolling, mostly for the worst, but sometimes for the better.

Let's begin by asking a big question. What is the economy for? And how do we know if it is succeeding? There is a confusion of signs.

Before the great economic crash of 2008, waiting lists for the ultra-rich queueing to buy petrol-hungry supercars were getting longer. Pity, for a moment, the frustrated plutocrat who might have had to wait five years to become the proud owner of a Rolls-Royce Phantom Drophead Coupe. To many, it was a great success of wealth creation. The car cost $412,000 and, driven in the city, will creep through the congested streets for just twelve miles on a gallon of petrol. Instead of triggering a cultural shift, the crash appeared to lay the foundations for unprecedented audacity and shameless greed. In October 2008, even when the cost of the crash was estimated to have reached a bewildering $2.8 trillion (that's $2,800,000,000,000) with hundreds of billions allocated from the public purse to support reckless financial institutions, management from banks implicated in causing the crisis were still intent on paying senior executives multimillion-dollar annual bonuses.

All the time, the real world grew more perilous as the prospect of potentially imminent and irreversible global warming grew closer. Casting an eye at the world economy, the share of the poorest in the benefits of global economic growth, already pitifully small, has dwindled in the last few decades.

A little less than half of the world's population, a staggeringly large number of 2.7 billion people live on the equivalent of $2 per day or less.[3] At that level of income, you'd need a little more than a Christmas bonus to afford the Rolls-Royce. In fact, saving every cent and spending on nothing else, you'd need to live to be around 600 years old.

We have been living at a time of unparalleled financial wealth, even as the mighty Anglo-Saxon British and American economies are wracked by credit (or rather, debt) crises, brought on by banks conjuring too much money into existence. Astonishingly, over 97 per cent of humanity's financial wealth is estimated to have been created in just 0.01 per cent of recent human history.[4] Yet the distribution of that wealth is tragically unequal. In the last decade, for every $100 of growth, only $3–4 worth found its way to those 2.7 billion. And in its wake lies a depressingly familiar trail of environmental wreckage, set disproportionately to undermine further the livelihoods of the poorest.

Money should never be the measure of all things, but we cannot dismiss the hardship that results from a level of income that, if endured in the UK, would be the equivalent of surviving on the minimum wage while having sole responsibility to support an extended family of at least 18 other people.

A growing literature explains how the world got to this point,[5] and at the end of the book I discuss some of the options available to enable us to move forward in a more progressive manner.

In the meantime, let's make a wild assumption that the purpose of the economy is to meet everyone's basic needs and lay the foundations for us all to have relatively long and happy lives, and to do so while not causing irreparable harm to the planet's biosphere upon which we all depend. This means that the economy needs to be trebly efficient. It must be efficient at producing things we *need* (but not, note, necessarily *want*, and the things that we need are most definitely not all material). It must then be efficient at making sure that people can get access to and afford the things they need – which could just as easily be more time with their families as something electrical to plug in.

Finally, efficiency must be measured against achieving all these things set within the unavoidable environmental limits of living on an island planet. The ultimate test could be summarised as, 'How good is the economy at delivering the opportunity for long and happy lives, that don't have to cost the earth?' How, actually, we might do this is discussed at the end of the book.

1

A Short Walk to Venus

The fantastic game of monetary cutthroat was described as the process of 'thrift and accumulation'; the outright fraud as 'enterprise'; the gilded extravagances of the age as colorless 'consumption.' Indeed the world was so scrubbed as to be unrecognizable.

Robert Heilbroner, *The Worldly Philosophers*, 1953[1]

Venus: her principal attributes are a scallop shell and dolphins (she was born from the sea), a flaming heart, torch and magic girdle (to kindle love), and the red rose (stained with her blood).

*Hall's Illustrated Dictionary of Symbols
in Eastern and Western Art*, 1994[2]

Venus is a planet much like earth. But you wouldn't want to live there. You couldn't. Having a 'sister' planet might make earth feel less alone in the incomprehensible vastness of space. But Venus' differences should be enough to make us tighten our grip on our own, still oddly hospitable home.

Venus and earth share roughly each other's size and heftiness. Venus is our nearest neighbour, passing closer to earth than any other planet. Though, at 39 million kilometres away, you won't feel the breeze as it passes. When Venus does go by every 584 days, it also disappears from view, turning its dark side toward us, lying too near the sun.

Until space exploration began in the 1960s human knowledge of the planet's surface was arrested at the 'made of cheese?' level. Dense cloud cover prevented real observation. People speculated that the clouds hid a lush tropical world. A world where all the possible forms of life were fuel to fantasy. But the planet, the brightest celestial body in the night sky after the moon, has always been a muse. It was an early navigation point for finding out where we lie in the galaxy. The planet fed mythologies in ancient civilisations worldwide. Study of Venus supported the Copernican revolution that reshaped our view of the solar system. It forced us to realise that we were not the centre of creation.

Now it stands as a silent warning to respect the arbitrary fluke of earth's liveable atmosphere – a fragile balance of gases that makes human society possible. Behind this warning lies a new revolution in thought, every bit as radical as Copernicus'. It holds another view that will set fundamental boundaries around how we live. It leads also to a profoundly different way of seeing the world. Compared to recent decades, it shows a world turned upside down, one where the global rich are seen to be massively in debt to the poor and not the other way around.

When in 1962 the Marina and later the Venera space probes, respectively from the United States and the former Soviet Union, began investigating the surface of Venus, it became obvious that we would not soon be shaking hands with our planetary neighbours. Beneath the thick clouds of sulphuric acid, temperatures on the planet's surface were over 400 degrees centigrade. Considerably higher, about double, the heat you would use cooking anything in a household oven. Research revealed that Venus was so hot because it had experienced an extreme greenhouse effect. The same effect that, to a lesser extent, earth is experiencing right now.

The greenhouse effect is exactly what it sounds like. The atmosphere acts like a greenhouse trapping heat that would otherwise radiate away into space. Some greenhouse effect is a good thing. It is necessary to create the conditions for life. Too much, however, like too much of many otherwise good things, can be fatal for fragile species like ours.

Venus is closer to the sun and has a denser atmosphere. The powerful greenhouse gas, carbon dioxide, is its most common atmospheric molecule. All of these help make Venus hotter than earth. Some believe that both planets when young may have had similar atmospheres, the result of volcanoes belching out gases. Yet today they could barely be more different. On earth the atmosphere contains 78 per cent nitrogen which is not a powerful greenhouse gas. Venus' atmosphere, on the other hand, contains 96 per cent carbon dioxide, which is a potent greenhouse gas.

The difference is life. Over millions of years the carbon that was once in Earth's atmosphere has been removed and stored. Today it exists in mostly stable forms like fossil fuel deposits such as coal and oil and in the limestone left behind by organisms. But, that life is fragile. And we are reversing the process that gave us the environment in which we now live with relative comfort. Humankind's overuse of its planetary oasis means that species of life on earth are becoming extinct at anywhere between 1,500 and 40,000 times the natural background rate.[3] At the same time our economic dependence on fossil fuels means that we are returning the powerful greenhouse gas, carbon dioxide, to the atmosphere around one million times faster than natural processes removed it.

1. The solar system drops a hint. A heatwave conspires with the rare celestial event of Venus passing across the sun in the summer of 2004 to help educate one of the world's major financial centres, London, about the prospect of global warming.

Now, a confession. Hopefully this chapter's title – A short walk to Venus – caught your attention. It intends to summarise and focus the planetary predicament in which we find ourselves. A situation is always more clearly visible when seen in contrast. But there is both less, and more, to the invocation of Venus than an informative comparison of different planets' atmospheric gaseous composition. Calling up Venus, or her Greek synonym Aphrodite, also has a metaphorical purpose. In mythology the goddess has many incarnations. She is not merely the standard-bearer for simple love or beauty. The reference books say she was a fertility goddess whose domain embraced all nature, plants, humans and other animals. Only later did she become, 'the goddess of love in its noblest aspect as well as in its most degraded'.[4] Inadvertently, Venus-Aphrodite steps forward from her giant sea shell as an emblem for our age. She symbolises, on one hand, a world of natural resources, inescapably the wellspring of our economic wealth. And, on the other hand, she represents the desires that drive both our necessary and our more profligate, destructive behaviour patterns.

There is an amount of consumption of natural resources that is necessary to meet basic human needs. For centuries it has included the burning of ancient bottled sunshine in the form of coal, oil and gas, to produce energy and also, unfortunately, the guilty greenhouse gas, carbon dioxide. This pollution could be called 'survival emissions'. But there is also conspicuous consumption, a term first coined more than a century ago by Thorstein Veblen in a critical and dryly satirical account of the social forces behind America's emergence as a global economic superpower. His book was called, appropriately, *The Theory of the Leisure Class*. When we burn these stable stores of energy so that we can play with sports utility vehicles and heat the private swimming pool, it leads to what we might cautiously, while invoking the images of Venus and Aphrodite, call 'luxury emissions'. The sexual overtones are curiously appropriate. Different incarnations of the great goddess stood for: 'pure and ideal love', the 'impious', as well as 'lust and venal love'.

As a child I remember a sleazy man who worked for my father's small business. The firm had the unenviable task of promoting innovations in the world of semi-conductors and microprocessors. The employee hit upon the idea, which to him was startling and original, of photographing a collection of products in the company of a topless, local teenage model. The photo-shoot had a backdrop of generic tropical paradise, painted by a street corner Botticelli more in the style of house decoration than fine landscape. At the time I thought hard, but could not understand the possible connection between the girl and the product.

Look anywhere in the British, European or US media and you will find advertisers offering you the promise of fulfilling love affairs with anything ranging from cars to double-glazing, and small white collectable limited-edition china ornaments. The apparently weightless service-led economies of the industrialised world are, in reality, heavy with rising consumption and related greenhouse gas emissions.[5] Advertisers are the cheerleaders for environmentally destructive conspicuous consumption. Even the largest encyclopaedias lack words to describe the full list of unnatural relationships commercially on offer. It takes time to work out that the basic false promise of consumer societies is that the act of superfluous shopping is also an act of lasting sensual fulfilment.

In this way, in an economy still almost wholly dependent on fossil fuels, and their inconvenient side effect of global warming, our strongest life force is deliberately linked with a behaviour that is inadvertently our most destructive. Back to the parallel with Venus. In fact nobody knows precisely how the complex interactions in our biosphere will respond to global warming over coming centuries. We could be surprised in a few good ways, and many very bad. Earth is unlikely to develop an atmosphere as hostile to life as that on Venus either in our lifetimes or even in the distant future.

But the problem is that it doesn't need to. Because life becomes very unpleasant for many millions, and impossible for many millions more, long before life is entirely unsupportable. We are now at the beginning of a game of climatic roulette where, already, we are second-guessing the behaviour of natural systems over which, for all our cleverness and technological sophistication, we have virtually no control. Exactly how fragile are we? According to the late pioneering Brazilian environment minister, Jose Lutzenberger, our situation is much more delicate than we usually credit:

> The range of temperatures within which life can exist and flourish – that is, the range of temperatures that makes biochemistry possible, the chemistry of proteins, carbohydrates, hydrocarbons, nucleic acids, the building of living cells and organisms, which is also the range in which water can coexist in its three physical forms, liquid, gaseous and solid – is extremely narrow when compared with the temperatures that prevail in the universe at large.[6]

Temperatures range from close to absolute zero in deep space, 273 degrees centigrade below zero, up to hundreds of billions of degrees centigrade in the 'furnaces of imploding stars'. Lutzenberger invites us to imagine this temperature range as a line where each degree measures 1 millimetre. The line would stretch for hundreds of thousands of kilometres reaching beyond the moon.

All the forms of life on earth could survive on only about 10 centimetres of that line. People could live comfortably on only a fraction of that. A step either side of our few centimetres of tolerable temperature range is a step into oblivion. So now we must walk with care because global warming is the journey we are embarked on. That is why the precautionary principle is so important, because what we stand to lose, simply, is everything.

SITTING UNCOMFORTABLY?

I am not. I am writing by the side of Loch Shiel in the West Highlands of Scotland, staying in comfort at the house of relatives. But even here there are inescapable reminders of what it means to live in a warming world. In the volatile Mesolithic period starting about 10,000 years ago after the last ice age, sea levels first rose dramatically by at least 5 metres as huge amounts of water entered the seas from the retreating glaciers.

They then gradually fell again as the land lifted up, relieved from the weight of the ice. Scotland is littered with archaeological evidence of human settlements from that time, old beaches, cliffs and coastlines high above where they are today.

What should someone make of such information? Should we take comfort? The planet eventually found the different, more tolerable, balance we now enjoy. Our ancestors survived, after all. Or, should we take the opposite of comfort? Because history means that we know what the biosphere is capable of. It has been there before. A sea level rise of just a few metres would submerge most of the world's major capitals. It would take tens of thousands of years to restore a more benign atmospheric equilibrium.

But regardless of global warming, human cleverness has found many other ingenious ways to make life for millions less comfortable than it needs to be. Often, invisible lines connect an international obstacle course of events such as colonialism and apartheid, and economic icebergs like the debt crisis affecting the majority world, and the power of multinational firms that litter the modern world's landscape. To really understand what is happening those connections need raising into view.

One such avoidable cause of discomfort and, inevitably, death has been the orthodox debt crisis of poor countries. In the late 1990s one child was being born into unpayable debt every second in a way that bore all the characteristics of a new kind of slavery.[7] I say orthodox because there are other burdensome debts that go unacknowledged, and there is now a new debt to shame the old. It is the ecological debt of climate change. Why call it that? For two reasons. First because we are spending, or rather burning, more of our fossil fuel inheritance than we can afford to in the sense that the atmosphere cannot safely absorb the resulting pollution without being disrupted. And second, considering that the atmosphere is a global commons which everyone alive has an equal claim to, some of us are using much, much more than our equal, safe share. Global warming is consequently an ecological debt that, in scale, will ridicule the convoy of international meetings of

governments and financial institutions that have, over a
decade, disingenuously claimed to be freeing poor countries
of their unpayable conventional foreign financial debts.

THE IN-TRAY OF AN OFFICE IN WASHINGTON DC

It had been a bad day that morning in the Washington DC
office of World Bank employee Axel van Trotsenburg. Axel was
in charge of the Bank's efforts towards writing off the foreign
debts of a small number of very poor countries. But things were
not going well. Few if any countries or people had received a
dollar of debt relief.

Worse than that, there was a rising tide of suspicion that the
Bank and its brother organisation, the International Monetary
Fund (IMF), weren't serious about ending the debt crisis.
Instead of winning maximum relief for the largest number of
countries, they were foot-dragging because, as creditors, they
had no self-interest in seeing the debts written off. Even more
cynically, it appeared to many that the deal was being used to
dump a package of widely discredited pro-big business ideas
on the countries, with little consideration of whether or not
they would work.

But that day Axel was a popular man. His postbag was full.
For a typically invisible civil servant in a global financial
institution it should have been reason to celebrate. The
international campaign to end the debt crisis, best known
under the collective banner of the Jubilee 2000 Coalition,
had turned him and his colleagues at the IMF into minor
celebrities, doing radio and TV interviews and being quoted
in newspapers. But his mail on this occasion was enough to
spoil anyone's breakfast.

An eight year old schoolboy had sent him a postcard asking
him why he was killing poor people in Africa? In fact he had
dozens of cards all questioning the Bank's handling of a
debt crisis that, according the United Nation's Development
Programme (UNDP)[8] was responsible for the avoidable deaths
of 7 million children a year. Money that could have been
invested in health and childhood development was instead

being allowed to pay back the governments of the rich world and their Washington DC-based financial institutions.

By 2001, five years on from the launch of an enormously hyped debt relief programme cumbersomely called the Highly Indebted Poor Countries Initiative (HIPC), the leaders of the world's most powerful countries had met every year, and the financial institutions twice a year, to discuss and implement debt relief. The story was spun to the media repeatedly after these meetings that the poor countries debt crisis was virtually, and then definitively, solved. In the summer of 2001 it became apparent that something had gone disastrously wrong. All 23 countries that had qualified for HIPC, from an original list of 41, were returning to having 'unsustainable debt burdens'. They were broke in other words. In spite of winning limited debt relief for a handful of countries, everyone's best efforts had failed. The poorest countries in the world were back to square one. Possibly the problem was that their debts simply weren't big enough. Unlike the Latin American debt crisis of the 1980s that bankrupted several US banks and, it was feared at the time, threatened the whole western financial system, the poorest countries' outstanding, unpayable foreign debt, mostly African, stood at around $350 billion, too small to worry the powerful and demand action. By 2003 only eight countries had seen any of their stock of debt cancelled.

At the same time that one debt crisis remains painful and unresolved, the different dynamics of a whole new debt crisis are emerging and turning the pattern of the old crisis upside down and inside out. The reason is as simple as the implications are huge. Our debt to the ultimate storehouse of value – the planet's atmosphere – is growing so large that we face environmental bankruptcy.

Centuries of global economic development have witnessed two striking phenomena: first, a huge expansion in the size of the global economy, and second, a dramatic divergence in the way that wealth is distributed. Wealth 'creation', though more properly often 'appropriation', has been based significantly on the exploitation of natural resources. From the early days of globally ambitious European empires, the gold and silver of Latin America kept old Europe economically afloat and financed its adventures. And, for at least the last two centuries the black gold of our fossil fuel inheritance has driven the expansion and divergence of the global economy.

Now, the fact that the rich are taking more than their fair and safe share of a finite resource has an extra, potentially catastrophic dimension. Observed climate change and better scientific understanding of environmental limits, coupled with new international commitments to poverty reduction, mean that the enormous ecological debt run up by the rich takes on a new global importance. Thinking in terms of ecological debt it is possible to imagine a great reversal of centuries of expanding use of finite resources like fossil fuels, and of the growing divergence between rich and poor, to one of 'contraction and convergence', a term first used by Aubrey Meyer of the London-based Global Commons Institute.[9] This means, in other words, finding an answer to how the global economy can both work within natural limits and fairly distribute its benefits.

A WORLD TURNED UPSIDE DOWN

But with sorrow we observe that, contrary to the ... repeated advices formerly given by this meeting against an inordinate pursuit after riches, too many have launched into trades and business above their stocks and capacities; by which unjustifiable proceedings and high living, they have involved themselves and families in trouble and ruin, and brought considerable loss upon others.

Quaker epistle, 1732[10]

Global warming is spilling over – seas over defences, rivers over banks and one issue over another. A paradigm shift is emerging not from politics or ideology, but from a deep fissure opening up between two great continental plates – on one hand, the way the world does business, and on the other, the limited tolerance of the earth's environment.

The shift will occur over coming years in stale conference halls that shelter a jumble of international negotiations. It will happen at ministerial meetings of the World Trade Organisation (WTO), and as the United Nations tries to drum up finance to pay for a long list of international targets designed to reduce poverty. It will happen at talks on climate change, at meetings of the self-appointed Group of Eight (G8) industrialised countries, at meetings of the World Bank and IMF and even in the policy playgrounds of the bureaucratic global elite such as the World Economic Forum and Bilderberg group.

The reason for the impending change is alarmingly simple. Rich countries' unequal use of the global commons of the atmosphere is running up a gigantic ecological debt. That debt and climate change itself create an entirely new context for dialogue between nations and different social groups, and for our lifestyles and the promises that our political leaders can realistically make to us. As poor countries become increasingly aware of the issue they will question the legitimacy of the authority that rich countries and their financial institutions exert over them. They will probably seek compensation. They will almost certainly challenge the continuing status quo of unequal global wealth distribution, powered, as it is, by the parallel unequal use of our once-in-an-era fossil fuel inheritance.

But the shift goes deeper. A plan to tackle climate change cannot succeed unless it concedes each individual's fair claim to the atmosphere. Over time, equal property rights in the air above our heads will mean a historic realignment of wealth and opportunity based upon the real economy of tangible resources. Many of us get trapped in a shrinking moment in which the media focus our attention on ever smaller details of human behaviour, removed from context and detached from an awareness of the history that we are making. This makes it difficult to see, or remember, that some reassuring precedents do exist for the lifestyle changes and curbs on rampant consumerism in rich countries necessary to tackle ecological debt. Whisper it, but perhaps the only viable way to deal with global warming will also be a means to spread prosperity more evenly around the world.

THE MEANING OF DEBT

And his lord was wroth and delivered him to the tormentors till he
should pay all that was due unto him.

Parable of the ungrateful servant

What kind of debts do you have? Unpayable emotional debts
to friends? Debts of favour that you 'owe' until they get called
in? Or, financial debts to banks or loan sharks? Of all the ways
that you can go into debt none is as fundamental, potentially
disastrous and unrecognised as ecological debt. The world's
wealthy, high consuming minority probably can't believe
their luck.

Every debt has a story. But the narrative running along the
spine of all debts dictates that they should be paid back. And,
in more recent history, paid back with interest. The price of
non-payment is high. A poor country not paying its foreign
debts becomes a financial pariah state, isolated and denied
international assistance. A financially excluded individual
driven into the arms of unofficial money lenders faces physical
abuse or worse. Bankruptcy or prison hangs in the air for
most ordinary people. Only political leverage or the right
connections supply a keep-out-of-jail card.

But nobody counts ecological debt, even though it threatens
the biggest storehouse of value we possess, our home planet.
Ecological debt doesn't have to be paid back in the conventional
sense. No matter how much in the red an individual or
country becomes, nothing happens to make them change
their behaviour.

It gets worse still. The defining western story of our time
tells us that the more we consume, the happier we will be.
The more we go into ecological debt – in other words the
more we consume over and above our fair shares per person
of the environment's carrying capacity – the more fulfilled
we become. Imagine the scene, a suicidal alcoholic goes to
a doctor and is prescribed a bottle of whisky and loaded
gun. Melodramatic? Up until now, climate change has been
mostly a consequence of levels of human consumption in rich

countries. In spite of the sophistication of the information age, all our economies still overwhelmingly depend on dirty, slimy, dusty, fossil fuels. In terms of dependency, it seems even the wealthiest civilisations have travelled less far than they think from the warmth gained crouching over wood fires in caves or behind improvised wind breaks in forest clearings. And someone else is paying the price.

Speaking in March 2001, Bangladesh's environment minister said that if official predictions about sea-level rise are fulfilled, one fifth of her nation will vanish underwater, creating 20 million 'ecological refugees'.[11] Would the rich countries be prepared to take them as environmental refugees, she asked?

Ecological debt reveals a world turned upside down. It's a place where costs get passed on barely questioned from wealthy ecological debtors to cash-poor environmental creditors. It's a world full of paradox in which sober suited government officials and financial commentators decry the economic folly and irresponsible behaviour of the poor countries that account for most of the globe. Warnings of moral hazards get raised if money is given or if debts are cancelled too easily.

But it's also a world in which the *Financial Times*, club paper of the economic elite, can produce and win awards for a magazine called *How to Spend It* . A glossy extra to go with the newspaper specifically to help the confused over-wealthy with the difficult task of losing their money. In this world, anyone lacking the desire for conspicuous consumption or who fails to build status with material possessions carries a whiff of betrayal. They are the class traitors in an age of triumphant individual wealth accumulation.

But all of this may be about to change, and change will be an understatement. An awareness that modern economies can alter fundamentally the ecology upon which they depend began to emerge much longer ago than most people realise. It started with a pungent whiff in the nineteenth century.

2

The Chemist's Warning:
a Short History of Global Warming

In order to protect the environment, the precautionary approach shall
be widely applied by States.

Rio Declaration, signed in June 1992 by 178 governments

'Climate is what you expect, weather is what you get'. In the twenty first
century, climate is what you affect, weather is what gets you.

Myles Allen, *Nature*, 2003[1]

The smell caused by a careless, young trainee chemist in a
Swedish town in the second half of the nineteenth century was
nothing compared to the lasting stink his ideas would cause
as a full-grown scientist.

Working as a lab assistant, Svante Arrhenius (pronounced
Arreneous) was asked by another chemist to dispose of a vial of
liquid containing a deeply malodorous substance.[2] Arrhenius
was cycling home before he realised that he'd forgotten to do
what was asked. Unwilling to cycle back, he threw the vial
away by the roadside. Underestimating exactly how vile was
the liquid in the vial, it leaked and a nauseating pall fell over a
significant area of town. An investigating committee failed to
find the cause and the smell was blamed on freak meteorological
conditions. Ironically, it was Arrhenius' prediction of a far more
serious and long-term meteorological condition that was to
earn him his most important place in history.

Born in 1859, Arrhenius was the first person to link explicitly
the massive burning of fossil fuels, used to power the economy,

with potential large changes in the earth's climate. He was the first man, properly, to predict global warming. Today we may all be playing catch-up in our attempts to understand the implications of climate change, but by how far is not commonly appreciated. Arrhenius made his prediction in 1895 in a paper that he gave to the Stockholm Physical Society called 'On the Influence of Carbonic Acid in the Air Upon the Temperature of the Ground'.

It is almost impossible to believe that the warnings have been with us this long. The Kyoto Protocol, the first international agreement to tackle global warming, only gained the support of enough countries to become legally binding in late 2004.

A Swedish colleague remembered Arrhenius only after a day of pondering, but even then not his connection to climate change. How many names, for how many reasons, cascade down the years to us? Soldiers, politicians, writers and artists, but the man who foresaw perhaps our greatest collective challenge to civilisation has been as obscure to the general public as a complex chemical equation. More amazingly, Arrhenius made his quietly apocalyptic discovery (although he thought it was anything but at the time) not as part of his main research but merely while dabbling in his hobby of climatology.

The man who stumbled upon the likely fate of the planet had as many problems getting his mainstream work accepted (work which was later to earn him a Nobel Prize) as the reality of climate change later had in finding official acceptance. Not until the 1960s would the prospect of human-caused global warming begin the slow march to consensus in the scientific community. History was to repeat itself over two different time scales, once for Arrhenius the man and once for global warming.

Arrhenius' original academic research in the 1880s was so far beyond his tutors' comprehension that he was only grudgingly given a scraped, fourth-rank pass for his doctoral dissertation. What he discovered was that when certain substances called electrolytes are dissolved in water they can separate and take on different electrical charges, positive and negative. Such solutions could see their freezing point lower and their boiling point raise. All sorts of consequences flowed from his discovery relevant to biology. They ranged from the use of serums, to the human digestion and the role of toxins and anti-toxins. The earthly application of his theory belied its wonderfully esoteric name of *electrolytic dissociation*. It wasn't until later in the 1890s, with the discovery of electrically charged sub-atomic particles, that people took him seriously. And, after that, only in 1903 that he was given the Nobel Prize.

As a man of an age in which the approach to academic research had yet to be confined to rigid paradigms in which academics work like battery chickens with little room to manoeuvre, Arrhenius let his mind wander. It wondered, for example, about the *aurora borealis*, or northern lights. It wondered about the even more fantastically named, and still debated, theory of *panspermy*. Arrhenius thought that life could have come to earth, and gone to many other places as well, as a result of living spores spreading through the universe under the force of radiation pressure. Finally, and most importantly for us, he predicted that the build up of 'carbonic acid' in the atmosphere, what we call today carbon dioxide, as a result of economic activities that relied on burning fossil fuels, mostly coal in his day, would lead to global warming.

Arrhenius' climatic work was built on the research of many other scientists. He openly attributes the coining of the idea 'greenhouse effect', the key description of global warming, to an aristocratic mathematician, Baron Jean Baptiste Joseph Fourier, of the French Academy of Sciences, in a reference dating back to 1827. He says Fourier 'maintained that the atmosphere acts like the glass of a hot house, because it lets through the light rays of the sun but retains the dark rays of the ground'.

Another important precursor to Arrhenius who met a tragically ironic end was the Irish scientist John Tyndall.[3] Born in 1820, Tyndall didn't make it to university until his 30s. He worked as a surveyor in Ireland before being sacked following complaints about his treatment of the Irish, and moving to England. There he worked for several years on the construction of the high speed transport network of the day – the railways.

As the railways spread across Britain like frost across a freezing pane of glass, guided by the surveyors' instruments, so did consumption of what fuelled them, the fossil fuel coal. Between 1845 and 1852 alone there were 4,400 miles of railway track laid in Britain. It represented an 'almost perennial conquest over the power of nature', to one Lord.[4] The industrial revolution was pumping, literally, full steam ahead. And so was Tyndall's career. Its path was itself about to make connections that would be vital for the later elaboration of our understanding of global warming.

In the year that Arrhenius was born Tyndall started to study the atmosphere and the way that different gases were capable of absorbing heat to different degrees. While many gases seemed alike in that they were 'colourless and invisible' he saw that heat passed through them in very different ways. Gases like oxygen and hydrogen appeared transparent to heat while water vapour and carbonic acid (carbon dioxide) contained heat. Most importantly he noted that the latter absorbed more heat than the atmosphere itself. This meant that they acted like the sheets of glass in a hot house.

Tyndall also, like Arrhenius, found time for his hobbies. In common with the odd digressions of other uncontained, eclectic men of his time, Tyndall left an improved design for the foghorn as part of his legacy. By the late 1880s he was suffering increasingly from insomnia and had effectively retired. To fill his time he joined the lobby that was opposing the Liberal Prime Minister Gladstone's efforts to promote Home Rule for Ireland, successfully as it turned out. That little bit of political skirmishing helped to leave a legacy of over a century's murderous conflict that we live with still today. Tyndall also had a redeeming civic verve for the promotion of industrial safety measures in everything from coal mines to naval navigation.

His work would eventually help us predict when an unsafe dose of greenhouse gases was being injected into the atmosphere. But Tyndall's own life ended in tragedy, ironic only on reflection, when his wife accidentally gave him an overdose of the medication, chloral, that he took to help treat his sleeplessness.

By the time Arrhenius wrote his now increasingly famous paper, it was already understood that the presence of water vapour and carbon dioxide prevented the kind of freezing temperatures on earth that would be hostile to life. But Arrhenius went further. He realised that enough new carbon dioxide was now being released into the atmosphere to make a significant difference to the ground temperature of the planet. Also, he realised that 'modern industry', human economic activity, was chiefly to blame: 'the slight percentage of carbonic acid in the atmosphere may, by the advances of industry, be changed to a noticeable degree in the course of a few centuries', he wrote.[5]

With a degree of luck and good judgement – he missed a few things out, forgivable considering the technology then available – he made predictions that were remarkably accurate, and close to some of the best guesses available today. He calculated that increasing the concentration of carbon dioxide in the atmosphere by between two and two and a half times would increase temperatures by 3.4 degrees centigrade. The panel of scientists known as the Intergovernmental Panel on Climate Change (IPCC), who advise governments in climate change negotiations, in the 1990s estimated a range of 1.5 to 4.5 degrees centigrade, more recently revised upwards.

In all his pictures Svante Arrhenius looks dour and serious. His round face, wide hanging moustache and respectable suit, all carefully groomed, make him into an oddly anonymous face from his age. He could have sat in almost any wood panelled smoking room in Europe or America and not been noticed. His expression might be the result of the arduously slow photographic processes of the time. Or it could be something else.

Early on, Arrhenius the chemist was largely ignored by his peers and teachers. The 'disgrace' of the work that would eventually earn him the Nobel Prize blocked any early

2. Swedish chemist Svante Arrhenius looking serious with good reason. At the end of the nineteenth century he was the first to credit economic activity with the potential significantly to change and disrupt the balance of the atmosphere.
(Photographer unknown)

professorships. But the experience didn't seem to embitter him. He was in love with his subjects. One night while hosting a dinner party, the aurora borealis began to show above the house. The chemist insisted his guests accompany him outside where he could explain in reverential detail how the natural phenomenon occurred.

However, the potential consequences of the second time that Arrhenius was ignored, a rather longer period roughly between 1895 and the 1960s, were, are, serious enough to make anyone look depressed in a photograph. Until the 1960s, a time when the world was waking up to other environmental problems, the idea that human actions could do anything so fundamental as change average global temperatures was dismissed as implausible. Now, of course, we know different.

The silence on the issues for over half a century wasn't quite absolute. Just before the serious distraction of the Second World War, in 1938, G.S. Callendar resurrected Arrhenius' theory about fossil fuel-driven global warming. He, too, met with an incredulous scientific community. And Callendar was lulled into a false sense of security, deceived by the economic effects of the Great Depression, in believing that increasing industrial efficiency had actually stabilised the level of production of greenhouse gases.[6] During the 1950s more sophisticated models of the working of the atmosphere were developed and in 1958 it was discovered that a greenhouse effect was responsible for the searing temperatures on the surface of the planet Venus.

About a decade later new calculations suggested that doubling CO_2 in the atmosphere would increase global temperatures by around 2 degrees centigrade. In 1968 the potentially catastrophic effects of the Antarctic ice sheets collapsing was pointed out. More research showed how vicious circles of warming could occur as, for example, the loss of ice sheets reduced the ability of the earth's surface to reflect heat, further warming the surface and accelerating the retreat of ice sheets. Environmental awareness in the western world was generally on the increase following the publication of works like Rachel Carson's *Silent Spring* in 1962 which opened with the words of Nobel Peace Prize winner Albert Schweitzer, 'Man has lost the capacity to foresee and forestall. He will end by destroying the earth'.

Then came the green 1970s. It saw the birth of many of today's household-name environmental organisations like Greenpeace and Friends of the Earth, and the spread of green political parties motivated by the notion that preserving a habitable planet was a precondition for any other political project and so should form the basis of any manifesto. E.F. Schumacher, a former economist for Britain's National Coal Board, wrote the classic text of environmental economics,

Small Is Beautiful, in 1973. The Club of Rome published the seminal, much criticised, tale of depleting natural resources *The Limits to Growth* in 1972 (subsequent research showed them to be more right than wrong), and the same year *The Ecologist* magazine published its famous rallying cry '*A blueprint for survival*'. At the time, even among these groups, there was far more concern over the fact of using-up all the oil than its consequences in global warming. Perhaps most relevant of all to the idea of ecological debt in this wave of publishing was a book edited by Herman Daly called *Toward a Steady-state Economy* that also came out in 1973.[7] In it Daly quotes three questions posed two years earlier by the American Association for the Advancement of Science, and still unanswered today:

1   How to live on a *finite* earth?
2   How to live a *good life* on a finite earth?
3   How to live a good life on a finite earth *at peace and without destructive mismatches?*

The earth, looked at through the lens of physical science and biology, he goes on, is a steady-state open system characterised by a shifting, but self-balancing equilibrium, 'Why not our economy also?' The prevalence of the opposite notion in the dismal science of economics, a system based on infinite growth yet mortally reliant on finite resources, is what creates the conditions for both ecological debt and a systems collapse.

After the 1970s warnings were then revised upward for how much the planet would warm if CO_2 concentrations in the atmosphere doubled compared to pre-industrial levels, and new studies emphasised the serious contribution to global warming that a group of carbon-based chemicals called CFCs, and methane and ozone, could make. By the end of the decade in 1979, coinciding with the second great energy crisis, the US National Academy of Sciences already warned that a doubling of CO_2 could raise temperatures by between 1.5 and 4.5 degrees centigrade. The basis for urgent international action was becoming more concrete. Today a still-emerging consensus suggests that a 2 degrees centigrade rise above pre-industrial levels is a maximum limit beyond which costs and damages become intolerable and potentially irreversible. For people living on low-lying islands or in coastal and river communities such a rise would likely be too high. It seems the writing has been in the sky for some time.

Nevertheless, in this cursory history, almost another decade passes before the groundbreaking IPCC is established in 1987 to study global warming and advise governments engaged in negotiating any future agreement on the problem.[8] Its formation followed a key conference held in Villach, Austria in 1985. It was the same year that a hole in the ozone layer above the Antarctic was discovered. Suddenly everyone was looking up, and looking worried. Surprisingly even conservative political leaders like Britain's Margaret Thatcher, Ronald Reagan and George Bush senior in the US went public with concerns. Thatcher, however, remained committed to a growing, car-based fossil fuel economy and Bush's administration put pressure on leading NASA scientist Jim Hansen to alter his stated concern and, for the benefit of the US Congress, to cast doubt on the greenhouse gas to climate change link. Hansen refused, and the ensuing scandal did even more to raise public awareness.[9]

In politics most panels and committees are created to give the illusion of action, thus excusing those in power from actually doing anything about the problem in hand. When reports emerge they tend either to exonerate officials or get quietly shelved. But the first report of the IPCC in 1990 was different. It presented enough of a consensus, and worried enough governments, to lead to a call for an international convention to stop global warming. The convention was agreed at the Earth Summit in 1992. Although it was good on the principles of what to do, it lacked targets and timetables and the world has been arguing over them ever since.

The Third Assessment Report of the IPCC predicted that over the course of the twenty-first century global average surface temperature will rise between 1.4 and 5.8 °C. Sea levels may rise between 9 and 88 cm. Their report also allowed for long-term, large-scale and catastrophic events related to dramatic sea level rise, in the event of either the West Antarctic ice sheet melting, or sustained local warming over Greenland.

Climate research establishments like Britain's Hadley Centre, part of the government funded Meteorological (Met) Office, point out that 'feedback' mechanisms in the environment are hard to predict. For example, trees absorb carbon dioxide, which is positive, but global warming could trigger forests to die. At that moment the trees change from being a 'sink' that soaks up carbon, to being a source that releases more of it into the atmosphere, therefore accelerating warming. The Hadley Centre researchers speculate on the possibility of runaway climate change that would significantly worsen current predictions. New work by them incorporating so-called environmental feedback mechanisms suggests that, 'The rise in global mean surface land temperature between 2000 and 2100 is around 3 °C greater ... compared to the previous model estimates'.[10] Their observations about how and, as importantly, when the climate responds to the build up of greenhouse gases reveal the potentially catastrophic contradiction at the heart of efforts to stop global warming. Politics is short-term, remember 'a week is a long time.' But climate change is long term, as the Hadley Centre points out, 'the long lifetime of atmospheric carbon dioxide [means] that much of the change over the next few decades is already built into the climate system from present day emissions and those from the last few decades'.[11]

There were two causes for concern in 2004. A team of 300 researchers completed a four-year-long assessment for the Arctic Council, a body made up of the eight nations with territories in the Arctic, and reported that the northern ice cap is warming at twice the global rate. Consequences could include a further acceleration of global warming.[12]

The second piece of bad news came from a mountain top observatory on Mauna Loa in Hawaii, run by the US National Oceanic and Atmospheric Association. The observatory has been making measurements for nearly 50 years and is considered one of the most reliable sources for information. In 2004 for the second year running, and without there being any separate natural phenomena to explain it, there was a sudden jump in the concentration of greenhouse gases in the atmosphere. Baffled for a specific explanation, speculation grew in the research community that this could be an early sign of the environmental feedback mechanisms beginning to kick in.

The man who started making the measurements in 1958, Charles Keeling, still works in the same field. He was reported saying, 'The rise in the annual rate ... is a real phenomenon. It is possible that this is merely a reflection of natural events like previous peaks in the rate, but it is also possible that it is the beginning of a natural process unprecedented in the record'.[13]

HOW FAR UP THE CREEK HAVE WE PADDLED?

Now, after more than two centuries of intensive and unrestrained fossil fuel burning, humanity's free lunch on the climate is over. During the last century the earth's average surface temperature rose by about 0.6 °C. Past and current pollution levels already commit us to a rise of up to 1.5 °C. That means that there is very little room for manoeuvre if the rise is to be held under 2 °C. Far from restraining our greenhouse gas emissions, projections from the International Energy Agency forecast the supply of coal, oil and gas increasing by over 70 per cent in the world energy mix between 2001 and 2030.[14]

After so long, the global economy has developed a fossil fuel addiction. This creates two problems. First, as with any narcotic addiction there is damage to the body, in this case the planet's biosphere, observations of which are now unavoidable. But the second problem has suffered from cry-wolf syndrome. Since the crude, early predictions of natural resource depletion, introduced by works like *The Limits to Growth*, were hard to prove it has been easy to dismiss subsequent warnings. But the issue has not gone away. And, as the oil runs out, managing the profound cold-turkey that will affect all major economies will take us into wholly new territory. At the turn-of-the-millennium there were major protests over fuel prices across Europe that shocked and threatened governments. But over coming decades these will have seemed as threatening as a dog asking for a walk. Without concerted efforts to prepare public opinion, and with private interests like the road lobby prepared to disrupt transport networks over relatively small fuel tax rises, the coming fuel shocks could easily leave countries ungovernable.

In the year I was born, 1965, discoveries of new oil sources peaked. As I approach my 40th birthday the growth in oil production is also peaking and about to begin its long decline.[15] A fluke of history has aligned my life with the apotheosis of the great fossil fuel economy. A century shot through with conventional war ends just as an indefinite battle with the climate begins. That battle is matched with an equally destructive struggle that will be caused as rising demand for fossil fuels meets declining supply. In economic terms – remember the global economy is around 80 per cent dependent on fossil fuels of which oil accounts for nearly half – that means a big crunch.

In 1998, adding together expected total world energy demand over the next few decades with known or anticipated available fuel sources, the International Energy Agency noticed there was a gap between supply and potential demand. To fill the gap it used something called 'unidentified unconventional' fossil fuel equivalents. But this fuel didn't actually exist, it was an exercise in creative accounting to stop policy makers from panicking. Looking ahead for the next few decades, uncertain comfort is available from projections that fill the supply–demand gap, but with fossil fuels that have only a 5 per cent chance of discovery.

I grew up in Britain during the optimism and euphoria of North Sea oil field discoveries. Evening TV news programmes broadcast pictures of filthy but heroic looking oil men working on towering sea platforms. We were given guided television tours of east coast Scottish towns enjoying the boom that oil wealth brought. I didn't realise then that the writing was already on the wall. Britain was to squander its oil wealth like the dissolute son of an aristocratic family drinking and gambling away his inheritance.

The moment at which production reaches a maximum and starts to drop off is called the Hubbert Peak after the geophysicist King Hubbert. In 1956 he correctly predicted when US oil wells would pass their peak. The reason this moment is so important is because it sets in train a domino effect with impacts on the climate, our lifestyles and the economy. The moment that production and demand head in opposite directions we can expect a sudden price explosion. The poorest oil importing countries will be hardest hit. But the impact on general global peace and security will probably be terrible as the world's dominant and heavily oil dependent countries like the US go to even further lengths to guarantee access to cheap fuel. For example, the International Energy Agency predicts that, even in a best case scenario of maximum diversification and technological advance, by 2030 Saudi Arabia and its immediate middle eastern neighbours will provide for two thirds of the expected increase in demand for oil.[16]

Globally, natural gas is expected to hit its Hubbert Peak about a decade after oil. A worrying likelihood is that, as oil production declines, governments will switch to coal. Coal is cheap and there is much more of it than oil and gas. But it is also much more polluting. For every unit of power produced, coal will belch out around one third more carbon dioxide than oil and nearly two thirds more than gas.

But there will be other major effects. Oil powers about 90 per cent of the world's transport system. Farming, and thus our food supply, is already threatened by global warming. But it is also very heavily dependent on oil for production of fertilisers and pesticides. As oil production dives so will the output from conventional high-input farming. More than 10 calories out of every 11 from farm products are subsidised by oil.[17] So, as we become more greedy for a shrinking oil supply we may also become hungrier in the real sense.

WHY EFFICIENCY AND 'TECHNO FIXES' WON'T WORK

The only get-out clause for business-as-usual would be if efficiency improvements and conservation gains could win the necessary cuts in CO_2 emissions.

The case is put that markets will sort out the problem. Price mechanisms will drive greater resource conservation. Technology will drive efficiency and no limit need be put on conventional growth. Each proposal has a fatal flaw. Price signals, like politics, work on a different, much shorter, time horizon than grand shifts in the balance of the environment. In climate terms the warning lights will come on only when the patient has already, and probably irretrievably, passed the critical stage. Relying on price alone also disproportionately hurts people living in poverty.

Because of this time gap, and the way that the current system undervalues or 'discounts' the future, a time lag of several decades has already opened up between expected demand for energy and the ability to meet it with renewable sources.[18] Under market mechanisms and with distorting public subsidies that favour dirty fuels there has been insufficient incentive to build a sector that will be essential in a relatively short period of time.

Crucially, there is also a strict limit to efficiency gains that technology can deliver. Astrophysicist Alberto di Fazio calculated how much increasingly efficient machines and production methods can do to hold-off climate change and he came to pessimistic conclusions. He measures that the global economy doubles roughly every 17 years.[19] Currently, the correlation between the size of the global economy and CO_2 emissions is, he says, 'astoundingly high ... practically total correlation'.[20] To make the planet fit for human life, CO_2 in the atmosphere was converted by natural processes into fossil fuel reserves over the course of 180 million years. According to di Fazio, humanity is converting fossil fuels back into the atmosphere 'a million times faster'.

Mainstream economists and policy makers seem to assume that efficiency can grow indefinitely. They believe that technology has all the answers. This notion allows them to believe that CO_2 emissions can be cut without either renouncing fossil fuels, or limiting conventional economic growth. However, even under the most unlikely, optimistic scenario, bringing us unimaginably close to the walls of the laws of thermodynamics, the best that technology can do is not very much at all. Remembering that in climate change we need to think in terms of geological time scales and the 'long-now', in the very best case, maximum efficiency gains would delay reaching a particular higher concentration of greenhouse gases by just 24 years. A more realistic outcome of global best efforts, taking account of the difficulty of collective political action, would be only a 'negligible delay'. Trusting to efficiency will not allow 'any significant or appreciable control of the coming climate crisis'. From a strictly technical perspective di Fazio concludes that, 'either we switch to non-fossil fuel sources of energy [which will take decades] or we limit the world industrial product, or both in some proportion'.

None of this, though, has stopped the desperate search for techno fixes. Both British and US governments' solution of choice is to look for technological rather than political and economic answers. The international climate talks in Milan in 2003 were littered with workshops, press conferences and brochures piled high on stalls about what science could offer. Most suggestions were, sadly, either temporary or daft. They ranged from fast-growing genetically modified trees that would soak up carbon dioxide, for a short time at least, to squirting CO_2 into cavities under the sea or storing it in frozen form as giant golf balls.

For these reasons it is becoming clear that the early days of climate change will have to be, by necessity, the same thing as the dying days of conventional economic growth. If there is any doubt about the precariousness of our situation, a visit to the metaphorical coalface of climate change demonstrates what is at stake.

Canaries carried in cages were an early safety innovation in Europe's rapidly developing, but extremely dangerous coal mining industry. Their sensitivity to the lethal gases that accumulated underground turned these small, yellow and previously carefree birds into icons of early warning. That's why Leo A. Falcam, President of the Federated States of Micronesia, said, 'Our early experience with the real consequences of global warming should be the canary in the coal mine', adding that,

'The climate change that threatens the existence of Pacific islands was not of their making. There is very little that they can do to prevent further loss'.[21] In late 2001 I went to Tuvalu on behalf of the *World Disasters Report* to see how they were coping.

3

The Heaven Bursters:
Tuvalu and the Fate of Nations

Tuvalu – uncomplicated by possessions, uncorrupted by machines, peaceful, happy contentment.

Tourist leaflet

'I'm Dreaming of a White Christmas' played in the transfer lounge of the airport in Fiji in the South Pacific. It would have to be a vivid, convincing dream. Early in the morning the day was already beginning to warm and lighten the island to reveal a lush, green character. The air was an assault of unfamiliar smells, disorienting with promise.

I was nervous. Before travelling I'd been told how internal connecting flights on the island had crashed inexplicably. I'd also been told of the time that a pilot on the flight to Tuvalu had, on a visit to the toilet, locked himself out of the flight cabin. That was the journey I was to take next. Already a reluctant and guilty, needs-only flier, my prejudices were being reinforced. But when, after two hours of flying, without crashing the twin propeller plane approached its destination, it was the land below, not us, that seemed fragile and impossibly vulnerable. In places like Tuvalu, the first steps on the short walk to Venus are being taken.

Funafuti, the main island of Tuvalu, was curled up in the sea like a shaving of pale wood and looked as if it could be washed away as easily. It was difficult to believe that people had survived there already for around two millennia. Its landing strip is the largest single-purpose piece of land on any of the islands that make up the nation. However, even a short stay revealed that the runway is anything but single-purpose. With a handful of planes flying in and out each week, the local population use it to stroll and drive down. They sleep on it during typically hot nights. And dogs use it as a perfect lazing ground at anytime.

I arrived in Funafuti, Tuvalu's main administrative centre, as I do in any new place, tired and slightly unsure of myself. I was almost as far from home as it was possible to be, and had been warned by colleagues about my local contact who, true to form, failed to show up to meet me. But the island's only hotel at the time had a four-wheel drive pick-up truck which, trustingly, I got into, carrying my luggage. I was then driven just 80 yards to the hotel's front door. How small and how vulnerable the island was would be driven home to me several more times during my stay.

My first appointment was with Paani Laupepa, the senior government official who represented Tuvalu at international talks on climate change. I phoned Paani to confirm our meeting not realising his office was also only a few yards away. But he wasn't there. He'd taken the day off to celebrate his particular island's festive day. Tuvaluan's first loyalty is to their home island. But before I could worry about arrangements falling apart, the voice that answered the phone interrupted, 'Can I help instead, I am the Environment Minister'.

The Minister said he wasn't busy, so closed the office, took the afternoon off and drove me around the island on its expensive new road, then being laid by foreign contractors. At some points the new road was almost as wide as the island. A few forlorn coconut palms sprouted either side. I'll come to the road later. The extreme shortage of land is brought home by another problem unfamiliar to most Europeans: where to bury your dead relatives? At one end of Funafuti the sea is already eroding the main, small burial ground. As a result people have taken to incorporating graves into the fabric of their homes.

When the people of Tuvalu first encountered Europeans they gave them the name 'Palagi', pronounced *palangi*. Victorian

3. On Funafuti, Tuvalu's main island, the little land available for
burying family members is at risk from an encroaching sea.

travellers translated the word to mean 'heaven bursters'.
Unquiet foresight fills the name now that climate change, a
bad spell escaped from the Pandora's box of the rich world, is
disrupting the lives of the people of the region.

A tourist leaflet produced for the benefit of the couple of
hundred annual visitors invites the interested traveller to
'Tuvalu – uncomplicated by possessions, uncorrupted by

machines, peaceful, happy contentment'. Like most adverts, it is guilty of misdirection.

During spring tides the airport runway floods on Funafuti. In 2000 for the first time in living memory at high tide it flooded for five consecutive months. Alone it could be a climatic anomaly. Coupled with disrupted rainfall, more frequent cyclones, erosion and rising temperatures it has led the government to ask neighbouring countries to consider welcoming a gradual relocation of its people.

Still rusting in Funafuti's lagoon is the wreck of a large fishing boat that fruitlessly sought shelter during a hurricane in 1972. The island was flattened. Miraculously only a handful of people died. To prevent being blown out to sea people tied themselves to trees. The island recovered. But during the 1990s Tuvalu suffered seven cyclones. UN regional disaster expert Charlie Higgins thinks that because of climate change countries in the region could be slipping into a series of events from which there is no escape: 'The frequency of extreme weather related events will increase, their intensity will increase, and as these events increase, the countries will really be in a cycle that they can't break out of'.[1]

Tuvalu has virtually no exports with which to earn hard currency. The two things it does provide to the wider world are a small but steady flow of trained merchant seamen from the local training college – an export which brings its own problems when seamen return from long voyages bored, cash rich and sometimes carrying sexually transmitted diseases – and the other export is stamps. Yes, stamps. In a large hut near Funafuti's library and modest government buildings a team of busy people stick brightly coloured special issue postage stamps, each one exploring a different theme, onto envelopes to post to eagerly waiting collectors in Britain and elsewhere. Two special issues in recent years put Tuvalu's predicament into context. One marked the country's win in the lottery of the modern age, selling rights to its internet domain name '.tv' for around A$30 million. The other raised the issue of global warming, showing how Tuvalu is trapped in a uniquely

4. Special editions of stamps are one of Tuvalu's few exports. Celebrating significant events, these two are oddly linked. One shows the domain name .tv won by Tuvalu in the great international lottery of the information age. But as it cashes in on its virtual domain, the greenhouse effect stamps show its real domain is in danger of being lost.

modern paradox. Just as it has rented out its virtual domain, it is in danger of losing its real one.

'In the past we really enjoyed the environment. It was fresh. Now the population is growing with the business-minded way of thinking and the western way of life. The environment is degrading and degrading and degrading', says Mataaio Tekenene, Environment Officer for Tuvalu. 'And perhaps there are more negative impacts which are not obvious yet. Both climate change and development are killing the island'.

Disasters and a challenging environment are nothing new to the Pacific. But two trends are closing-in to make people's livelihoods more precarious. Climate change and pressures from conventional development such as people crowding into housing in hazard prone areas are significantly increasing vulnerability. Places like Tuvalu reveal these threats and challenges in microcosm. Their fate is echoed around the region and around the world.

THE PARTICULAR VULNERABILITY OF SMALL STATES

Tropical Cyclone Trina struck the Cook Islands in early December 2001. Heavy rains and strong winds hit with very little warning. 'I have never seen the seas as high as they were the last few days', said Nikki Rattle of the Red Cross. 'Many low-lying areas were flooded. The supply of local fruit and vegetables is ruined'. International flights stopped, roads were ripped up and an odd mixture of Christmas festivities and first aid workshops were cancelled. On the island of Mangaia local people said flooding was the worst since 1977. Normal life comes to a standstill when extreme weather events hit small nations.

A single cyclone, Kina, hit Fiji in 1993 and caused the re-deployment of one third of the government's budget to pay for urgent reconstruction. Drought in Papua New Guinea caused an estimated US$100 million damage in 1997, while floods killed over 2,000 in 1998.[2]

The small size, lack of resources, economic dependence and relative remoteness of small island nations makes them especially vulnerable to so-called natural disasters. A 'degradation of traditional coping measures', normally relied on by people in remote communities is considered by the United Nations Development Programme (UNDP) to be making the problem worse. Bad and volatile terms of trade, coupled with capital flows and national income that are unstable also increase vulnerability. Small states are disproportionately affected by fluctuations in increasingly open trade and capital markets. Dependence on exports of agricultural crops adds to their 'susceptibility to external shocks' says UNDP.

Moreover, new and fundamental threats to low-lying nations are emerging. Five countries are made up entirely of low-lying atolls: Kiribati (pronounced *Kiribass*), the Maldives, the Marshall Islands, Tokelau and Tuvalu.[3] A number of factors make these places the most vulnerable of all small island states. High population densities, high ratios of coastline to land area, narrow underground freshwater lenses easily contaminated by sea water, and ecological systems destabilised by beach mining, grove clearance for house building and land and sea waste dumping, are all common problems.

Less well understood is that a rise in the temperature as well as the level of the sea is a serious threat. Coral growth maintains natural sea defences and preserves the fish habitats essential to the local diet. But the reef-building corals die when temperatures rise beyond a narrow band. Too little research hampers a clearer understanding of local coral health in Tuvalu. Temperature changes and storm surges linked to global warming remain the biggest threats.

Tuvalu attracted attention in 2001 when news emerged that the government was preparing for the worst in the face of climate change and rising sea levels. According to officials the government has had to adjust its planning horizon from one of 80–100 years to between 50–60 years, or to within the lifetime of the next generation. The dramatic shift of focus changed the approach to climate change from one which could be infinitely deferred. Now it is integrated into every planning decision, and every decision taken by a parent on behalf of its child, according to senior government representative Paani Laupepa.

After having a proposal for special immigration status rejected by Australia, Tuvalu negotiated a deal with New Zealand whereby a number of its citizens would be accepted each year effectively as environmental refugees. Tuvalu only has a population of around 10,000, and the arrangement is projected to last for between 30 and 50 years. In response to criticism that they are admitting defeat and 'giving up' by taking the precautionary approach and planning for gradual relocation, Paani Laupepa responds, 'We have to plan for the future, any responsible government would do that'.

For others the threat is even more immediate. Carteret, part of Papua New Guinea, is similar to the circular atoll home of many of Tuvalu's population. But rather than a gradual relocation, 1,500 people from Carteret had to move suddenly. One islet in the Carteret group was cut in half by rising sea levels. More are facing the same fate on the island of Takuu, 170 km away. Flooding destroyed houses, washed away shoreline and ruined the compost pits central to the island's garden farming. But more than land can be lost in the process. As people are relocated and their culture diluted, a unique heritage is lost. Settled in long-standing communities, the Takuu islanders developed the ability to sing 1,000 indigenous songs from memory. That is threatened by the break up of the community just as much as homes and crops. Global warming's impact on heritage worldwide is another disaster beginning to happen.[4]

THE WEATHER REPORT

Hilia Vavae is director of the Meteorological Office on Tuvalu. She has worked there since 1981. Her expertise marks her out as special. Hilia was approached in the street by a woman she didn't know who noticed a bandage on her foot. 'Get it mended', said the unknown woman, 'you are the most important person in Tuvalu'.

As a result of problems with data and the complexity of drawing definitive conclusions from different trends, she says that few things about climate change are certain. But Vavae is confident that between 1950 and 2000, 'Temperatures indicate a general warming through the period. In the 1980s only in February did the low-lying areas get flooded, and not very much. But since the late 1990s, and especially now, the frequency of flooding has tremendously increased. Last year we were flooded in November, December, January, February and March, its quite unusual'.

A consensus has emerged among the research community that sea levels are rising across the Pacific at a rate of approximately 1 mm per year. That figure disguises, however, much greater chaotic fluctuation of tidal lows and highs in the short and medium term. Without action to halt climate change expected sea level rises will inundate and displace lowlands, erode shorelines, worsen coastal storm flooding, and increase salt intrusion into estuaries and freshwater aquifers.[5]

Globally, nine out of the ten warmest years on consistent records going back to 1860 occurred since 1990 according to the World Meteorological Organisation. Since 1976 the global average temperature rose at a rate around three times faster than the century-scale average.[6]

The 1990s saw a marked increase in the frequency of tropical cyclones for Tuvalu. In common with other islands of its type Tuvalu is naturally dependent on rain-fed drinking water, but rainfall patterns are also changing. Overall there has been a decrease in rainfall, but that is coupled with disruption which causes both more periods of drought and periodic inundations.

In spite of the focus on sea level rise, experts like Eileen Shea of the East West Centre and Paani Laupepa in Tuvalu are critical of the obsession with it. The issue is complicated by the movement of the land. Some suggest that fears for the region are exaggerated if the land is rising on its continental plate in such a way that it compensates for rises in sea levels. A team of scientists from GeoScience Australia set up a series of GPS (Global Positioning System) stations during late 2001. Over a five year period they plan to clarify what is happening to absolute sea levels, taking account of land movements. But what they will not be able to predict accurately are rates of future global warming and sea level rise. Yet whatever happens to sea levels, all the other impacts related to global warming present a long list of inescapable threats.

One worry is the change in cyclone seasons as they become more unpredictable. Local people understood the normal, more regular patterns and were able to prepare. But now people on the island believe the patterns are changing. On two or three islands storm surges have ruined the Taro pits used for growing the local subsistence crop. Once polluted with salt water the pits take at least a year to recover. Droughts can last for three or four months. But they become a problem after only two or three weeks. On most of the islands the groundwater is not drinkable according to the Environment Ministry. They say that local people have a taste for rainwater and that groundwater is brackish by comparison. But there is not enough capacity to collect and store rainwater.

Most people with conventional jobs in Tuvalu work for the government. On a small island nation still strongly embedded in subsistence lifestyles there is no other major employer. Seluka Seluka, who works for the government on climate change, pointed out that a strong cyclone-proof house can be built for A$30,000, but questions whether it is sensible to spend such amounts in the face of the increasing impacts of global warming. Similarly, Kakee Kaitu, senior assistant secretary in the Prime Minister's Office, dismissed engineering solutions to coastal vulnerability: 'Sea walls don't solve anything. We tried them to stop coastal erosion, now you go back and the walls are gone'.

In addition to all the practical difficulties there can be unexpected problems in the path of those working to raise public awareness of global warming.

'GOD PROMISED NOAH: THERE CAN BE NO MORE FLOODS'

Also working for the government, Poni Favae organises and runs workshops on Tuvalu's outer islands. They are well attended and the older people, mostly, are full of questions. But then the difficulties begin. 'The problem is the local church belief that there won't be any flood. They say that God promised Noah', says Favae about the biblical story of the great flood and its aftermath. 'We have workshops where we try to explain to people the opposite. We say that God is not sending this flood, it is a human cause'. So, preparing people for more frequent disasters is another problem.

A fashion emerged to put money into complex computer modelling systems aimed at improving early warning. Though interesting for researchers, it's a top down approach and can be useless to vulnerable villagers for whom flashy computer graphics can be meaningless. Options in the face of an approaching storm are limited for most people anyway.

If a household on a small island gets a cyclone warning very simple, practical action is usually taken. Under their own initiative villagers seal plastic containers and barrels containing food and drinking water. Any tree branches overhanging houses will be cut and coconuts that could fall onto roofs removed. Tall trees are usually allowed only at a safe distance from village housing. Posts may be sunk into the ground and basic windbreaks set up, made of matted palm fronds from the coconut trees. A combination of posts and tree trunks may be used to give extra support by lashing them together with the houses' support beams.

Government assistance tends to concentrate overwhelmingly on picking up the pieces after a disaster, so even when warnings are available, people are usually on their own as the storm approaches. Because of the remoteness of many communities they are often left that way for days afterwards as well. In an atoll nation like Tuvalu, the outer islands are up to three days' sea journey from the main administrative centre, Funafuti. Then, the government had just a single boat to provide assistance which, anyway, was not always available.

Public education materials can take on a bare, pragmatic flavour. The National Disaster Management Office in Fiji produces a poster, also reproduced as an office calendar. It reminds people that 'Disaster Do Happen. ARE YOU PREPARED?'. After that general reminder there follows a series of cartoon pictures accompanied by simple words of advice. The suggested actions are: 'TSUNAMI – RUN', 'EARTHQUAKE – DUCK', 'FIRE – DON'T PANIC' and 'FLOOD – EVACUATE'.

By declaring the 1990s the International Decade for Natural Disaster Reduction the United Nations was perhaps setting itself an impossible task. The accumulated impacts of climate change set the initiative like a minnow against a flood tide. We now know that even if the concentration of greenhouse gases in the atmosphere were stabilised immediately, global warming would continue for decades.

After a decade of trying to improve organisation and co-ordination of government services in advance of disasters, to raise public awareness and develop national disaster management plans, a lot still remains to be achieved. 'Most plans emerged from standard models. They didn't emerge from the particular circumstances of the country. And, therefore, they don't guide appropriate actions', says Charlie Higgins, the

United Nation's regional disasters officer. His concerns were echoed by Seo Seung Chul, of the International Federation of the Red Cross: 'Many government plans are unworkable. They get written by Australia or New Zealand not by people on the ground. The plans are not understood or shared among government departments. They also don't have the financial resources to carry them out. They're good on paper but most wouldn't work'.

Even though vulnerable people are often left to save themselves, there is no substitute for commitment, organisation and resources directed by central government. Hurricane Michelle hit Cuba with winds of 216 km per hour. In spite of over 20,000 homes damaged and nearly 3,000 wrecked, only five lives were lost according to disaster expert Dr Ben Wisner. When the weakened weather system hit Central America 10 died and 26 people went missing. Wisner believes that the crucial difference was the carefully planned and timely evacuation of 700,000 of Cuba's 11 million population: 'This is quite a feat given Cuba's dilapidated fleet of vehicles, fuel shortage and poor road system. It was possible only because of advance preparations and planning, a cadre of local personnel, trust in warnings given and cooperation with the Red Cross'.[7]

At least theoretically, authorities in Tuvalu use a simple formula to help people plan for disasters: hazard *times* vulnerability equals risk. But this didn't prevent some odd planning decisions. One large generator provides the electricity for Funafuti. But the generator is located on the ocean side of the island's runway, the area most exposed to the open sea and most prone to flooding. Today the vogue is for 'participatory disaster preparedness'. The community draws maps of vulnerable places and people, such as the homes of the young, sick and elderly, as well as potentially hazardous locations like latrines, deep water spots or even areas of long grass hiding snakes. Other initiatives have sought to collect and catalogue traditional coping strategies that are being lost due to development. Traditional practices are embedded, for example, in the stories ('mo 'olelo') chants ('mele') and dances ('hula') of native Hawaiians.[8] New models for effective community participation are also drawing on older models such as the Hawaiian 'aha council in which people solve problems and plan by dialogue and shared decision making.

Indigenous cultures offer broad stable frameworks for decision making in an increasingly unstable world. This is embodied, for example, in words such as the Carolinian 'meninkairoir', meaning taking the long view, and the North American First Nation people's concept of considering the impact of any decision on seven generations, those past and yet to come.

MODERN LIFE IS RUBBISH

'In the past people had land, trees, the tools they need and the knowledge from ancestors. It was all they needed to survive. You never used to see the difference between rich and poor, now you can', says Mataaio Tekenene from Tuvalu's Environment Department. 'The shift to a modern lifestyle, a western lifestyle is making people more vulnerable to the climate. They have lost their ways of coping and managing'.

It is often argued that environmental problems will evaporate with the wealth brought by conventional economic development. One view holds that development inevitably reduces vulnerability to disasters. It follows from the fact that more people in poor than rich countries suffer death and injury from comparable disasters. But several of development's dynamics in this region, and in others, have precisely the opposite effect.

Mining, forest clearance and cash crop farming increase soil erosion, river sedimentation and the risk of flooding. Since 1975 there has been a 50 per cent population growth. Growing populations mean more people at risk. More people mean more houses, farms and other infrastructure open to extreme weather events and geological threats.

Population growth is accompanying a drift of people from rural areas and outlying islands to urban centres. A lack of land and decent housing has seen an increase in vulnerable squatter settlements. The high demand for housing and the cost of land encourages building in areas more sensitive to flooding, tsunamis and storm surges. In the Solomon Islands, Papua New Guinea and elsewhere, new settlements are built on plots subject to flooding and landslides.

Tourism is encouraged as one of the few regional opportunities for conventional economic development. On Fiji, tourist developments grow on exposed coastal strips. The typical location of tourist centres means that tourism is uniquely vulnerable to climate change. At the same time, the development of tourism creates its own particular pressures that impact on the resources available to local people. Because of the industry's susceptibility to both political, economic and climatic factors its growth also creates new economic insecurities. In late 2001 the number of people flying dropped dramatically after terrorist attacks on the United States and Fiji's industry was hit hard by its most recent military coup.

The ideas underlying conventional development can also unintentionally increase a community's vulnerability to floods and storms. Securing the basics of life in the event of a disaster traditionally rested among the islands on a kind of social and economic organisation geared toward co-operation and sharing. Orthodox development, however, is based on the market approach of maximising personal gain and competition for profit.

Detailed studies of island economies based on sharing and gift giving, such as Nanumaea, one of Tuvalu's islands, show that highly co-operative and mutually supportive communities grew out of this fundamentally different way of organising an economy. The increasing intrusion of a competitive and acquisitive economic culture has a direct effect. According to anthropologists Keith and Ann Chambers, 'In a sharing system, maintaining supportive social relationships is so intrinsic to the exchange process that short-term tallies of material benefit are meaningless. As a result, sharing equalises access to resources across a community and serves as a socio-economic levelling mechanism'. In comparison, say the Chambers, profit seeking enterprises pushed by aid projects, 'all support the weakening of sharing obligations', that are central to coping when disaster strikes.[9] Without understanding what holds the fabric of a community together no strategy to adapt to climate change can succeed. 'Community cohesion, evocatively dubbed "unity of heart" by Nanumaeans, is often regarded as fundamental to entrepreneurial development', the Chambers write. 'There seems little recognition, however, that communal values are at odds with the individualistic orientation of capitalistic-based development'.

Development pressures are not new, and are nearly always disruptive. Ever since more regular contact with Europeans and Americans in the middle of the nineteenth century, the people of Tuvalu have been drawn 'inescapably into the complex commercial system of their visitors'.[10] Slavery and the copra trade characterised the early encounters with the commercial system. The slave traders were known as Blackbirders. Boats would arrive from the coast of South America and capture almost entire villages and communities. They were taken off to work in mines and plantations. One visit by Blackbirders took 250 people from the island of Nukulaelae, leaving only 65 behind.[11]

Today, alcohol, urbanisation, land shortage for housing and gardens, a consequent shortage of local foods and the twin problems of increasing dependence on cash bought goods and 'unemployment' are common problems in Tuvalu. 'Increasingly all the islands are dependent on imported food', says Mataaio Tekenene. 'The older generation say it is bad, expensive and brings new diseases like heart attack and diabetes. And that the food is not fresh. I support the older people but we cannot escape from it. We have become dependent'. These changes are significant also for the way they affect a community's ability to respond to disasters.

Current social change in Tuvalu shows how co-operative behaviour can be lost. On the increasingly westernised main island of Funafuti, 'They don't share things in the same way. They won't share outside the family', says Sunema of the Tuvalu National Red Cross Society. 'On the islands [which are less westernised] they help each other, they help everyone. When there is a disaster you need things'.

One of the largest items of expenditure in Tuvalu's budget when I visited was a road development programme described by the Minister of Finance as, 'A substantial claim on the public finance'. The department in charge took nearly one third of the annual budget. Spending on the road came to A$6 million. In spite of a housing shortage, only A$200,000 was spent on building new homes and renovating existing ones. The priority seems even stranger considering that the whole island is flat, has a speed limit of 15 mph, and you could walk from one end to the other in about one and a half hours. Traffic accidents are an unwelcome new phenomenon. At one end of the island the road's final destination is a fetid rubbish tip. Tuvalu's Environment Officer complains that, 'Things have been done without proper consultation. Now it's too late, nothing can be done. The building company had already arrived before we could raise our concern'.

During the Second World War Funafuti's subsistence agriculture was all but destroyed when American servicemen built a runway for their aircraft, now the airport, on the largest available strip of land. Before it had been a maze of pulaka gardens. Europeans and Americans failed to understand the importance of subsistence crops. 'At least all the mosquito-bogs have been filled in', was a comment made at the time. The legacy is a lasting dependence on imported rice and flour.

Traditional Pacific agriculture is thought to lie behind the historical resilience to disasters of many islands in the region, especially weather-related incidents like cyclones. During the 1990s Samoa was hit by two '100 year' cyclones and the loss of its main crop, taro, due to disease. Instead of famine Samoa recovered. Its resilience is attributed to the traditional food production system which uses a wide diversity of crops bred over generations to be hardy and grown together in a robust mixed crop pattern. The breakdown of such systems across the region is causing, says the UNDP, 'repercussions on food security and vulnerability to other disasters'.[12]

However, new development objectives are attempting to correct the historical error of the runway construction and raise food security in the increasingly disaster prone region.

Turning to self-reliance and self-sufficiency, based more on sustainable agriculture, is seen as the way forward but is also under threat from commercial agriculture. Peter Waddel-Wood, of AusAID, the principal donor for many small Pacific states, explained: 'Our focus is on self-reliance and self sufficiency because of the particular problems of the region'.

A handful of basic crops, though with hundreds of varieties, provide the basic diet of people in the South Pacific: banana, coconut, breadfruit, taro, pulaka (a popular variety of taro), squash, yam, cassava, papaya, sweet potato, paw paw, fish, pork and chicken. Some varieties are more storm resistant than others. There are over 470 varieties of sweet potato alone from highland areas. But many of these well-adapted varieties are under threat from the push to commercial mono-crop type farming. Dr Jimmy Rogers, a regional expert on agriculture, highlights why this is a danger: 'Mono-cropping is OK if you can avoid disasters, but you can't avoid disasters either natural, or economic in terms of fluctuating prices'.

'THERE I HAVE NO LAND, THERE I AM NO ONE'

It is easy for urbanites in rich countries to underestimate the importance of land to Pacific islanders, and hence the deep personal and cultural significance of its loss. A woman from Kiribati explained, 'We can't just move to another country. I would love to go to Fiji. But there I have no land. There I am no one'.

There is almost universal acceptance in the region, however, that large-scale movements of population are inevitable. Down by the edge of Funafuti's near-perfect lagoon local woman Seinati Telaui sits talking about the dilemma facing her and her people: 'Climate change is one of the driving forces making people migrate. Even though they want to stay in this free and beautiful life, parents are planning for their children [to leave]. They see there is no future'. But there are great obstacles in preparing to adapt to new large-scale movements of environmental refugees: the rigid order of nation states and the lack of flexibility in the designation of refugee status.

People like the UN's Charlie Higgins are convinced that in the face of climate change some countries will cease to exist altogether. It raises numerous questions about how the international community should respond. Paani Laupepa in Tuvalu expresses a desire to preserve national integrity, even if it means doing it somewhere else: 'I think we could have a state within a state, that has to be negotiated with other governments. The concept is not a bad one, it is a good idea. It will enable us to preserve our sovereign integrity'. In spite of his diplomatic caveats, it's clear that there are some obvious candidates for consideration in Tuvalu's case: 'The northern part of Australia would be best, it is closest to [the climate in] Tuvalu. New Zealand is cold [but] we have 1,000 in New Zealand already'.

The view is challenging in a region where Australia is already accused of acting against the spirit of the Refugee Convention.[13] Conflict and climate change are increasing pressures for relocation. Yet instead of an increasingly flexible international community capable of absorbing these pressures, an already ossified order of large nations is becoming more restrictive. 'What has changed', says Higgins, 'is the rigidity of the international system'.

Once land has been lost, will a residual nationality be able to persist, or does there need to be a new category of 'world citizen'? Could such a status be created in acknowledgement of the fact that climate change is a collective problem and requires a collective solution? Will it be acceptable to displaced populations just to struggle for greater recognition as 'environmental refugees'? In the event of a full-scale national evacuation there are as yet no plans to deal with an abandoned country's exclusive economic zone, its territorial waters and nationhood.

Few things could be more sensitive than carving out new territory to create space for a nation. A process will be needed to handle such dilemmas that carries at least the stamp of legitimacy of the UN's General Assembly. Poni Favae picks up the point: 'The UN has the IPCC but it has no equivalent panel to talk about migration'. But he thinks the argument can become too esoteric: 'If everyone is thinking about migrating, then others will join them. But how will they live? We are a subsistence people'. Yet plans must be made. 'The government has decided to take a precautionary approach', says Paani Laupepa. 'We have to plan now for the future'.

There is an ironic twist to Tuvalu's tale. Australia is still seeking an unfortunately named 'Pacific solution' for dealing with refugees. One among many small island nations, Tuvalu was approached by Australia to 'hold' its unwanted refugees after Tuvalu's own polite request had been turned down. But it gets even stranger than that.

The story of fellow Pacific island Nauru is a parable of failed development. Its history contains a convoluted tale of calculated colonial exploitation following the discovery of valuable phosphates in the island's centre. Exploited by all-comers, the island is now an environmental wreck, mostly broke and dependent on imports for most things (see chapter 12).

Nauru came to international attention in 2001 when it was persuaded to accept refugees intercepted at sea on the way to Australia. Human rights group Amnesty International described their conditions of confinement a year later as inhuman. In response, the Australian Minister for Immigration likened their imprisonment to a holiday in 'paradise'.[14] Nauru's fame coincided with the death of its phosphate mining industry. So, as Nauru accepted refugees that were destined for comfortably rich, high-polluting, climate change treaty rejecting Australia, expatriate mine workers from threatened little Tuvalu were having to leave Nauru and its exhausted phosphate mines. These workers were faced with the option of either emigrating, or returning to Tuvalu whose government was negotiating a deal for the gradual relocation of its own people.

Tuvaluans are not to be messed with, though, as one early European trader discovered. He was caught using the drinking well on Niutao, an outer island, as a toilet and didn't live to explain himself. Now, as the rich world continues to use the atmosphere as its toilet, countries like Tuvalu are in the vanguard of finding new ways to seek legal redress. That, though, will not stop global warming in the foreseeable future.

Sadly, long forgotten promises are coming true in Tuvalu, even if they were made by mistake. Victorian missionary Rev A. Murray recorded the stumbling efforts of Elekana, an unfortunate early pastor. Elekana went to the island of Nanumaea, part of Tuvalu, intending to say that he was going to 'turn the islanders from heathenism to Christianity'. Sloppy translation meant he actually promised to 'turn the island upside down'. Horrified islanders believed him and he was chased at spear point, barely escaping with his life. Today a combination of climate change and orthodox development are finally delivering on Elekana's inadvertent pledge.

The problems experienced by Tuvalu are the trials of a modern day canary in a warming world. But they also highlight how we need to rethink basic assumptions about human progress. First, because there will be no progress if the consequence of pursuing it is global warming. And second, because in almost everything we do from now on we will have to adapt to climate change.

4

The Great Reversal of Human Progress

He that dies pays all debts. I defy thee.

Shakespeare, *The Tempest*

I pondered all these things, and how men fight and lose the battle, and the thing that they fought for comes about in spite of their defeat, and when it comes turns out not to be what they meant, and other men have to fight for what they meant under another name.

William Morris, *A Dream of John Ball*[1]

Europeans and Americans dream of Jamaican beach holidays. For those who actually get there, met off the plane by steel bands and coached directly to all-inclusive resorts, none gets to meet Elsie. She was the reason I was there.[2]

Elsie was a grandmother several times over. On her knee a baby called Growth screamed. Elsie's daughter had denied she was pregnant complaining instead that she merely had a 'growth'. The baby would get a proper name one day, but for then, Growth stuck. I asked Elsie how many grandchildren she had and she laughed and said, 'A whole lot of them'. Elsie said she was 61 years old but, although it seemed unkind to think so, she looked a lot older. She survived by making and selling small amounts of charcoal, and working at a cleaning job once a week.

In her house – a wooden shack with two beds where she lived with three generations of her family – there was no running water or electricity. For privacy their yard was protected by sheets of rusting metal fence. A couple of other houses stood nearby. The way that the lanes around her house were divided up into yards gave rise to the infamous 'yardy' tag taken on by organised Jamaican gangsters. Thin wires wriggled down from overhead power cables to many of the other yards, each containing two or three huts-cum-houses. Stealing electricity was common but potentially lethal among the flimsy wooden buildings. House fires were frequent, another cost of poverty. Only official home owners got legal access to services like electricity. Most of Elsie's neighbours were squatters in the eyes of the law, even if they had lived there for decades.

Baby Growth was not the poorest of the poor in Jamaica when I went there to gather evidence at the height of the Jubilee 2000 debt campaign. But in a country drained by foreign debts, divided by enormous inequality and imploding with violence, if Growth lived up to her name it would be a triumph against all odds.

To get to Elsie's place you drove down a tarmac road that cut through the zinc fencing and dust lanes of Bennetlands, one of Kingston's downtown 'communities'. Compared to many other roads in the area it was a good one. But it was also the sort of road that the local middle classes feared to drive down after dark.

On a bend in the road that the project took its name from, the poorly funded S-Corner clinic provided a range of basic services to the local community: a health clinic, school classes, access to drinking water and, in the absence of a proper public sewage system, help with sanitation. They even ran a modest nutritional scheme encouraging people to grow their own food to eat and sell. But before the clinic could even begin to carry out its heroic tasks, it had another problem.

The community S-Corner served was not just poor and lacking amenities, it was riven with violence. The clinic could only function by first brokering peace treaties between local warring factions. It was doctor, teacher, plumber, engineer and peacekeeper all at the same time. Also, the clinic wasn't the result of well-meaning charities parachuting 'good works' into the area. It grew as a result of local people who moved into an abandoned building and organised things for themselves, negotiated with the building's owners and got the clinic going.

But rather than working to support such courageous local people, global governance, in the shape of the World Bank and IMF, worked implicitly against them. As the former chief economist of the World Bank Joseph Stiglitz wrote, the IMF 'undermines the democratic process by imposing policies'.[3]

According to Angela Stultz-Crawle, the Jamaican woman who ran the clinic, under pressure from the IMF the money available for social programmes in Jamaica had halved. S-Corner was already picking up the tab for people who had fallen through the threadbare government safety net, but they, too, only had half the funds they needed. She wrote to the government's Ministry of Health asking for more support and got a letter in reply that read: 'We are so sorry, we wish we could help, but as you know we have to be paying debts, that is why we cannot help. We empathise with your situation but we cannot do much more than what we are doing'.

Here, in microcosm, was what J.M. Keynes described with deceptive simplicity as, 'the economic problem': the struggle to meet basic human needs and lift people out of the struggle for subsistence. Jamaica was far from the poorest of countries. But even there, towards the end of the last millennium, were symptoms of the world's collective failure to organise its affairs to solve the economic problem. They were symptoms repeated thousands of times in projects and public services in dozens of countries, often regardless of the fact that, with political will, the necessary resources were not very far away.

At the time I was in Bennetlands, for every dollar the government spent, nearly half, 46 cents, went on debt service. Unemployment was high. HIV infection rates were doubling every two years. It was getting harder and harder for the country to earn a living from its principal exports like sugar and bananas due to a long-term downward pressure on prices, in spite of the fact that the island was rich in natural resources and should have had no problem.

Angela saw the consequences of skewed spending priorities every day at first hand: 'There's the reduction in health programmes, reduction in education, in roads, in lights. Just walking around you see people living in dirt yards, scrap board houses. It is repaying. Everyday you hear the government come out and say "Oh we have met our IMF deadlines, we have paid", and everyone claps. These people don't know anything. Had it not been for local people's resistance to these things, their own innovativeness, they would have been totally devastated'.

Somehow in international relations we have arrived at a situation where 'debtor' is a term synonymous with economically weak Third World countries. And 'creditor' refers to the apparently shiny efficiency of the rich, industrialised nations. Those terms are more than merely economically descriptive. They carry weight and moral judgements. Debtor equals feckless, dependent and largely incapable. Creditor means supportive, generous, trustworthy and solid. The words have taken on these meanings in direct contradiction of reality.

The US, for example, a spider at the centre of the web of the international financial community, behaves with the pompousness and faux piety of an old high street bank manager. At the same time, however, it is simultaneously the world's biggest economic and environmental debtor. Debt is about power, politics and how you play the system. But with the rules the way they are, the system is about to break down.

Conventional Third, or majority, World foreign debt dominated the debate about the future for poor countries at the end of the last millennium. A campaign was born that took its name from the old practice of 'jubilee' in Judaism. Once in every 50 years people were set free from their debts. It was meant to stop particular families or communities getting caught in a debt trap and all the social problems and division that result. The campaign was called Jubilee 2000 and started in a shed on the roof of a Third World development group where I was working near Waterloo in London. In just a few years it gathered 25 million signatures in support of cancelling unpayable poor country debt.

In many ways, however, it was less a debate of elaborate policy exchanged between sophisticated experts, and more like the camp theatre of silent movies. Wide-eyed, innocent campaigners pleaded on the streets and in the conference

venues for the lives of the desperately poor and indebted, while
Victorian stage villains from the World Bank and IMF sniggered
and said life wasn't that simple.

Millions signed petitions. Thousands attended demonstra-
tions. Dozens of reports were written (I know, I wrote several).
And what was the result of the biggest international mobilisation since the anti-apartheid movement? Officials made a
U-turn in policy. They decided that the debts of the poorest
countries were, indeed, unsustainable and designed a labyrin-
thine mechanism to deal with it. In July 2001 Jubilee Research,
a successor to the Jubilee 2000 coalition campaign, published
a report called *Flogging a Dead Process*.[4]

Of the original 41 highly indebted countries, 39 that were
functioning states would still require total cancellation to
stand any chance at all of meeting poverty reduction targets.
In spite of winning some limited debt relief for a handful of
countries to be spent on health and education, and building
an international campaign movement, a harsh judgement
would say that everyone's best efforts had failed. The poorest
countries in the world were back where they started. Many
were even further behind.

A DEBT IS A DEBT?

A debt is a debt, isn't it, no matter what the circumstances,
and should always be repaid? That is not the lesson taught by
history. The past indicates that if you have either power or
strategic importance it is remarkable how the rules will bend
to your will.

Britain, for example, still has an unpaid debt of around $14.5
billion owed to the US from the time of the First World War.
The last payment was made in 1934, not a penny has been seen
since. Unlike the more recent debts of very poor sub Saharan
African countries, Britain's debt is quietly forgotten. Other
European countries including France and Italy owe another
$18.5 billion.[5] The English have, in fact, been welching on
debts for a lot longer still.

England was one of the first countries to default on international loans right back when Italy laid claim to inventing the precursors of modern banking. In the fourteenth century Florentine banks lent money to the English king to finance his wars against the French. When, in 1327, it was time to repay, Edward I declined. As a result, the Bardi and Peruzzi Banks collapsed. Add another century and the Medici Bank, in spite of the family's 'colourful' reputation for intimidation, had to swallow the bad debts of England's Edward IV.

J.M. Keynes pointed out that, 'The majority of the countries which were heavy borrowers abroad during the 19th century frequently escaped from it by defaulting more or less'. The long-established Barings Bank was made famous in the 1990s when its greed for profit led to its spectacular collapse after allowing the trader Nick Leeson to run up hundreds of millions in debt. But that wasn't its first foray into high risk games with credit. In the first half of the nineteenth century it lent money to states in North America that, in 1842, defaulted. But then, creatively, to get its money back Barings financed candidates in the state elections of Maryland that stood on a promise of debt repayment. They won. Another debtor, Mississippi, didn't repay and as recently as 1980 banks in London were still pursuing 138 year old loans.

For several centuries debt was held in check in the western world by religious principles. Lending and charging interest payments were considered morally wrong by the Christian church. Usury was high crime. Then during the Renaissance, as trade increased and more people had need to borrow to finance deals, 'religious scruples yielded in normal fashion to pecuniary advantage', commented J.K. Galbraith.[6] In some respects it has been downhill ever since. Christian objections were won round by the argument that money was a productive asset in the same way that a cow or woodworking tools were. If someone lent you money, they were missing out on other benefits they could get from their money, and should be compensated. It mattered less at a time when cash was not the dominant form of exchange. Now it matters a lot.

Debt-based economies with weak financial regulation have emerged since the nineteenth century to display distinctly unpleasant characteristics. People with money tend to get more of it, because they can set the terms on which it is lent. So, gaps between rich and poor get bigger. The poor pay more to borrow. Consequently, our social landscape has been scarred with debtors prisons and loan sharks, with people losing their homes and pensions. In poor countries hopelessly mired in obligations to service ultimately unpayable debts, we've seen the destruction of health and education services.

Mainstream lenders can be hard to distinguish from the men touring council estates with a wad of notes and baseball bats. Interest charges of over 200 per cent for small loans to private individuals in Britain are not uncommon. In Muslim societies charging interest is still considered wrong. A handful of British banks make special mortgage arrangements available for Muslim families. However, even in these cases, instead of interest charges, a fee is commonly payable which roughly approximates to the prevailing interest rate.

The last half of the twentieth century has been characterised by the strategically important friends of rich and powerful countries having their debts written-off, and poor, strategically unimportant countries being bled dry to repay their – often illegitimate – 'debts'. Germany was given postwar debt relief in 1953 around four times more generous than that offered to the least developed countries in Africa during the 1990s. After Suharto's military coup, Indonesia got hefty debt relief in 1969. Egypt was well treated after the Gulf War of 1991 as was Poland during the death throes of the Cold War. By contrast, the Archbishop of Capetown said in 1997 that, 'The external debt of developing countries has become an eternal debt'.[7]

'Blessed be the young, for they shall inherit the national debt'. Former US President Herbert Hoover's words echo still as the US national debt, the world's biggest, surpasses $5 trillion. If it wasn't for the free ride gifted to the US, currently holder of the world's reserve currency – and the way that it means it can borrow low and lend high – the US today would be up a stinking creek with no method of propulsion. But we shouldn't gloat over the US bubble economy. We should worry. Over the last couple of decades, the huge growth of assets in the US economy has gone to a tiny, rich minority. The enormous debts that kept the economy going, however, were racked up by the poor.[8] Ironically an unpayable debt crisis in rich countries early in the new millennium has brought the global economy to a precipice of instability. Michael Lewis in a classic account of 1980s excess in the money markets, *Liar's Poker*, revealed how we fell for faux-macho corporate bluster during a period of intense corporate mergers: 'The take over specialists did for debt what Ivan Boesky did for greed. Debt is good they said. Debt works'.[9] Exactly how wrong they were – as usual, though with a few exceptions – only became apparent afterwards.

Without ever really accepting that they were really dealing with the symptoms of a huge economic failure, world leaders and the rest of the international community did, finally, try to get their heads around some solutions.

THINGS CAN ONLY GET BETTER?

A song called 'Things Can Only Get Better' became a temporary national anthem in Britain in 1997. It was adopted by the Labour Party in an election campaign which led to the end of nearly two decades of Conservative Party rule. But an assumption of steady, if faltering, human progress has long been at the heart of western civilisation.

In the wider world, the final few decades of the last millennium saw the emergence of a unique, if frequently disingenuous, international consensus among governments. An end to global poverty and the harsh struggles of people like Elsie and Growth was to become the focus of nations working together, and through their appointed agencies like the World Bank. At least since the controversial appointment of the American government official Robert McNamara as president of the World Bank in 1968 commitment to poverty eradication has been a necessary matching accessory to most gatherings of heads of state. The problems of countries like Jamaica, and others even poorer in Latin America, Africa and

Asia, were supposed to be consigned to history. McNamara's reign at the bank did much to rehabilitate his public image, sullied by his hawkish role in escalating US military aggression in Asia around the time of the Vietnam War. But, in fact, between 1968 and 1981 when McNamara was president less than 10 per cent of World Bank loans went to areas generally understood to target poverty directly, like health, education and supplying clean water.[10] The gap between reputation, rhetoric and reality has remained, soaked deeply into the grain of the world's negotiating tables and the well-meaning words of politicians.

By the beginning of the 1990s, things were still not going well. The Cold War and the legacy of the Soviet and American superpowers fighting proxy wars in poor countries had left the world in an unstable and conflict-ridden mess. Far from poor countries enjoying a 'peace premium' after the collapse of the Soviet Union, their loss of geopolitical importance had the opposite effect. At this time the rhetoric of the 'war on terror' was still far off. With all the money supposedly freed up from military spending that was no longer needed in a world with only one superpower left, aid was supposed to increase. But it didn't. Aid shrank throughout the following decade. Also, a commercial debt crisis that hit Latin America in the 1980s gave way to a public debt crisis in Africa and elsewhere in the 1990s. Something drastic needed to happen in the build-up to the new millennium.

The United Nations, thawed by the end of the Cold War, seeing its opportunity took a big, deep breath and, beginning with the Earth Summit in Brazil in 1992, turned the 1990s into a political railroad with stops every few minutes for another major international conference of unquestionable importance. Along the line which stretched around the world's great cities from Beijing to Copenhagen there were conferences where civil servants and activists gathered by the thousands to talk about the planet's prospects for, among other things: drinkable water, equality between men and women, social development, human rights, urban living conditions, having enough to eat, cancelling the debts of poor countries and finding money to pay for it all.

The final challenge fell to a gathering in the city of Monterrey in 2002, just before the tenth anniversary of the original Earth Summit held in Brazil. It was problematic and indicative. Diplomats use language with great subtlety. For months nobody could decide what to call the gathering. Whether it was a conference, a summit or just a meeting would convey different levels of political commitment to the outcome. Agreeing on 'conference', in the event it proved largely irrelevant as only a dribble of new resources was actually pledged.

Issues thrown up by the special UN conferences spilled over into the regular meetings of the G8, a club of the world's self-appointed most powerful and important countries, and into other get-togethers of the World Bank, IMF and the WTO.

Had all the money spent on business-class travel, hotel and restaurant bills instead been put into a separate fund and wisely spent, it's just possible that the problems may have been solved anyway. But as J.K. Galbraith observed of senior bankers and politicians in the United States at the time of the Wall Street crash in the late 1920s, it is important for important men to convene important meetings about important issues, to show that they are important, and to reassure the public that something is being done. But, then, as now, the most substantial thing to happen was usually the meeting itself, not anything that came out of it.

However, many of the conclusions from ten years of well-meant conference hopping were gathered together into a mini-manifesto to improve the lot of the world's poor. Eventually known as the Millennium Development Goals they became the focus for aid agencies and pretty much everyone else involved at the international level in tackling poverty. Heads of state and government declared at the UN in September 2000: 'We will spare no effort to free our fellow men, women and children from the abject and dehumanising conditions of extreme poverty'.[11] Mostly meant to be achieved by 2015, the goals are:

1   Eradicate extreme poverty and hunger.

- Reduce by half the proportion of people who live on less than a dollar a day.
- Reduce by half the proportion of people who suffer from hunger.

2   Achieve universal primary education.

- Ensure that all boys and girls complete a full course of primary schooling.

3   Promote gender equality and empower women.

- Eliminate gender disparity in primary and secondary education, preferably by 2005, and at all levels by 2015.

4   Reduce child mortality.

- Reduce by two thirds the mortality rate among children under five.

5   Improve maternal mortality.

- Reduce by three quarters the maternal mortality rate.

6   Combat HIV/AIDS, malaria and other diseases.

- Halt and begin to reverse the spread of HIV/AIDS and halt and begin to reverse the incidence of malaria and other diseases.

7   Ensure environmental sustainability.

- Integrate the principles of sustainable development into country policies and programmes; reverse loss of environmental resources.
- Reduce by half the proportion of people without sustainable access to safe drinking water and basic sanitation.
- Achieve significant improvement in the lives of at least 100 million slum dwellers, by 2020.

8   Develop a global partnership for development.

- A range of commitments by northern countries to address trade imbalances, debt, aid and development financing, and intellectual property rights.

Plans were drawn up, aid programmes reshaped and more global civil servants clocked up even more air miles flying around the world to spread the good news. For anyone interested in how the world has staggered towards running itself, the very different treatment given to social and environmental issues on the one hand, and economic issues on the other, is interesting.

The former are generally seen as 'soft' policy best kept in its natural setting of community groups and non-governmental organisations (NGOs), while the latter, economic issues, are 'hard' policy best managed by the real powers of government, finance and big business. Agreements to uphold social and environmental goals are typically voluntary. There is no real penalty if a country decides not to play ball. If, however, a country doesn't live up to a trade deal or to the letter of its arrangements with the international financial institutions like the IMF it will very quickly find itself in the global dock. Trade sanctions and blacklisting by the international bankers await countries which try to go their own way where the global economy is concerned. The global environment, on the other hand, is deemed worthy of only voluntary, ad hoc attempts to look after it.

The most noble and moral ambitions of the international community that are condensed into environmental agreements, campaigns to cancel Third World debt and to raise people out of want and suffering tend to emerge from people and community groups agitating outside government, at the grass roots level. But reading press reports can create an impression that such groups are disruptive or anti-progress. The Secretary General of the United Nations, Kofi Annan, points out, however, that, 'Those labels overlook the pioneering role of NGOs on a range of vital issues, from human rights to the environment, from development to disarmament. We in the United Nations know that it was [NGOs] who set the pace'.[12]

The family of international economic agreements, on the other hand, that have so far demonstrably failed people in poverty, such as those overseen by the WTO and others such as the North American Free Trade Agreement, emerged out of close collusion between big business, big finance and government. At the infamous meeting of the WTO in Seattle in 1999 the US organisers had a large help desk for the world's media. Any journalist who had an enquiry could go to them. There they had a reference book with contacts offering spokespeople to comment on any issue that emerged. Very late one night, when the negotiations were deadlocked and the press room was empty, I took the book from behind the desk and leafed through. There were pages and pages of contacts for every imaginable big business and trade association, from American chicken farmers to car makers. Human rights organisations, unions and environmental groups, however, were nowhere to be found. In the eyes of the US government they clearly had nothing useful to say.

Not only do efforts to tackle poverty suffer a lack of teeth. They suffer perhaps the greatest oversight of our time. Because throughout all these earnest and self-important attempts to get our international act together, one thing was significantly overlooked: global warming.

The failure to account properly for the impacts of climate change make a mockery of more than a decade of political efforts. Agreeing bold new goals for nations collectively to pursue was a great achievement. But, as these challenges to the goals show, without a realistic plan to stop climate change they may be a complete waste of time.

THE MILLENNIUM DEVELOPMENT GOALS[13]

Goal – Lifting People out of Poverty

There is a target to halve between 1990 and 2015 the proportion of people living in poverty – defined as those whose income is less than $1 per day. Measuring poverty like this creates its own problems. Quality of life can, for example, be very good in a community which looks poor because it doesn't use cash for many of its transactions, preferring instead other forms of barter and exchange. And quality of life can be very bad in more cash rich societies which have less community spirit, more crime, loneliness and polluted environments.

However, to address the system using its preferred counting method, global warming makes the sums go horribly wrong. Disasters stemming from the climate tend to target the poor and keep them that way. Over 90 per cent of so-called natural disasters are climate-related and over 90 per cent of the people affected by them live in poor countries. Single extreme weather events can devastate whole economies. Hurricane Mitch hit Central America in 1998. In a couple of days it destroyed three quarters of the annual earnings of Honduras, and set the country back decades in terms of progress according to its prime minister. Farming was wrecked and virtually all its crucial banana plantations were flattened. According to the UN Environment Programme economic losses due to 'natural' disasters are doubling every ten years. Small recurrent disasters, working like a low level war of attrition, are also devastating over time. Mitch was just one of more than 700 disasters to hit the region between 1980 and 1998.

Insurance companies need to plan ahead. What they are seeing when they do looks disastrous. Andrew Dlugolecki, a former director of global insurance giant CGNU, plotted the rising trend of economic losses from disasters, most of them climate-driven, against likely global economic growth over the coming decades. He came to the astonishing conclusion that some time around the middle of the 2060s, that is to say during the lifetimes of people alive today, economic losses would outstrip global income. In other words, the world economy will have been bankrupted by 'natural' disasters. And, Dlugolecki's projections were conservative because they did not allow for the possibility of accelerated, or runaway, climate change, a scenario that many in the research community consider highly likely.

A one metre sea level rise, possible within the next century or so, would, for example, displace 80 per cent of Guyana's population and impose costs equivalent to ten times the country's annual earnings. A more modest 50 cm sea level rise would, ironically, bankrupt oil-rich Venezuela. The country could simply not afford either to protect its coastline or to replace everything that got washed away.

Goal – Making Sure People Have Enough to Eat

By 2015, again, the intention is to halve the tally of around 800 million people in the world who don't get enough to eat. Now, it is true that the world produces more than enough food for everyone to be well fed. The fact that they are not is testimony to governments' penchant for economic ideas that look good on paper rather than work in practice. Where the lives of poor people are concerned, the winds of laissez faire markets still blow strong. The poor are still expected to fit in with markets rather than the other way around. But redistributing the wealth of resources that we do have is a bit like gardening, it requires intervention and management. Unless, that is, you don't mind your garden being overrun with a couple of multinational corporate superweeds that get lucky and take over the vegetable patch. Unfortunately radical pro-poor market reform, which would involve things like giving people a fair share of land, is nowhere globally on the cards. And climate change stands to make the task of getting dinner on the table a whole lot harder.

Generally speaking under global warming wet areas will get wetter, and dry areas drier. This is particularly a problem for places like Africa. During the great floods in Mozambique in the year 2000, the worst for 150 years, the lowlands of the Limpopo river were inundated for three months. Sometimes flooding can be a good thing. In the short term it can benefit crops like rice. But Mozambique's floods lasted so long that the UN Food and Agriculture department said there had been a 'complete wipe out of plant genetic resources'.[14] Everything was destroyed, seeds, food stores and all the crops in the field.

Ironically historical records show that total annual rainfall across Africa has been declining since 1968. When the rains come either not at all or all at once, the problem is either the devil of drought or the deep blue sea of flood. Over the past 25 years the Sahel has experienced the most 'sustained decline in rainfall recorded anywhere in the world within the period of instrumental measurements' according to the IPCC.[15] The great famines of the 1970s and 1980s had many political causes as well. But as the land becomes drier, smaller and smaller political sparks can start the fires of famine. During 2002 12 million people in southern Africa faced hunger and disease due to a crisis driven by two years of drought.

Most farming in sub Saharan Africa is fed directly by rain. Farming accounts for over two thirds of jobs and more than one third of the region's earnings. Farmers in the region have, over time, proved incredibly resilient to environmental changes. But global warming stands to push them over the edge.

Crop yields are projected to fall by one fifth in a region where 200 million already go hungry. In Britain people spend 12 pence in every pound on food. In sub Saharan Africa the figure is the equivalent of between 60 and 80 pence. Climate change could create the worst of all worlds. Local food prices are driven up due to scarcity. Expensive imports are then bought with declining revenue from the sale of Africa's cash crop exports, which are grown instead of food for local consumption.

Goal – Getting Children into School

Another goal is to make sure that every child goes to primary school. What threat could climate change pose to this impressive aim? When Hurricane Mitch struck Central America, one quarter of the countries' schools were flattened. Wherever more extreme weather events and rising sea levels threaten centres of population they also threaten education. Then, of course, there are the hidden threats. Hunger, disease and forced migration all make schooling difficult if not impossible. Global warming promises more problems with all three. A hungry or sick child makes a poor pupil. A child on the move is difficult to teach.

Around one half of the world's population lives in coastal areas threatened with upheaval due to sea level rise, for example along the coasts of Bangladesh and Vietnam. Bangladesh fears that in coming years it could see 20 million people displaced due to global warming. In the mid 1990s it was estimated by Norman Myers of Oxford University that there were already 25 million environmental refugees in the world, and that the figure could increase due to climate change to around 150 million by the middle of this century. As farms fail in a warming world, famine could create 50 million environmental refugees in Africa alone by 2060.

At the moment people who are forced to flee for environmental reasons get none of the protection given to people fleeing political persecution or wars. They are seen as second-class refugees. A drought devastated Afghanistan for three years from 1998 leading 80,000 people to flee to neighbouring Pakistan. But the Pakistani authorities argued that because they were fleeing a 'natural' disaster they did not deserve refugee status. This meant that they were not entitled to help from the relevant UN agencies. Those who fled were effectively starved back across the border. It's hard to imagine giving all children a decent, basic education if millions of them are running from the effects of a disturbed climate, while at the same time international law fails to give governments at home or abroad an obligation for their care, protection and education.

Goal – Giving Women a Better Deal

This goal promotes equality between men and women, and seeks to give girls as good a deal at school as boys. But, under the status quo climate change is likely to make life more difficult. Whatever is bad for poor communities will be bad for women. Stuck with 'traditional female roles', in other words doing all the work on the farm and in the household, women will bear the greater burdens that global warming dumps on the poor.

As greater pressure is placed on already stretched government budgets by the costs of climate change, the poorest members of the community, who already have least access to health and education services, in other words women, will become poorer and more marginalised.

Goal – Sorting Out the Health Problem

Here is a sweeping set of targets that are all vulnerable to climate change. They seek to cut by two thirds the number of children who die before their fifth birthday, to reduce by three quarters the number of women who die as a result of childbirth, and to stop and reverse the spread of major killers like HIV/AIDS, malaria and other diseases.

However, the former chair of the IPCC Robert Watson said, 'Projected changes in climate could lead to an increase in the number of people at risk of malaria of the order of tens of millions annually'.[16] Locations where mosquitoes and tsetse flies can thrive will change, in turn introducing the diseases they carry like malaria, dengue and yellow fever to new populations. Epidemiologist Andrew Dobson of Princeton University was quoted in *Science* magazine saying, 'Climate change is disrupting natural ecosystems in a way that is making life better for infectious diseases. The accumulation of evidence has us extremely worried. We share diseases with some of these species. The risk for humans is going up'.[17] Research from a group of UN organisations estimated conservatively that global warming was responsible for 150,000 extra deaths in the year 2000.[18]

Many dangers cross over from other problems associated with global warming. For example, we've already seen the threat to people's ability to feed themselves. Hungry, malnourished people are also more susceptible to disease. Poor people are also more vulnerable to disease. The difference of infection and survival rates concerning HIV/AIDS between rich and poor countries demonstrates that the illness is, to a significant degree, a disease of poverty.

Drought, too, pushes people to drink from ever more unsafe water sources. Climate change could be setting in train a domino effect that topples the weakest members of global society. Floods and storm surges contaminate drinking water supplies. Floods driven by the El Niño phenomena along the east African coastline brought cholera in 1997/98. There was also an outbreak of rift valley fever, which jumped the species boundary from cattle. Warming temperatures also mean that some diseases which would normally die off in the cold of winter may now proliferate more aggressively. It looks like a warmer world means a world more prone to illness.

The problems are not isolated to poor countries. In 2003 a sudden heat wave that coincided with national holidays in France led to around 15,000 deaths above the seasonal average, and a possible further 20,000 across Europe. Rising heat-related deaths will particularly affect the world's burgeoning mega-cities which, because the way that they are built up interrupts the natural exchange of heat between the ground and the atmosphere, already create 'hotspots' that are warmer than the natural background temperature.

Goal – Clean Drinking Water, Sorting Out City Slums, and 'Sustainable Development'

In a rather throw-away fashion, and without really thinking through the consequences, this goal calls on countries to 'integrate the principles of sustainable development' into country policies. It also aims to halve the proportion of people who do not have reliable, safe drinking water by the year 2015, and to improve the lot of 100 million slum dwellers, somewhat arbitrarily by the year 2020.

To begin with, and as a fundamental test case, the first point would require all countries to play their part in a global plan that stood a realistic chance of stopping climate change. Such a plan is the foundation stone of anything that can call itself sustainable development. And yet, as described later in this book, it is very far from the international target that the world has today, set by the Kyoto Protocol.

The aim of increasing access to safe drinking water is also fatally compromised by global warming. Around 1.3 billion people are estimated to lack sufficient drinkable water. With growing economies and rising populations that figure is expected to double by 2025. Worryingly, worldwide water consumption rose twice as fast as population over the duration of the last century. Scenarios for climate change suggest that, in spite of more extreme storms and rainfall in some areas, in many arid and semi-arid regions of the world water supplies will decrease drastically. Asia's great rivers like the Tigris, Euphrates, Indus and Brahmaputra are expected to experience a one quarter drop in flow. At the same time more and more people are expected to cram into Asia's mega-cities, putting even more pressure on existing water supplies. India's capital Delhi may exhaust freshwater reserves by 2015 and two thirds of China's cities already face serious shortages.

Most of the world's mega-cities are coastal or river-based and are uniquely vulnerable to climate change and sea level rise. Across Asia urban populations are rising between four and five times faster than rural ones. The pressure on quality of life in big cities is already unbearable for millions even without global warming. Pumping groundwater at unsustainable rates can also worsen the problem by causing subsidence. As desalination plants become more necessary for drinking water, and slum dwellers need to be moved away from particularly vulnerable areas, the costs imposed on developing countries become still more of a burden.

Largely illegitimate financial debts, cruel in their consequences, blocked human progress for many countries over recent decades. Looking ahead, though, it is the inescapable ecological debts of the rich that threaten our collective future. And these debts have deeper roots than they are often credited with.

5

Ecological Debt

debt *(noun)* what one owes to another: what one becomes liable to do or suffer: a state of obligation or indebtedness: a duty: a sin *(bible)*; **debt of honour** a debt not recognised by law, but binding in honour; **debt of nature** death.

Chambers English Dictionary, 1989[1]

It was not the metal but its consequences, and these were not at all mysterious.

J.K. Galbraith, *Money: Whence it Came, Where it Went*, 1975

In a small wooden box with a snugly fitting hinged lid I kept a tiny coin collection. As a child I liked the way the box shushed when closed as the air compressed, and sucked as the lid opened. The coins were like keys opening the past, tarnished and nearly black. Victorian one penny pieces looked up more than a century old, impossibly remote in time to a child. Cold sour-tasting metal sat in my hand as proof of the existence of history. The coins unlocked the real world too. Innocent, exotic tokens from countries separated by unimaginable distances. Proof of quite other lives. The faces staring from the coins were once motherly and fatherly. Reassuring presences with authoritative writing around the rim, a name and a year. Certainty fixed like a nation's flag, unquestionable.

But as well as telling stories the coins also lied. They kept secrets that our teachers hid from us. When I opened the box as an adult the whispering of friendly ancestors and the wisps of unvisited continents were replaced by the smell of betrayal. Had I known how to read them, the coins used to run-up and

5. James Gillray's classic satire of 1805 on colonial powers, France and England, carving up the world for their own ends: 'The plumb-pudding in danger; – or – State Epicures taking un Petit Souper'. (Courtesy of the National Portrait Gallery, London)

pay-off debts also held dark stories of suffering, obligation and worse.

Now I look at them and feel queasy. As if I have unwittingly harboured terrorists and war criminals among my childhood memories. The Spain of the fascist dictator General Franco looks up from my palm. Here's a one franc coin from German occupied France on which the words *Liberté, Egalité, Fraternité* have been replaced with *Travail, Famille, Patrie* (work, family, fatherland), much more solid Nazi values. There's a phoenix rising on a ten drachma coin from the time of the Colonels, the right-wing military regimes in Greece established after a coup in 1967. The small change of Queen Victoria's British empire also washed-up in my little wooden box along with one of her cousins. A tiny ten centime coin from Leopold, King of the Belgians. It links us directly to another dark history which is part of the story of ecological debt.

Just as it is possible to look at something very familiar, like a childhood coin collection, and see it very differently with the benefit of experience, so it is possible to look at the world afresh with a simply altered perspective. School taught us that the emergence of the modern age, with its particular balance of power between nations and between rich and poor, was a largely benign process. In the absence of any other explanation we were left to assume that wealthy, advanced industrialised nations became so because they contained better, brighter people full of natural endeavour. But open the box of ecological debt and a different story escapes.

Belgium. Why is it so special? It is a country oddly caught between being a very large car park and the geopolitical centre of the modern age. For an English adolescent growing up in East Anglia – a flat area in the lower-middle right of the United Kingdom – Belgium was often the first taste we had of independent foreign travel. The scent of freedom turned a journey by tired train and heaving ferry into something exotic. Before cheap short-haul flights became available, and the centuries-long promise was realised of a tunnel beneath the channel between England and France, the continent was separated by the blinking strip lights and oily, petrol smell of ferries. Night time crossings on uncomfortable bright nylon chairs, and the struggle to keep nausea at bay from the ferry's deep lurching, were the trial and prelude to an opening adult world.

Napoleon Bonaparte gave us the concept of small man syndrome: an individual driven by his reduced physical stature to over-achieve in other ways. At certain moments in its history Belgium exhibited a similar phenomenon, small country syndrome. Belgium had a head of state, Leopold II, who helped spark the scramble for Africa's natural resources in the nineteenth century. It played host to the twentieth century carve-up of the Middle East's oil reserves. Today, Parc Leopold in Brussels backs on to the buildings of the European Parliament. Brussels is home to the rest of the machinery of the European Union, the principal economic counterbalance to otherwise largely unchallenged US power.

Belgium and its fellow former European imperial powers, together with their haphazard colonial projects, offer a window onto the history and emergence of ecological debt. It is a debt that has emerged alongside two unmistakable trends. On the one hand, the massive expansion of the global economy. And on the other, a dramatic divergence between rich and poor.

> The modern age opened, I think, with the accumulation of capital which began in the sixteenth century. I believe that this was initially due to the ... treasure of gold and silver which Spain brought from the New World into the Old. (J.M. Keynes, 'The economic possibilities for our grandchildren', 1930)[2]

Although he would not have thought in these terms, John Maynard Keynes made the point that the modern age was triggered by the Old world running-up an enormous natural resource debt with the New. In reality of course, in terms of deep historical human migration patterns, the New world was often just as Old, as it were, as the Old.

'From that time until today the power of accumulation by compound interest ... over two hundred years is such as to stagger the imagination', wrote Keynes. For reasons that will become obvious in the context of climate change, his view of the magic of compound interest is a useful, if underrated, warning.

Writing in 1930, he points out that the pirate turned 'Knight of the Realm', Francis Drake, robbed the Spanish robbers in 1580 using his ship the *Golden Hind*, to remarkable and lasting effect. Out of the share of the spoils taken by Queen Elizabeth I she was able to pay off England's foreign debt, balance the country's budget and have left over a substantial £40,000 sum in hand. The Queen invested in the Levant Company whose profits gave birth to the East India Company and, to simplify the story, hence the British empire. Keynes took an envelope and did a few sums. That £40,000 cash in hand, invested at 3.25 per cent compound interest, subsequently equalled the total value of England's foreign investments at various times, up to the point of Keynes' writing. By then in 1930, £1 brought home by Drake would have been worth £100,000. Today, that original, single pound would have turned into £1,032,701.[3]

Also, today, the ironically named 'positive environmental feedbacks' that are likely to accelerate climate change have become the compound interest of ecological debt. And, lest we in the already industrialised north think that we have got away with our earlier expropriation of majority world wealth and natural capital, we haven't. Someone has noticed.

Guaicaipuro Cuautemoc, a Latin American Indian chief, in a letter to 'all European governments', asked for his continent's money back:

> Paper after paper, receipt after receipt, signature after signature show that between 1503 and 1660 alone, 18.5 thousand kgs of gold and 16 million kgs of silver were shipped in San Lucar de Barrameda from America.[4]

The gold and silver, he concluded, must be considered as the first of several 'friendly loans', granted by America for Europe's development. Any other way of seeing 'such fabulous capital exports' would 'presuppose acts of war'. It was, he said, a 'Marshalltezuma Plan to guarantee the reconstruction of a barbarian Europe'. To repay in weight of gold and silver, now popular again in these deflationary times, and using the 'European formula' of compound interest would require an amount whose weight 'fully exceeds that of the planet earth'. However, any shame, apology or display of remorse on the part of the 'borrowers' seems still to be missing. On the contrary, the Old world and their descendants are prepared to go to court to claim and keep their stolen property.

Early in 2003 news emerged of a French galleon, the *Notre Dame de Deliverance*, once in service to the King of Spain. It had sunk in a storm off the Florida Keys on 1 February 1755.[5] It sailed from Havana loaded with 'treasure' dug from the mines of Peru, Colombia and Mexico and was heading back to fill the vaults of the Spanish King Charles III. Seventeen chests of gold bullion, over 15,000 gold doubloons, 1 million 'pieces of eight', 24 kg of silver and more silver ore, 153 gold snuff boxes and countless more items of silver, diamond jewellery and other precious stones were sitting at the bottom of the sea. In deep sea limbo, the wealth estimated to be worth $2 billion was long-lost to both the land of its original owners, and the Old world plunderers.

Media interest was aroused not, though, by yet further historical evidence of systematic colonial theft, but by claims and counter claims for the sunken cargo. The US-based Sub Sea Research company claimed to have located the wreck and was seeking salvage rights. But the Spanish government was 'almost certain' to claim the *Deliverance* under a Treaty of 1902 it has with the US. The French, too, as owners of the ship, were thought to be in with a chance. The countries not even mentioned in the haggle over the 'treasure' were those countries from whom the wealth was taken. It shows, perhaps, how deeply we have internalised and accepted the 'natural logic' of history's negative redistribution of wealth between continents to our, northern, advantage. It also shows how invisible are the real ecological and economic debts that have paid for the unequal world we live in today.

The observations are more than historical point scoring. According to economist J.K. Galbraith, 'Discovery and conquest set in motion a vast flow of precious metal from America to Europe'. Prices rose in Europe in response to the increase in supply of 'the hardest of hard money'. A combination of high prices and low wages freed up enormous amounts of capital for investment. These prices, notes Galbraith, rather than the tales of the conquistadors, 'were the message to most Europeans that America was discovered'. Some view that the influx of gold and silver *per se* gave birth to European capitalism. Galbraith prefers to emphasise that the consequences of the lustrous metals, rather than the metals themselves, were more important.[6]

Temples in America were looted of precious objects but it was the rape of the earth, principally for silver, that was most significant. Mines in Mexico and Peru were principally important. Most of this action was over by 1630 with the richest ores already exploited. But just under a century and a half of wealth extraction had been enough to refloat some of the Old world's great powers, previously made almost bankrupt by constant warring. Max Weber estimated that 70 per cent of Spain's and two thirds of other European nation's earnings from this time went to finance war, which also meant, of course, more colonial conquests.[7]

What happened between Europe and Central and South America in the sixteenth and seventeenth centuries, in terms of the way that it opened up enduring gaps of wealth and wellbeing between continents, was, rather than being historically isolated, the start of what a criminal psychologist might today call, 'repeat offending behaviour'.

'If the history of British rule in India were to be condensed into a single fact, it is this: there was no increase in India's per capita income from 1757 to 1947', observes Mike Davis in *Late Victorian Holocausts: El Niño Famines and the Making of the Third World*.[8] In Britain, on the other hand, per capita incomes rose 14 per cent between 1700 and 1760, 34 per cent between 1760 and 1820, and 100 per cent between 1820 and 1870.[9]

In a period during which the British empire expanded to become, for a time, the dominant global power, India, its 'jewel' in the imperial crown, stagnated economically according to Davis. In the last 50 years of the nineteenth century, when the empire was at its peak, income in India actually dropped by an estimated 50 per cent. From 1872 to 1921 the average Indian's life expectancy fell by one fifth.

Britain re-engineered India's economy towards cash crops for export. Opium, cotton, wheat all pushed out the farming of crops for local consumption. Grain exports went up from 3 to 10 million tons between 1875 and 1900. These were also years that included the 'worst famines in Indian history'. Forests were felled to build a railroad infrastructure vital for the new, crude, extractive economy. Cash, too, was a major export as the empire's merciless demands continued to bleed the country for taxes, even during times of famine. And famines there were, aplenty.

British rule was not without its internal critics. Lt Col. Osborne commented in 1879 that to the great mass of people, the English official was hard, mechanical and enigmatic, 'a piece of machinery possessing the powers to kill and tax and imprison'.

As the new economy dismantled established coping mechanisms, dispossessed great swathes of the population, and took away many of their customary rights, the population became much more vulnerable to 'natural', climatic disasters. Their increased exposure to a harsh climate walked hand in hand with increased integration into the world markets and a 'dramatic deterioration in their terms of trade'.

Explaining how the global economy expanded and diverged in this period both shows why millions more died in climate-related disasters such as famines than was necessary, and describes much of the 'origins of modern global inequality'. It shows also why it is still the case that, without radical changes, the poor, majority world stands to suffer disproportionately in the face of inevitable global warming.

Differences in wealth were minimal between the major civilisations of the eighteenth century. Research by Paul Bairoch led him to conclude that: 'It is very likely that, in the middle of the eighteenth century, the average standard of living in Europe was a little bit lower than that of the rest of the world'.[10]

Table 5.1 Shares of world GDP (%)

	1700	1820	1890	1952
China	23.1	32.4	13.2	5.2
India	22.6	15.7	11.0	3.8
Europe	23.3	26.6	40.3	29.7

Source: Angus Maddison, 1998[11]

As with India, China's slide from world economic prominence was helped by a major shove from Britain's gunboat economic diplomacy. Notably it happened around their forced incorporation into the opium trade with British India.

But both former (and emerging future) world powers gave up their positions only slowly and 'grudgingly' up until 1850.

The fact that India and China appeared to stand still, and then slide back, had less to do with the natural, indigenous dynamism of European capitalism and the liberating power of the free market, than with the fact that their competition was 'forcibly dismantled by war, invasion, opium and (in the case of Britain) a Lancashire-imposed system of one-way tariffs'. Davis points out that even if account is taken of internal cultural and political factors, from the end of the eighteenth century, 'every serious attempt by a non-Western society to move over into a fast lane of development or to regulate its terms of trade was met by a military as well as an economic response from London or a competing imperial capital'.

So much for Asia and Central and South America. Africa's turn was coming and with it, Belgium's as well, to furnish us with a shocking, but not untypical case-study, of naked colonial exploitation.

For centuries the Old world – in this case Europe – had been taking slaves from the Older world – Africa. If they survived transit, and millions did not, they were put to work on colonial plantations producing sugar, tea and tobacco around the world. In 1695 Bristol sugar merchant John Carey described slavery as 'the best Traffik the Kingdom hath ... as it doth occasionally give so vast an Imployment to our People both by Sea and Land'.[12] A member of parliament argued that the abolition of slavery would be 'ruinous to the colonies and commerce of the country'.[13]

Here is another kind of debt still waiting to be settled, one that demands more than embarrassed apologies from western world leaders as they visit the old slave ports of the west coast of Africa. Slavery remains an unsettled historical account that, like ecological debt in the form of global warming, is heading for the courts.

Apart from the slave trade, until the mid-1870s Africa was, for Europeans, still largely unexplored. Then, between 1876 and 1912, according to Thomas Pakenham, the scramble for Africa was complete.[14] Five European nations – Britain, Germany, Italy, Portugal and France – had sliced up Africa 'like a cake' and swallowed the pieces. It was an experience that the continent still suffers from today. Africa is home to the majority of the world's least developed countries, and is still tyrannised by conflicts directly related to the old, imperial power play.

Many of the half-myths that drew the Spanish to America also stirred the European imaginations in Africa. Once again, according to Pakenham, 'there were dreams of El Dorado, of diamond mines and goldfields criss-crossing the Sahara'. In the Congo, for example, the French imagined a cornucopia of natural resources: ivory, rubber, maize, copper, palm nuts and lead. The salivation was inspired by reports from a British explorer, Lt Cameron, in January 1876. He had been in central Africa and reported that, 'The interior is mostly a magnificent and healthy country of unspeakable richness'.[15] It was not to stay that way for long. King Leopold II of Belgium's subsequent reign of terror and pursuit of riches in the Congo remains, even today, a murderous, suppurating historical sore.

Rubber from the Congo made millions for Leopold. In the late 1890s over 1,000 tonnes per year were exported. Demand was high because in Europe Mr Dunlop had invented the pneumatic tyre to soothe the vibrating behinds of the travelling public. At home in Brussels Leopold spent his proceeds on building a fabulous baroque palace which he turned into a museum of central Africa. It still stands today only a short ride on tram number 44 from the city centre. Together with promises of social reform the story seemed dream fulfilling, benign and adventurous. The museum has only reluctantly and recently conceded that its benefactor's role in Africa was less than praiseworthy. Still the truth is hard to find on the museum walls, so powerful are the myths of innocent adventure and benevolent motivation. Leopold's weather-stained statue stands proud in an otherwise barren grass courtyard. Old-fashioned galleries line the walls inside decorated with poorly painted African landscapes. Assorted dead wildlife is rigidly perched against blocks of yellow and green for grassland, dark green and black for forest. A stuffed elephant lumbers on display. Visitors have thrown coins around its feet as if the animal was a wishing well. Even if it was, it's too late for the people

6. Leopold II's statue at the museum of Central Africa in Brussels, Belgium, built with the proceeds from the Congo rubber trade. It stands in a bare grassy courtyard, weathered and as stained as his legacy in Africa. And, as if it was scratched by ghosts, even this picture returned from the camera shop with a bleached, dripping stain on the print.

of central Africa who must have wished that Belgium never discovered the rubber trade.

Leopold, cousin of Britain's Queen Victoria, evidently wasn't just 'enjoying a slice of this magnificent African cake' (his words),[16] he was also cooking the books. The Congo rubber trade, it emerged, was based on murderous forced labour. Edmond Morel, a Quaker-influenced reformer who at first held conventional, supportive views of colonialism, found the trade to be 'legalized robbery enforced by violence'. Shocked at his discoveries in Leopold's private fiefdom he observed, 'It must be bad enough to stumble upon a murder. I had stumbled upon a secret society of murderers with a King for a croniman'.[17] It transpired that whole populations were being set impossible targets to collect rubber. Workers were 'encouraged' by the sight of their friends and family being summarily shot for under-performing. To save on bullets they were made to stand in a line and a single bullet shot through them. Others had ears and hands cut off. Pakenham records that soldiers collected the body parts by the 'basket load' to prove they were not wasting ammunitions. Farms were abandoned to collect rubber, leading to widespread hunger and starvation.

Some might dismiss the story of Leopold's Congo as an aberration. But tales from the textile wars between Britain and India also record the severing of thumbs to debilitate Indian textile workers. Stanley, of Dr Livingstone fame, earlier boasted that during his expeditions of 1876–77 he had, 'hurled himself down the Congo like a hurricane, shooting down terrified natives left and right'.[18] And, the year that Leopold's atrocities became the subject of serious public debate, the same production method was beginning to earn profits in French Congo, and Germany was pre-occupied with the extermination of the Herero people in south west Africa. In 1867 the discovery by an African shepherd of diamonds on the Veld was to transform South Africa and the British involvement in it. Again, the legacy lives on there as it does in the Congo. The recent war in the Democratic Republic of Congo is estimated to have cost 3 million lives. In 2003 an independent panel of the United Nations reported that multinational companies in collusion with governments were profiteering from the exploitation of natural resources like gold and other minerals. The plunder is alleged to be fuelling ongoing conflict.[19]

UNCTAD, the UN specialist body on trade, regularly shows in its *World Investment Reports*, that more than a century on, the

7. The shadow of colonialism is still over Africa. This advert produced by the Belgian branch of Amnesty International starkly comes to terms with the lasting destabilisation of a continent. Its reference to the twin towers invites us to consider the region's ongoing tragedy with the same respect felt towards the wounds of the United States.

major focus of the small amount of foreign direct investment going into Africa is still to extract its mineral and natural resources – oil from Nigeria and Angola, diamonds still and even a rare metal, tantalum made from coltan, needed for the manufacture of mobile phones.[20] When Joseph Conrad wrote *Heart of Darkness* (1902), says the writer Sven Lindqvist, the dark heart he was describing was not that of Africa the continent, but the souls of the European conquerors.[21]

There is another ecological tale to tell about the history of colonialism and the wealth divergence between nations. The story is told by Alfred Crosby in his book *Ecological Imperialism: The Biological Expansion of Europe, 900–1900*.[22] It shows how the conquering colonial nations took with them plants, animals and diseases that, as much as any of their weapons or religion, both directly and inadvertently displaced the people that they found in the lands they took control of. In *Guns, Germs and Steel* anthropologist Jared Diamond points out how the prior distribution of certain animals and plants that were easier to domesticate and cultivate, coupled to the greater geographical ease with which technology spread in some parts of the world than others, goes a long way to explain the contemporary global imbalance of power between nations.[23] These initial advantages helped lever the emerging colonial powers into a position from which they could benefit further from the natural resources they found in their supplicant lands. Very broadly speaking these events also set a pattern of unbalanced advantage in world trade from which the majority world is still struggling to escape.

There were huge profits to be made from the plants the colonists found and put to their own use – coffee, tea, opium, cocoa, rubber, coca, tobacco and potatoes, to name a few.[24] Imagine what the wealth of the majority, developing world would have been today if they had been able to apply the modern, broad-based patent protection system to these natural resources now insisted upon by industrialised countries. If for no reason other than to illustrate the indefensibly restrictive nature of contemporary intellectual property laws, such sums should be done. Upsetting the natural balance still further, and yet another aspect of ecological debt, today we also have to account for the impact of climate change on the rich diversity of plant and animal life. We are currently falling over the cliff of a mass extinction event. The science journal *Nature* reported threats of extinction for potentially more than one third of land-based plant and animal species by 2050 as a result of global warming.[25]

All of these are important. And the way that the modern markets for commodities are still controlled (it would be more honest to say 'fixed'), goes a long way to explain why the gap between rich and poor has persistently grown. The debt of climate change, however, proves to be the biggest, most life-threatening and urgent to address of all the ecological debts.

The consequence of this history emerges in simple statistics from the annual *UN Human Development Report*. Income gaps between people living in the richest fifth of countries and those living in the poorest fifth have steadily diverged.

Table 5.2   Ratio of Richest to Poorest Fifth of Countries

Year	Ratio
1820	3:1
1870	7:1
1913	11:1
1960	30:1
1990	60:1
1997	74:1

Source: UNDP 1999

One problem is, especially in more recent years, that orthodox neo-liberal theory predicts that exactly the opposite should happen.

'Convergence', noted the World Bank's 1995 *World Development Report*, 'is a notion dear to economists, who like its close fit with theory and abhorred by populists in rich countries, who see it as a threat to their incomes. Past experience, however, supports neither the hopes of the former nor the fears of the latter'. It goes on to observe, 'Overall, divergence, not convergence, has been the rule'.[26] The leading economic forecaster Paul Ormerod makes the same case in *The Death of Economics*.[27]

Recently, an intense debate has raged about the precise effects on overall poverty, and the gaps between rich and poor, of the past two decades of the accelerated (if partial), unmanaged movement of money, goods and services around the world. A key attack on critics of economic globalisation is that they are wrong to say that the global gap between rich and poor is growing.

Commentators like Clive Crook of the *Economist* and Martin Wolf of the *Financial Times* are, generally, fans of the benefits of trade and financial liberalisation as part of globalisation. They make the case that if you measure income not by US dollars (the nearest thing we have to a truly global currency) but by another measure called 'purchasing power parity' (PPP), which takes into account the different local costs of living, actually the gap between rich and poor countries is closing. And, therefore, globalisation must be working. But this argument is fundamentally flawed for several reasons.

First, dollars are an important measure in their own right, especially where economic globalisation is concerned. Whenever poor countries engage with the global economy they have to use dollars: to pay the service on their foreign debts, to conduct international trade, and, notably, to buy oil to run their domestic economies if they are energy importers.

Second, the percentage of population in the least developed countries (LDCs) living on less than $2 per day has remained effectively static over the last 35 years – while the wealth of the already industrialised countries has grown hugely – but the actual number of such poor people has more than doubled from around 211 million to 449 million. Their average daily consumption also marginally fell.

Robert Wade of the London School of Economics concludes that there is overwhelming evidence for the rise in global inequality.[28] Comparing several different methodologies for measuring income inequality based on both market exchange rates and PPP he says: 'the strong conclusion is that world inequality has risen ... [and] a rising share of the world's income is going to those at the top. Moreover the absolute size of the income gap between countries is widening rapidly'. Comparing the incomes of the richest 10 per cent of the world's population with the middle, and the middle with the poorest, global income distribution has become much more unequal over the past two decades.

Yet there is another story, which suggests the situation is even worse. And it underlines how inequalities within countries have worsened as a mirror of the situation between nations.

These arguments concern assets. The last three decades have seen an explosion in financial assets, like shares, which have been mostly captured by an already wealthy global minority. In the US, for example, since 1983 almost all the increase in wealth has accrued to the richest 10 per cent of the population. Also, crucially, almost all of the increase in debt since 1983 has accrued to the poorest 90 per cent of the population, while very little debt has accrued to the richest 10 per cent. In the UK the bottom 50 per cent of the population now owns only 1 per cent of the wealth, while in 1976 they owned 12 per cent. The dominant economic system's incentive structure, instead of 'trickle down', is causing a 'flood-up' of resources from the poor to the rich. So, as finance outstrips the real economy, and when we include assets as well as income in the equation, the gap between rich and poor is even bigger.

ECOLOGICAL DEBT – WHERE DID THE IDEA COME FROM?

Like most ideas, the notion of ecological debt emerged over time. No one person can claim credit for it. As is common in the history of ideas, many people thought about it unaware of others doing the same. In the mid-1990s I was deluded into believing my own originality when it occurred to me that the ecological debts of the rich were a perfect counter to the smug mismanagement by rich country dominated financial institutions of poor country financial debt. Others of course had, and were, thinking similar thoughts. But Britain was home to the rapidly growing Jubilee 2000 debt relief campaign and here it was absent from the debate.

Orthodox financial debt is often about the abstract world of finance. Remember the magical accounts of energy firm Enron, its accountants Andersen, and European consumer goods giant Parmalat, to name only a few companies who were crushed by experimenting with debt's dark forces. Ecological debt, on the other hand, is a lens through which to see how our real natural wealth is used and abused.

Debt in its money form is one of the few grand organising devices. It keeps people in place today, chained to desks and jobs they often hate, in the same way that the local Lord and the power of the church kept people tied to a plot of land in feudal times. Although debt is as old as human civilisation, there is something very different about its scale and ubiquity in our modern lives, both financial and ecological.

Up until about 30 years ago the way money was created and moved around was fairly controlled. Then, like a farm animal that escapes into the wild and breeds to pest-like proportions, things got out of control. 'The process by which banks create money', wrote Galbraith, 'is so simple that the mind is repelled'.[29] Financial assets include things like bank loans, mortgages, shares and bonds – mostly invented money, lent into existence.

In 1980 assets like these in five of the world's richest countries were already worth around $20 trillion, about five times their combined national incomes. Just 20 years later the figure had leapt to an amazing $140 trillion, ten times their combined incomes. This is a picture of a world living on money that has, quite literally, been imagined into existence.[30] While that might sound both esoteric and head-spinning, its consequences are very real. All that borrowing means that people consume more stuff and use up more natural resources.

We are accustomed to balance sheets showing cash as credit and debt but less so when it comes to natural resources. This is partly because of the still-powerful notion that nature is inexhaustible, a god-gifted income stream to the economy that doesn't need accounting for, and also because it is hard to know where to draw the environmental line and what is, and what is not, sustainable.

However, the balance sheets of ecological debt are now rising in prominence. They present a different picture of the world. They are informed by increasingly well-established norms on human rights, equality and international law governing the environment. Better scientific knowledge about the natural limits of the world around us and its life-supporting capabilities also plays a vital role. Other trends are influential too.

Modern international business is strictly controlled by laws protecting brand names, patents and other intellectual property. It is hardly surprising then that majority world nations now feel aggrieved that rich countries have, for centuries, systematically expropriated and exploited their natural resources and local technological innovations for profit, either without paying at all, as in the case of the bio-piracy of genetic plant, animal and human resources, or by paying too little, as is still the case with products like coffee, cotton and cocoa.

In the shadow of the now famously disastrous 1999 meeting of the WTO, Shri Murasoli Maran, India's Minister of Commerce and Industry, stood up to address a special United Nations conference devoted to trade. He decried the fact that

Britain had, while historically enjoying a guaranteed supply of cheap natural resources, by manipulating trade especially in textiles ensured that others would at best stand still in their development and at worst slip into reverse:

> India had supplied Europe with calicos and muslins, as China had supplied silks and satins. The cotton towns of Surat of India, Dhaka and Murshidabad of Bangladesh, which is now a least developed country, were described by Robert Clive in 1757 as just 'as extensive, popular and rich as the city of London'. What happened to the Indian textile industry was repeated in other industries. The native iron smelting industries of India that could produce six-ton 24 feet steel pillars at Qutab Minar 1,500 years ago ... were wiped out. That's how we lost out and became part of the 'Third World'.[31]

Making the same point at the same meeting in a less articulate but equally effective manner, an enterprising member of *Pâtissiers sans Frontières* landed a cream pie into the outraged face of Michel Camdessus, retiring head of the International Monetary Fund.

The general case for indignation is supported by the chronic long-term depression of commodity prices in international markets, markets dominated by northern multinational companies. Capping all of these, though, is the use of fossil fuels and the spectre of climate change.

Diverse debates on politics, history, the environment and society prepared the ground for seeing the world through the lens of ecological debt.[32] But what, exactly, is it? If you take more than your fair share of a finite natural resource you run up an ecological debt. If you have a lifestyle that pushes an ecosystem beyond its ability to renew itself, you run up an ecological debt. In short it is a different way of understanding economic relations that grounds us in the real world of natural resources. The stuff, in other words, upon which the myriad exchanges of markets really depend. The idea of ecological debt has several historical roots.

In the nineteenth century the patriotic observer of the British empire Robert Southey had a character in his *Letters from England* comment, 'all parts of the world are ransacked for the

Englishman's table'.[33] Writer George Orwell wrote in 1937 that for England to enjoy its material comforts, 'a hundred million Indian's must live on the verge of starvation'. Orwell began his working life in the Indian Imperial Police. In spite of his later radical reputation his early politics were ambiguous. He excused the 'evil state of affairs' because otherwise the empire would be thrown 'overboard' and England would become 'a cold and unimportant little island where we should all have to work very hard and live mainly on herrings and potatoes'.[34]

The 1960s saw a second Malthusian wave of anxiety about unsupportable population levels. It inspired Georg Borgstrom to shine a light on the 'ghost acres' that wealthy countries like Britain depended on in other lands to feed their people. Britain required an even larger plot of land overseas to meet domestic demand than it had under cultivation at home. Ivan Illich brought the two big themes of this book together in 1974, but unconnected to global warming. In *Energy and Equity* he said that a society based on low energy use and equal access to resources would, regardless of environmental collapse, be more convivial and supportive of democracy. 'A low energy policy allows for a wide choice of lifestyles and cultures', he wrote. 'If, on the other hand, a society opt for high energy consumption, its social relations must be dictated by technocracy and will be equally distasteful whether labelled capitalist or socialist'.[35]

In the late 1980s enquiries into equity and geographical carrying capacity introduced the language of 'environmental space'. At the start of the 1990s Canadian geographer William Rees began talking about 'ecological footprints'. It became possible to look at the size of a given 'hinterland' needed to support an industry or population. The late Indian environmentalist Anil Agarwal with colleague Sunita Narain applied a harder political edge in 1990 in *Global Warming in an Unequal World*, which exposed the wildly different degrees to which people in rich and poor countries pollute. They also wrote openly about what they called 'environmental colonialism'.[36]

The answers these enquiries threw up were often obvious. Rich people and big cities took up a lot of space – the resources of 'distant elsewheres'. They were like cars badly parked at a supermarket, crossing several slots and taking up more than their fair share of space.

Still reeling from at least a decade-long debt crisis, born of international economic chaos and commercial banks pushing loans onto countries at a time when interest rates were rock bottom, a handful of South American academics pointed to the exploitation of their countries' natural resources and started speaking about ecological debt. In the run up to the 1992 Earth Summit a group from Latin America and the Caribbean put together a report called *Our Common Agenda*. 'The industrial revolution was based in large part on the exploitation of natural resources in ways which did not reflect their true costs', they argued, concluding, 'the industrialised countries have incurred an ecological debt with the world'.[37] Such debts today get broadly defined to include pollution, theft of resources and disproportionate use of the environment. Ecuador is now home to a campaign to reclaim the debt.[38]

Strikingly, however, promising beginnings for a revolutionary idea came to little. After the initial optimism of people gathering together in Rio de Janeiro for the Earth Summit, worried about both the environment and social problems, it all drifted apart. Environmentalists went to environmental meetings and anti-poverty campaigners went to meetings of the World Bank and IMF, who usually meet together like tweedle dum and tweedle dee.

In spite of orthodox debt being top of the anti-poverty agenda at meeting after international meeting during the mid-to-late 1990s, and into the new millennium, both climate change as an issue, and ecological debt as a concept, were virtually nowhere. In 1999, frustrated with the dynamics of the debt debate, in collaboration with two friends I wrote a report called *Who Owes Who?*[39] which was well-reported in the British media. I took it to the annual meetings of the World Bank in Washington DC. Late the previous year 155 mph winds from Hurricane Mitch devastated Central America, and the event was still in people's minds. The Bank refused to cancel debts owed by the affected countries. At the time Nicaragua and Honduras were paying debt service at the rate of $2.2 million per day. The Honduran President, Carlos Flores, said,

'We lost in 72 hours what we have taken more than 50 years to build'.[40]

In a large open meeting with the World Bank's chief economist, Joseph Stiglitz, I put it to him that things were back to front. Shouldn't we, the rich world, be paying the majority world much more ecological debt service for the increasingly severe weather events associated with global warming than they were paying us for questionable financial debts that the Bank was equally responsible for? Laughter rippled around the room, some nervous, while others enjoyed the speaking panel's obvious momentary discomfort. There was no official answer that they could give.

Since Mitch struck, echoes of Central America's experience still sound. When Cyclone Heta flattened the South Pacific island Niue with winds of 185 mph in early 2004, the nation's Premier lamented it had wiped out 'whatever we have made in the past years'.[41] All mainstream projections suggest that the echoes will become more frequent instead of dissipating.

END OF THE FREE LUNCH

A growing awareness that there are global commons which provide 'public goods', like the capacity of the atmosphere and seas to absorb pollution, is waking people up to an important contradiction. There are things to which we all have an innately equal claim, yet which are currently very unequally used.

Where climate is concerned, there is now a good understanding of how much pollution the atmosphere can absorb before its balance is disturbed. The chief pollutant, CO_2, is fundamental because it is a by-product of what fuels the global economy. The two are hardwired – broadly speaking more economic activity means more CO_2, means more climate disruption. From this elegantly simple equation enormous consequences flow.

If a global commons like the atmosphere, to which we all have an equal claim, is being overused and corrupted by one group of people, they accrue an ecological debt to the wider community who also depend on the commons. There have been attempts to put cash costs to ecological debt.[42] But with global warming, the real debt is the concentration of greenhouse gases in the atmosphere that upsets the balance of the weather. While this does imply much needed compensation to developing countries for the ensuing damage, it importantly also demands a plan of action to eradicate the debt.

Conventional wisdom on the environment is a parody of attitudes during the global economic turbulence of the 1970s, when, on the international economic scene, 'debt was good' because interest rates were effectively negative. The same wisdom would conclude that ecological debt is good – if it knew such a thing existed – because there has been no obvious interest rate to pay. But, just as the brief moment couldn't last when petro-dollars made money too cheap not to borrow, environmental interest rates in the darkening cloud of climate change are set to explode skyward.

The reckless environmental credit boom is over and a huge ecological deficit has opened up. Recrimination is inevitable and the books have to be put straight for the planetary budget. Yet at one level there is a danger that the policies necessary to preserve a habitable planet could leave nations ungovernable. Fuel price riots in Europe were possibly only a foretaste of greater upheaval. Can we, in the industrialised world, accept the consequences of our ecological debts? It is time to look at the world upside down. How will it seem as we make the necessary moves to managing the world economy against new, inescapable physical realities? How will it seem as we try to maximise returns to all of us who are shareholders in the global environment, rather than the few who are shareholders in multinational corporations?

The tale of ecological debt in the modern age began with gold and silver. It was the beginning of a massive expansion in size, and a divergence between rich and poor, in the global economy. But the story moves rapidly on to the black stuff of fossil fuels, and how we came to be so uniquely dependent upon them. Only by understanding the dynamics of this addiction will we be able to break it.

6

The Carbon Debt

The meek shall inherit the earth, but not its mineral rights.

J. Paul Getty, US oil magnate

We hold these truths to be self-evident, that all men are created equal.

US Declaration of Independence

Recognition of the inherent dignity and of the equal and inalienable rights of all members of the human family is the foundation of freedom, justice and peace in the world.

Universal Declaration of Human Rights

In the early twentieth century roads were so bad, and petrol-driven vehicles so unreliable, that even oil companies moved their products around by horse and cart.[1] Less than one hundred years later airports and flight traffic are set for massive expansion. New runways and more and bigger planes are planned for Britain. London is the principal hub of flights in Europe and for those passing through to more distant destinations. In the century since the first powered human flight in December 1903 the global rich have become increasingly addicted to this least environmentally friendly form of transport. Ironically the Wright brothers, Orville and Wilbur from Millville, Indiana, formerly ran a bike shop, promoting the most environmentally friendly form of getting around. In a few generations, for those who can afford it, the exotic has become ordinary. A type of transport that forces you to use more than your global fair share of fossil fuels has become a lifestyle 'right', rather than a luxury. But some are beginning to ask questions.

On a summer night in London the audience at a fashionable modern theatre was becoming restless. They had been promised a show by a small group of performers. The lights went down, the performance began, but instead of the expected actors, they got me. The reason for the group's absence was carbon debt. Platform is a theatre company committed to ecological principles. They had been invited to tour several locations in the United States. James Marriott, one of the group's prime movers, didn't want to add to his personal ecological debt by taking a fuel-hungry transatlantic flight. He wanted to see if it was possible to travel differently. He would go by sea instead. Doing so he would take longer, several days in fact, and miss his appointment at the theatre. So the audience got me, reading the presentation that James and I discussed in the preceding weeks.[2]

If more people thought about what it took to fill the fuel tank of a plane flying across the Atlantic they would, perhaps, also think twice about flying. Thanks to a friendly, anonymous contact working in the oil fields off Britain's North Sea coast we know the journey that fuel itself takes.

To allow a 747 jumbo jet to take off from London to fly to the United States it takes:

- 30 minutes for oil and gas to rise 10,000 feet from the Lower Palaeocene sandstone layer of the geological strata underneath the North Sea. This layer was created about 67 million years ago.
- 2 days for the oil and gas to pass down the Forties Pipeline to Kinneil.
- 2 hours to separate the oil from the gas at the Kinneil separation plant.
- 2 hours for the crude to travel the 15 miles to the loading terminal at Hound Point.
- 17 hours to load the crude oil on to a 300,000 tonne tanker at Hound Point in the Firth of Forth.

- Another whole day for a tanker to sail to Coryton Refinery on the Thames Estuary in Essex.
- 120 hours for the crude to be refined into aviation fuel, as well as other products.
- 9 hours for this aviation fuel to pass by pipeline to the fuel depot at Heathrow airport.
- 15 minutes for a 747 to refuel its tanks at Heathrow's Terminal 3.
- Half an hour for the 747, bound for New York, to take off and, above the Irish Sea, achieve a speed of 555 mph and an altitude of 31,000 feet.
- This hydroscope takes under 10 days to run its course – for liquid to move from 10,000 feet below sea level to 31,000 feet above sea level, for a liquid hydro carbon to turn into a carbon-dioxide gas. For something laid down 67 million years ago to melt into air.

If among all the world's people we were to share equally a safe volume of greenhouse gas emissions, a single long-haul flight would take up one person's entire ration for several years. That's why this mechanical collapse of time and space is driving the accumulation of carbon debt. Millions of years evolving the fuel, shrunk to a few days' preparation and rapid consumption. The consequence? Climatic disturbance that will take thousands of years to correct.

If the part of the Gulf stream that warms large parts of northern Europe is switched off by global warming, a realistic possibility ironically plunging whole countries into an unfamiliarly cold climate, it could be 60,000 years before the old flow of warmer waters returns. Then it might seem rather short-sighted to have used 'saving time' as both the rationale and apology for increasingly energy intensive lifestyles.

'All life depends on plants', is the motto of the Royal Botanical Gardens at Kew, in London. Although the economy is obviously a subset of the environment, the alarming resilience of the opposite notion, that the environment is a luxury only to be afforded by successful economies, means that this simple point requires tedious repetition. It is very easy to forget that

– apart from the plants that give us drugs to heal, food to stop us going hungry, and chemicals and materials to make things with – the global economy is still more than four-fifths dependent on fossil fuels derived from plants, for energy.[3] Even mainstream debates among environmental economists about natural capital appear as an exotic fringe in the macho world of 'real' economics.

Yet, it is surprising how directly, and yet invisibly, the fates of our natural resources are interwoven with the self-absorbed human economy. For example, by peculiar coincidence, the financial loss to Africa due to its declining terms of trade on primary commodities – plant products and stuff dug from the ground – in little over a decade between 1980 and 1992 was around $350 billion (it has been much more since). This figure was more-or-less the same amount of unpayable debt held by the group of heavily indebted poor countries, mostly in Africa, that the Jubilee 2000 debt relief campaign mobilised to get written-off. Another example would be the direct link between land and income distribution. Numerous studies have found a direct link between unequal ownership of land and the income gaps between rich and poor.[4]

Just as the silver and gold of the Americas were the midwife and milk-full breast at the birth of western capitalism, and the systematic expropriation of majority world natural resources fed it through childhood, so the use of coal and the discovery of oil in the second half of the nineteenth century were the food and intoxicating liquor that marked industrial capitalism's passage from adolescence into adulthood.

AND SO TO THE BLACK STUFF

New machines and burgeoning empires were hungry for the frozen sunshine of coal in the mid-1800s. Europe was being transformed by industrial revolution. Great wealth was generated but at the same time people on both sides of the colonial relationship were brutalised by the process of change. The appalling conditions faced by miners in France were chronicled in Zola's novel *Germinal* (1885). In Britain about one thousand miners were killed each year between 1856 and 1886.[5] Wilfred Owen, the poet better known for his First World War writing, in his poem 'Miners' described the, 'moans down there / Of boys that slept wry sleep, and men / Writhing for air'.[6]

In France between 1850 and 1873 the production or use of coal leapt from 7 million tons to nearly 25 million. In Germany it went from 5 million to 36 million. In the United Kingdom, the dominant power of the day, it soared from 37 million tons to 112 million. In Belgium, too, it tripled.[7] Demand was being driven by new developments like the railways. In the 1840s Europe laid 13,000 miles of new railway, America 7,000 miles. In the 1870s the figure had risen to 39,000 and 51,000 miles respectively.[8] James Watt, who commercialised the steam engine, prophetically remarked 'Nature can be conquered if we can but find her weak side'.[9] But as Barbara Freese, a historian of coal, points out, 'In looking for nature's weak side, we found our own'.[10]

Throughout Europe for the duration of the nineteenth century, fuels like charcoal that could be renewed in the time it takes to grow a tree were being replaced by coal-based fuels that would take millions of years to replace. As mentioned above, one estimate suggests that today we are returning carbon to the atmosphere one million times faster than nature took to remove it.[11]

To produce iron in France in 1825, 194 tons of charcoal were used compared to just 5 tons of coke, the fuel produced by burning off the more volatile compounds in coal. Just 60 years later, France was using 1,600 tons of coke and just 29 of charcoal. The addiction had taken hold.

It has been fashionable over the last decade to point to an increasingly 'weightless economy'. The information age was supposed to reduce our dependence on raw materials. But where one of the *most* raw materials, carbon from fossil fuels, is concerned, the global economy just keeps getting heavier. Among rich countries alone between 1973 and 2001 energy supply from coal, oil and gas went up by a quarter.[12] Globally the rise was more than half.

Virtual shopping via the internet heralded the anticipated weightless economy. But studies of e-commerce in the Netherlands instead showed a significant increase of road traffic. Overall, pollution increased 28 per cent from 1975 to the end of the century in rich countries. In the US fuel economy in cars recently hit its lowest level for 20 years as technical improvements went into performance rather than fuel efficiency. There was virtually no air freight before 1950, now, by way of illustration, there is the equivalent to one tonne of goods travelling 100 billion kilometres by plane each year.[13]

Had they but known it at the time, the early industrialising nations were as successful in their disproportionate occupation of the atmosphere with carbon emissions, as they were in their military occupation of the terrestrial world. Up until around the time of the Second World War, they had managed this atmospheric occupation largely through exploiting their own fossil fuel reserves. However, from around 1950 another form of divergence occurred as industrialised countries became more and more dependent on energy imports. For so-called less developed countries the experience was a mirror image. From the same time, they began to produce more than they consumed.[14]

Using a World Energy Gini Coefficient (this rather exotic term, which has nothing to do with clouds emerging from bottles and granting your wishes, is simply a way of measuring inequality) Bruce Podobnik shows that for the second half of the twentieth century, with the exception of one decade, global inequality in energy consumption continued to increase in line with a long historical trend. By 1998, the wealthiest fifth of the world's population was consuming 68 per cent of commercial energy, and the poorest fifth 2 per cent. But the peaks and troughs of inequality paint an even more extreme picture.

A decade after the UN Framework Convention on Climate Change (UNFCCC) was signed, ranging from the US to Australia, Canada and across Europe, countries were, per person, pumping out more carbon dioxide than they were at the time of the Earth Summit in 1992. To put that into perspective, beginning from the stroke of New Year, as they sit down to their evening meal on 2 January, a US family will already have used, per person, the equivalent in fossil fuels that a family in Tanzania will depend on for the whole year.

Even with technological advances in energy efficiency, and the creeping introduction of renewable energy, there is still an incredibly close correlation between crude measures of economic wealth and the consumption of fossil fuels. Rich people pump more greenhouse gases into the atmosphere.

Unfortunately, until renewable energy goes mainstream, access to conventional economic opportunity and access to fossil fuels are more or less the same thing. It is a big problem. It means that there is no more fundamental issue than the distribution of wealth in a carbon constrained world economy.

Estimates vary, but scientists suggest that to stop dangerous climate change becoming irreversible, over the twenty-first century 60 to 90+ per cent cuts in greenhouse gas emissions will be necessary. Understandably, however, the majority world believes it has a right to become very much richer in the material things that the citizens of rich countries already take for granted. Without a radical change in how we manage the global commons of the atmosphere, this means one of three things. Either there has to be a massive reduction in rich country emissions, far beyond the scope of the current international agreement, the Kyoto Protocol, to give poor countries the environmental space to develop. Or, poor countries are simply to be denied the carbon-rich development path followed by industrialised countries. An instruction that, to a degree, they can simply and understandably ignore. Or, finally, the third option is that the engine of conventional development keeps running on carbon, and there is climatic chaos. In this case a radical or, perhaps, logical change of direction suddenly becomes an attractive option.

Yet it's easy to forget how relatively new this predicament is. The global economy's oil addiction is little more than a century old. It began in America at the same time that the use of coal for industry in Europe exploded. After early discoveries in Oil Creek, Titusville, Pennsylvania, in the US in the late 1850s, it wasn't until 1870 that John D. Rockefeller formed the Standard Oil Company of Ohio. No other single event bound the fate of economies as tightly to the fate of the environment and world politics.

In 1975 Anthony Sampson wrote his classic work, *The Seven Sisters: The Great Oil Companies and the World They Made*.[15] Where Britain was concerned, says Sampson, oil was, from the beginning, associated with 'national survival and diplomacy, and oil soon seemed part of the empire itself'. The firm Royal Dutch that later merged with and assumed control of the British firm Shell had 'origins belonging to the world of Conrad'. The Anglo-Persian Oil Company, which from its start enjoyed the special protection of the British government, later became Anglo-Iranian before changing again to become British Petroleum, now BP, one of the world's largest companies. During its early years, Sampson notes, the firm 'had a captive production, and a captive market, protected by the army in order to supply the navy'. In an echo of Drake's gold and silver, and his relationship with Elizabeth I, in the early 1920s BP was making handsome profits 'from which the Treasury collected its half', and from which Winston Churchill, then Chancellor of the Exchequer, boasted of the financial rewards the government received. Perhaps predictably, BP was resented by foreign, especially colonial, countries 'as an arm of government'.

In 1928 the greatest 'carve up' in fossil fuel history, known as the Red Line Agreement, divided up the oil resources of what was considered as the former Ottoman Empire in the Middle East, by granting hugely one-sided concessions to British and American oil companies. At a meeting in Ostend in Belgium (that country again), oil entrepreneur Calouste Gulbenkian literally took a red pencil and drew a line around Saudi Arabia, Iraq, Jordan, Syria and Turkey, at a stroke changing more than just their destinies. No participation, for example, was allowed in the oil concession for the government of Iraq, which had wanted a minor role in a partnership to exploit their oil. It became a source of lasting bitterness.

Certain places and events recur in history. During the First World War and the time in the 1920s when Churchill was feeling so smug about Britain's new oil income, two countries in particular felt the impact of the world's latest weapon of war: bombs dropped from the air. They were Afghanistan and Iraq. The reasons too, were similar. Britain wanted to control both uncompliant local leaders for political advantage, and any natural resources. In 1919 Kabul, Jalalabad and Dacca were bombed by the British under Arthur 'bomber' Harris, the man still criticised today for the extensive bombing of civilian targets in the Second World War. In 1920 the target was Iraq and the aim was to bomb a country only recently free from Turkish rule back into control by Britain and to attack from the air so as to avoid the need for a physical occupation force. The novelty of this approach led to 'wild confusion' among local people in Baghdad. A report described how: 'Many of them [the elderly, women and children] jumped into a lake, making a good target for the machine guns'.[16] In 1923, after further bombing in Baghdad, a more sympathetic officer, Lionel Charlton, reported in horror, after visiting a local hospital, the 'indiscriminate bombing of a populace ... with the liability of killing women and children, was the nearest thing to wanton slaughter'.[17] Arthur Harris on the other hand saw things more from the empire's point of view. Local people now knew, he said, 'what real bombing means, in casualties and damage; they now know that within forty five minutes a full-sized village can be practically wiped out and a third of its inhabitants killed or injured by four or five machines which offer them no real target, no opportunity for glory as warriors, no effective means of escape'.[18] Towns and villages from India to Iran, Egypt, Somaliland, Trans-Jordan, Southwest Africa and elsewhere all received similar treatment in the years after 1918 to teach them their place. It is a lesson that the modern imperial powers of the US and Britain are still teaching.

Unbalanced concessions between oil companies and host country governments, grossly in favour of the companies, were a particular feature of the late days of empire. Unsurprisingly the companies fell victim during the subsequent waves of national independence movements. In 1969 Libya supplied a quarter of western Europe's oil and used its position to break the companies' steel-grip and emboldened the Organisation of Petroleum Exporting Countries (OPEC) for the great confrontations in the 1970s with their old masters.

With geopolitical shock waves that live with us still, from Libya in North Africa to the almost permanent battleground of Angola, and mighty Nigeria, oil has been, and remains, the colour of struggle, conflict and debt; between rich and poor, between global north and global south.

In 2002 Nigeria was producing around 2 million barrels of oil a day. Crude oil accounted for 80 per cent of government revenue and 90 per cent of foreign exchange earnings. The approximate $11 billion earnings from oil sales, shared equally, would give each Nigerian about 27 cents a day. But Nigeria racked up financial debts of $5.6 billion at market rates under its military dictators. Just servicing its debts in 1999 and 2000 cost Nigeria $1.4 billion each year. Several mainstream banks including Barclays, HSBC and Merill Lynch were censured by City regulators for flouting anti-money laundering rules in relation to accounts linked to Nigerian dictator General Abacha. He stole an estimated $4 billion from his country. Other parts of Nigeria's debts are made up of foreign funded projects that have failed due to dependence on foreign inputs, equipment and technical support.

Nigeria, however, still has to keep paying with the revenue from its oil. At the same time the cost of environmental degradation in Nigeria, much of it in the oil producing Niger Delta, for a long time a playground of the likes of Shell, Mobil, Texaco and Chevron, has been put at $5.1 billion. By early 1998 around 14,000 compensation claims for oil-related damages had been presented by groups, individuals and communities to the Nigerian courts.[19] Harder to cost are the ethnic tensions exacerbated in the oil areas. The southern Delta State produces 40 per cent of Nigeria's oil. Violence during state and federal elections in early 2003, part of an ongoing struggle to control oil resources, left hundreds dead and thousands homeless.[20]

Only recently the world has been divided again by a conflict in Iraq with multiple causes, but among them, the control of oil certainly one. And in South America, the US has been happy to undermine the government of Venezuela, with fears over the price of oil a likely motivation.

Were he writing today with the benefit of hindsight and the knowledge of global warming Sampson might have written instead *The Great Oil Companies and the World They Broke*.

Almost all of humankind's fossil fuel emissions of carbon dioxide, the main global warming gas, have happened over the twentieth century. Coal dominated first, followed by oil. The use of natural gas took off in the 1970s. All along there has been an almost exact correlation between greenhouse gas emissions and levels of economic activity – they rise and fall together.

It is possible to see the changes in the life of a single family. James Marriott spent years looking at the oil industry and its impact on our lives. He worked out that his great grandfather was the first in their family to smell petrol. James was the first to travel in a car before he was born. His own parents are the first generation to spend their pensions on international air travel. Because of climate change, they also may be the last.

Aubrey Meyer of the London-based Global Commons Institute, likens the growth of emissions and concentration levels of carbon dioxide to watching an explosion in slow motion.

In particular, the sections of the global economy that have grown rapidly are also those that are most fossil fuel dependent, such as international trade. In the postwar period trade grew much faster than production. Between 1950 and the mid-1990s, while total world output grew by a factor of five, exports went up by over 14 times.[21]

Economic globalisation that depends on fossil fuels for its life's blood is also socially divisive – increasing risk and instability – and undermining the basic security needed for viable livelihoods and stable communities. Even the ultra-conservative former head of the IMF, Michel Camdessus, recognised that, 'Poverty is the ultimate threat to stability in a globalising world ... The widening gaps between rich and poor within nations, and the gulf between the affluent and the most impoverished nations, are morally outrageous, economically wasteful, and potentially socially explosive'.[22]

By making a few assumptions about what levels of equitable, global per capita carbon emissions are sustainable, it is possible to indicate where – by over or under-consuming – people are running up ecological or, more specifically, carbon debts and credits.

In 1998 I was working at the development agency Christian Aid. We had launched, with others, and were in the middle of the Jubilee 2000 debt relief campaign. At the time, oblivious to much of the background described above, and feeling that many of the orthodox foreign debts of poor countries were illegitimate anyway, I thought that global warming was the clearest case of a much more threatening and genuine debt crisis. Only this crisis reversed the typical roles of creditor and debtor. With Aubrey Meyer and Nick Robins of the International Institute of Environment and Development, I produced a graph comparing two groups of countries: the G7 nations, usually the 'creditors', and the group of highly indebted poor countries, the so-called HIPC nations (see Figure 6.1). It reverses the traditional roles. In ecological or carbon terms it shows that, per person, the mostly African HIPC nations are in credit, and the industrialised G7 countries are in debt.

Based on assumptions of the scientists of the IPCC, in 1995 to stabilise atmospheric greenhouse gas concentrations at a safe level implied a global, equal, per capita entitlement of about 0.43 tons of carbon. Typical US per capita carbon use in 1995 was 5.3 tons.[23] That represents a potential carbon debt for a single year of 4.87 tons per US citizen. The British government estimates that the damage-cost of carbon emissions related to how they disturb the climate – but not including their much larger general economic value – is in the range of $56 to $223 per ton of carbon (t/C). That means that just to account for the damage-cost of their unsustainable carbon use, each US citizen would have been liable to pay between $273 and

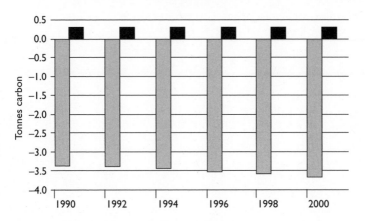

Figure 6.1 Carbon Debts of the G7 Nations (▢) Compared to the Carbon Credits of the Heavily Indebted Poor Countries (HIPCs) (■)

Source: Simms, *Who Owes Who?* (1999) Christian Aid

$1,086 each year for the privilege to pollute more than their fair share of carbon dioxide.[24] Nationally, for the US alone, at today's prices that implied a bill of between $73 billion and $290 billion: money that could be channelled to invest in sustainable development and the Millennium Development Goals for reducing global poverty. An assessment of the value of the G7 countries' economic output at around the same time as the calculations above, built on the foundations of unsustainable per capita carbon use, throws up a figure in 1994 prices of between $13 and $15 trillion.[25]

The economic costs of global warming are rising dramatically. The number of major climate-related and flood disasters quadrupled during the 1990s compared to the 1960s.[26] Resulting economic losses increased eight-fold over the same period. If that continues, as we've seen according to the insurance industry, by about 2065 we will be facing the bizarre situation whereby the cost of natural disasters driven by global warming will overtake the value of the gross world product. It is time, as they say, to try something different. It is vital that the global economy stages a rapid, managed retreat from its fossil fuel addiction because there is no other way to get off-the-hook from impending climate chaos.

WHO OWES WHO?

Industrialised countries still pursue highly indebted poor countries to pay off their foreign financial debts. They do so at great cost to the millions who subsequently go without vital health and education services. But this book argues that industrialised countries are themselves responsible for the much larger debt to the global community of climate change. The prospect of global warming introduces a level of environmental determinism that takes political debate beyond the usual contest over whether to put money into this or that particular budget. It takes us all into the theatre of mutual survival (or not, as the case may be). Put another way, if we don't get it right, we've had it.

Rich countries' reckless use of fossil fuels has created climate change. But it is poor people in poor countries that suffer first and worst from both extreme weather conditions related to climate change, and from the struggle to clear unpayable, and often illegitimate, conventional foreign debts.

My motivation to put ecological debt on the political agenda is not to put a price on nature, or its contamination, which is an inescapably fraught exercise. It is to set the parameters for a paradigm shift. The discussion is about how and why countries and people become impoverished and enriched, and at the expense of what and who. The crucial question is, who owes who? And further, what should be done about it? To date international attempts to manage the twin crises of ecological debt and foreign debt have exhibited a systematic bias against the majority world. In both cases, those with the least role in creating the problems bear the greatest burdens. And those most responsible for the crises appear to escape responsibility. The following brief comparison of leading efforts to tackle poor country dollar debt and rich country ecological debt reveals deep perversity and political failure.

A TALE OF TWO DEBTS: FOREIGN DEBT VERSUS CARBON DEBT – THE HIPC INITIATIVE AND THE KYOTO PROTOCOL[27]

How the international community has managed these two great crises – climate change and poor country debt – shows how confused our priorities are.

Who Pays the Price?

Carbon debt: the poorest people in the poorest countries suffer overwhelmingly the worst impacts of climate change. By 2025 nearly half of people living in developing countries will be vulnerable to 'hydro-meteorological disasters', otherwise known as floods and storms.

HIPC debt: the populations of the poorest countries pay for the debt through their taxes and through the loss of investment in schools and hospitals.

Who is Responsible for the Debts?

Carbon debt: historically, the industrialised countries of the rich world are almost entirely responsible for climate change.

HIPC debt: the debts that weigh heavily on the shoulders of poor people are invariably the consequence of collusion between elites North and South. That said, the scale of outstanding unpayable debt for poor countries is oddly similar to the amount they lost in declining terms of trade in a single decade from the early 1980s.

Who Controls the Process?

Carbon debt: rich countries drive the Kyoto Protocol and decide for themselves how much they should do to control climate change.

HIPC debt: rich countries and their appointed representatives in the financial institutions drive the HIPC initiative and decide how much poor countries should pay.

Are the Targets Adequate?

Carbon debt: the Kyoto Protocol proposes an average 5.2 per cent cut in CO_2 emissions for rich countries against 1990 levels.

The scientific consensus is that cuts of 60 to 80 per cent are necessary. Some, such as the head of UNEP, go further calling for cuts of 90 per cent or more. Britain's Secretary of State, Margaret Beckett, said that current US policy could leave their emissions 25 per cent higher in 2010 than in 1990, compared to the 7 per cent cut that the US agreed to in Kyoto.[28]

HIPC debt: notionally, HIPC will write off around one third of the debts of 23 qualifying countries. Debt experts Jubilee Research based at the New Economics Foundation (**nef**) estimate that 39 of 42 countries need 100 per cent cancellation plus a doubling in aid to reach the Millennium Development Goals.

How is Stabilisation Achieved?

Carbon debt: no official proposal in the international negotiations comes close to stabilising climate change.

HIPC debt: a macro-economic plan that imposes measures for economic stabilisation is a pre-condition to qualifying for conventional debt relief.

Is Adjustment Demanded?

Carbon debt: US citizens lead one of the most fossil fuel intensive lifestyles in the world. Yet the US administration dismisses as unacceptable any demand to change the American way of life in response to climate change.

HIPC debt: agreeing to fundamental economic adjustment is a pre-condition to qualifying for conventional debt relief.

Who Designs the Stabilisation and Adjustment for the Debts?

Carbon debt: for what little there is, the rich countries.

HIPC debt: rich countries.

Is it Legal?

Carbon debt: industrialised countries are setting up carbon trading regimes to help implement the Kyoto Protocol. However, you cannot trade what you do not own. Consequently, before there is an agreed global basis for allocating emissions entitlements, any emissions trading is effectively trading in stolen goods.

HIPC debt: the G8 industrialised countries control 49 per cent of votes on the board of the International Monetary Fund, and voting allocations are related to the size of financial contributions. In most electoral democracies paying for votes would be considered a criminal offence.

Using natural resource accounts, very poor countries are actually financing development in the rich world, not the other way around, and in several ways. They concede their environmental space and the economic opportunities it represents. They bear the environmental costs of development in rich countries through the physical and environmental damage caused by pollution and natural resource exploitation, and they have to meet the cost of adaptation to problems like global warming. Social upheaval, for example due to the creation of environmental refugees or through the conflict for control of natural resources, generates still further costs yet to be accounted for.

In many cases the payment of orthodox external debt leads to still further pressure on natural resources, especially where the prevailing policy paradigm emphasises export-led development strategies that are highly dependent on primary commodities.

Carbon debt in particular raises two questions for rich countries: how will the majority world be compensated for the carbon debt and its consequences, and how will rich countries balance their environmental budgets? The following chapters look at possible ways to tackle both.

7

Rationalising Self-destruction
(Or Why People are More Stupid than Frogs)

Video meliora proboque, deteriora sequor.[*]
> Sir John Simon, British Chancellor of the Exchequer, 1940

The pleasure principle is ... from the point of view of the self-preservation of the organism among the difficulties of the external world ... inefficient and even highly dangerous.
> Sigmund Freud, *Beyond the Pleasure Principle*, 1920[1]

Pliny the Elder has an Observation that nullum frequentius votum, No Wish more frequent among Men than the Wish for Death.
> Peter Ackroyd, *Hawksmoor*, 1986[2]

'Humankind cannot bear very much reality'
> T.S. Eliot, *The Four Quartets*, 1969[3]

Put a frog in gradually warming water – so the story goes – and it will let itself be cooked to death. Frogs are allegedly incapable of identifying the moment at which the temperature of the water around them becomes life threatening. Their central nervous system is incapable of receiving the necessary feedback, and then acting accordingly. As the poet Wilfred Owen wrote, 'warmth shall lull their dreaming lids'.[4] Frogs, it seems, perfectly present the predicament of humanity faced by global warming.[5]

---

[*] 'I see the right, and I approve it too, Condemn the wrong, and yet the wrong pursue'.

But, 'rubbish', say the people who know about frogs. 'If a frog had a means of getting out, it certainly would', according to the curator of reptiles and amphibians at the US national Museum of Natural History. 'They don't sit still for you', adds a professor from the biology department at Harvard University. 'It will jump before it gets hot'.[6] The story appears to be the pond equivalent of urban myth.

People, then, must be worse off than frogs. We sit around as the world warms, in full knowledge of what is happening and its likely consequences, and let it happen. Something deeper, therefore, must be going on and not just at the bottom of the frog's pond. Where better to start looking for 'deep' than in the original unpicking of the human unconscious by Sigmund Freud. He makes an interesting guide to irrational behaviour because he also lived through a period of enormous human self-destructiveness. It is still possible to visit the apartment in Vienna where Freud developed his ideas and treated his clients or, more properly, guinea pigs. At the heart of the defunct Austro-Hungarian empire you can still follow precisely the footsteps of the rich, aristocratic and disturbed who sought his help. Go through a doorway off the street into a cobbled passageway, up a grand staircase that doubles back on itself to the right and straight ahead. Ring a bell pressed over the years by hundreds of gloved fingers in search of self-awareness. Here is a good place to pause and speculate on why we as a species may be more stupid than frogs.

In order for the First World War to carry on for as long as it did, with an immense cost in human life, as well as tremendous economic and political costs, it was necessary for the slaughter to be 'rationalised'. This required not only the prior existence of complex psychological drivers, but also the mass mobilisation and manipulation of public opinion among everyone from intellectuals to the masses.[7] Once established, the case for war, just like the case for a society based on the unbounded consumption of non-renewable natural resources, easily withstands rational demolition by argument. 'It seems as if there were no progress in the human race, but only repetition', wrote Virginia Woolf in 1938 as the storm clouds of war gathered again in Europe.[8]

Many of Freud's theories have been discredited, but several of his insights have also stood the test of time. It might be unwise to take his and subsequent psychoanalytical conclusions too literally, but it would be foolish also to ignore them completely. They should be considered if only for the fact that some of the theories prove an uncanny fit with our current condition.

Assuming, for the moment, that we do not have a collective death wish (which may be a rash assumption), consider the lighter charge that we are simply in denial. Charles Ryecroft writes in his critical dictionary of psychoanalysis that 'denial of painful perceptions is a manifestation of the pleasure principle' and that all such painful perceptions therefore have to overcome resistance from the pleasure principle.[9] He then goes on to explain that the psyche avoids:

> Pain or unpleasure aroused by increases in instinctual tension and [does] so by hallucinating the satisfaction necessary to reduce the tension. Only later after the ego has developed, is the pleasure principle modified by the reality principle, which leads the individual to replace hallucinatory wish-fulfilment by adaptive behaviour.

In this literature *psyche* is another word for the mind, and ego is used in contrast to the id: ego meaning reason and common sense, while the id is to do with passions. The situation with regard to society and global warming could barely be described more simply. The pleasure principle doesn't mean that we are always actively pursuing pleasure and damning the consequences. It means, rather, that we actively avoid painful reality.

If society, then, has yet to develop its collective ego, or common sense, it is perfectly understandable, if not excusable, that its collective denial is yet to be modified by the 'reality principle'. And, also, that it has yet to develop effective 'adaptive behaviour'. Group therapy anyone? I believe it is more than coincidence that 'adaptation' is a key topic of debate in global warming. Ryecroft describes the 'reality principle' as the opposite of the pleasure principle. When it takes control, instead of avoiding painful reality, the individual seeks gratification 'by accommodation to the facts of ... the external world'.

Freud says of the pleasure principle that 'from the point of view of the self-preservation of the organism among the difficulties of the external world, it is from the very outset inefficient and even highly dangerous'. The emerging power of reason, he says, does not abandon pleasure, it just abandons 'a number of possibilities of gaining satisfaction' – such as driving fuel-guzzling sports utility vehicles perhaps, and taking round-the-world holiday flights – and it tolerates an amount of 'unpleasure' on a different, 'indirect road to pleasure'.

The pleasure principle in its fullest meaning, according to Freud, is so bound up in our 'hard-to-educate' sexual instincts that it frequently dominates the reality principle in ways that are harmful to the whole body. Freud believed the pains that the pleasure principle goes to great lengths to avoid are mostly 'perceptual', not tangible. Could it be that the feared pain at the heart of our resistance to life-changes necessary to combat global warming is also perceptual. And that in fact, as happened in the relatively recent past of most industrial societies (see chapter 10), the changes could instead bring some unexpected pleasures?

Growing up in apartheid South Africa Stanley Cohen became obsessed with the human ability to witness suffering and atrocity and yet not act against it. Haunted by what he saw there and elsewhere around the world he charted the different courses denial takes. He described how easy it is for people to be in a state of simultaneously knowing, and yet not knowing something.[10] Obedience to authority, the pressures of social conformity, acting out of necessity and the ability to separate out and compartmentalise areas of life, all play a part. Denial can be literal, interpretive or implicatory, he says. It can work at the personal, official and cultural level. Literal denial is a flat rejection that something is true or exists, 'there is no such thing as climate change, it is a conspiracy of self-interested scientists'. Interpretive denial might concede that something is happening but explain away its significance, for example, 'there is global warming but it's just part of a natural cycle'. Implicatory denial accepts the facts of an event or issue, but fails to acknowledge and accept their importance and the imperative to act on them. Hence we conclude, 'climate change is happening but it's nothing to do with me, why should I alter my behaviour'. Denial can also be passive, 'the withdrawal of attention, deflecting the gaze', or active, 'repudiation, rejection, negation, disavowal'.

On the Natural History of Destruction by author W.G. Sebald is a case study on the complexity and thoroughness of cultural denial.[11] It analyses how postwar German writers averted their gaze and chose to ignore war crimes committed against their people in the Second World War. Just because Germany was the aggressor it did not mean that its opponents were free to act with impunity against them. Even before the age of aerial warfare it was illegal under the 1907 Hague Convention to bombard, 'by whatever means ... towns, villages, dwellings or buildings which are undefended'. Yet so-called *strategic bombing* was precisely targeted at German civilians who could not defend themselves. In 1942, 37,000 tons of bombs were dropped mostly at night on residential areas in Germany. Official air force plans to escalate bombing in the next two years were expected to kill 1 million civilians, injure 1 million more and leave 25 million homeless.

British government officials responded, 'It is unnecessary and undesirable in any document about our bombing policy to emphasize this aspect, which is contrary to the principles of international law'.[12] Official denial, knowing without knowing. Controversy in Britain over respectful official recognition of one of the architects of strategic bombing, Arthur 'Bomber' Harris, continues to this day. British bombing of Hamburg killed more people, mostly women, children and the old, than all German air attacks against British cities put together.[13] In total, towards the end of the war the Allies dropped around 1 million tons of bombs on 131 German towns and cities killing 600,000 civilians and destroying 3.5 million homes.[14] Yet this wanton slaughter was for decades written out of German consciousness. Denial is not straightforward. Both victims and protagonists can conspire in it. It means that tackling denial about climate change will not be easy.

Cohen concludes that denial is not an aberration but the basic human condition. The exceptions are the occasions when people intervene in situations that do not affect their immediate material interests. Some of the paths of denial that we engage in and submit to that Cohen describes do not, however, preclude action on global warming. On the contrary. 'Authority' can direct actions; living in a 'climate friendly' way can become an act of positive social conformity once a tipping point of consensus is passed, or become understood as an act of necessity that over-rides other motivating forces.

But perhaps there are also darker forces at work in our rationalisation of self-destruction.

THANATOS, THE DEATH WISH AND PERSONAL TRANSFORMATION[15]

In the shadow of the First World War and in the run up to the Second, Freud thought and wrote about the death wish, or death 'instinct'. As with all terms in psychoanalysis, though, the idea is not as straightforward as it at first seems. As a result, it is also far more interesting.

The death instinct is not the same as a direct impulse towards self-destruction. Freud was a man with medical training and realised that even with the recent mechanical slaughter of millions in the First World War the notion that there exists in people a fundamental suicidal impulse could not be backed up with any scientific evidence. He did, however, observe that as life was a mostly conscious, one-way trip from birth to death there must be a psychological component to that journey. Somewhere a struggle occurred between the sexual instincts which strive to renew life, and knowledge of the slide towards mortality. There is a more subtle interpretation put forward of the death instinct. The death instinct, in this case, is the label given to what drives us towards personal transformation through the dissolution of the self. Anyone who doubts the existence of this common human motivation only needs to turn on daytime television and watch the parade of make-over programmes.

This formula is interesting because it bears the same signature as, some argue, the principal driver of modernity and the modern age. According to literary and cultural critic Marshall Berman, modernism's defining characteristic is the process of change through dissolution. He summarises the experience of modernity in the title of his highly original book, *All That Is Solid Melts into Air*.[16]

THE TRAGEDY OF DEVELOPMENT

There is something deeply Faustian in the pact civilisation has made to advance its material standards of living. Instead of a soul being sold for power and success, though, in the age of global warming a one-off fossil fuel inheritance that took tens, even hundreds of millions of years to accumulate, has been burned in a few human generations. In the face of global warming it is a kind of economic transformation through dissolution. And Faust is the literary character that Berman identifies as the classic spirit and architect of the modern age.

Whatever is considered modern is considered necessary and unstoppable. Even unaware we all struggle for the mantle of modernity. But the brightness can be blinding. In Goethe's famous tragedy there is a parable for development and the growth economy. Faust's character has many incarnations. His first self is the dreamer. But the dreamer is dissolved and Faust is transformed into the lover. Finally, in his last transformation and 'romantic quest for self-development ... he will work out some of the most creative and some of the most destructive potentialities of modern life; he will be the consummate wrecker and creator, the dark and deeply ambiguous figure that our age has come to call, "the developer"'.

Faust dramatises the central contradiction of the global economy. He is 'convinced that it is the common people, the mass of workers and sufferers, who will benefit most from his work ... [but] he is ... not ready to accept responsibility for the human suffering and death that clear the way'. Faust progresses, brutally clearing from his path whatever obstacles he comes across, even if they are the same people in whose name he builds. Here is a man both in 'denial' about his actions and driven by the transformative death instinct. The scenes of forced relocation that accompany Faust's work will be instantly recognisable to anyone who has seen the great modern dam projects of China or India.

Berman explains, 'Goethe's point is that the deepest horrors of Faustian development spring from its most honourable aims and its most authentic achievements'. Similarly, the promise of better lives flowing from unrestrained economic growth unwittingly unleashes forces (among them greenhouse gases) that do more harm than growth can repair and do good.

The aim of growth, wrapped in self-important modernity, ignores the cost of the means, and then loses sight of the original ends. Faustian development, 'entails seemingly gratuitous acts of destruction – not to create any material utility but to make the symbolic point that the new society must burn all its bridges so there can be no turning back'.

DENIAL IN ACTION

Nearly every disaster movie includes a particular stock character. In classic popular films like *Jaws*, *Jurassic Park* and *Robo-Cop* there is always a man in a suit who tries to hide simmering danger. The cover-up is usually because 'whatever the danger is' threatens somebody's money making scheme – the summer tourist trade, the new theme park, the infallible robot policeman ready to be marketed.

Climate change too has its small, dedicated cast of outright contrarians who say there is nothing to worry about. Some like Fred Singer from the University of Virginia and Richard Lindzen from the Massachusetts Institute of Technology have been paid consultants to the oil industry. Others like retired, British-based academic Philip Stott and Australian Hugh Morgan are linked to industry-backed, anti-environmentalist lobby groups.[17] But let's look in detail at two other characters in the global warming drama whose denial is more oblique and therefore more interesting.

Martin Wolf is a contrarian columnist who writes for the business paper the *Financial Times*. He appears as one of the suited figures in the 'movie' of the climate change debate. After the breakdown of talks on implementing the Kyoto Protocol at The Hague in November 2000, Wolf told his readers not to worry. The 'alarmists', he said, were wrong. His arguments covered most of those typically used in the business-as-usual defence. He made the common observation that the Kyoto Protocol was inadequate to make a real difference to global warming, ignoring that the Protocol was only ever meant as a first step towards building international political consensus. No journey can begin without a first step. Then he asserted that climate science was 'uncertain', and that 'we do not know what harm global warming will do'.[18] This is a case of interpretive denial. Because, at one level all science is uncertain. It works on the basis of probabilities and always leaves room for doubt. Accepted theories routinely get overthrown. On another level, as described earlier, considerable consensus has existed for some time on what global warming will do. It will cause trouble. A joint statement of 17 national science academies, ranging from the UK to China, Brazil and Australia, repeated in May 2001 what had been known for some time: human-driven global warming was 'evident' and would increase 'intense' weather events and 'drought'. It would damage 'agriculture, health and water resources'.[19]

But experts like these were dismissed as so-called 'alarmists'. They include staff employed at the Hadley Centre for climate research, part of the UK government's Met Office, and the insurance industry which also has made outspoken speculations on the possibility of global economic bankruptcy in the wake of a warming world.

Wolf then conceded that the 'obvious solution' is the option of a worldwide plan based on an 'equitably distributed set of property rights in the globe's absorptive capacity'. But, as the necessary global authority needed to carry out such a plan doesn't yet exist, he dismissed it. Implicatory denial: 'what's the point?' Happily defeated, he relaxed back into comforting ideological slippers, pipe and armchair. These tell him that conventional, fossil-fuel addicted growth, which created the problem, is also the best way to manage it.

A core but perverse logic filters through. We must keep growing in order to generate wealth, so that we can pay for the damage (in this case climate change) created by growth. Nothing, not even the loss of a habitable atmosphere, is allowed to interfere with the important business of business. Applied to a person, the logic runs that an individual must work until they make themselves sick, in order to buy the medicines needed to return to work. More simply, we must destroy the planet, to pay to put it back together. A cocktail of rationalisation and denial.

How can we unpick such confusion? Two core observations push through the paving stones of this hypnotic, downward spiral of reasoning. First, trusting to growth alone – given the unequal dynamics of economic globalisation – is both an inefficient and highly unreliable method to give the world's poor access to the resources they need to protect themselves from climate change. In the global economy wealth tends to flood up from poor to rich, not trickle down the other way. Also the poor suffer first from environmental degradation linked to growth and are most exposed to the extreme weather of global warming.

The second problem is the humpty dumpty factor. If we break the climate, can we put it back together again? There is now the real possibility of runaway climate change. The melting of ice shelves, death of vegetation and different factors feeding off each other point in the future to the submergence of the world's major capitals. Even the expected reality of warming based on the continuation of observed patterns creates the spectre of a problem beyond the capacity of humans to control.

Wolf then manipulates and reinterprets the precautionary principle. The precaution we must take, he says, is against turning our backs on 50 years of rapid growth which could 'more than offset the costs of any warming consequent on that growth'. Nothing tastelessly environmental is allowed to darken his brow, even renewable energy is rejected on the rational grounds that wind farms are 'hideous'. Hurricanes and nuclear reactors are by contrast presumably beautiful. Carry on as usual. The shark is dead. The android cop is safe. The velociraptor will not escape.

ATTACK FROM THE INSIDE – THE COMPLACENCY CODE

One of the most talked about assaults on the green movement in recent years came from the self-styled 'sceptical environmentalist', Danish statistician Bjorn Lomborg.[20] In the popular contrarian imagination he refuted every worry that environmentalists ever put into our minds. That, however, is not true. In his own words things look bleak. As a result of humankind's impact on the environment, he wrote, species are becoming extinct at a rate '1,500 times higher than ... natural background extinction'. Elsewhere '20 per cent of tropical forests' have disappeared. In countries like Nigeria and Madagascar that figure is 'well over half', and Central America may have lost 50 to 70 per cent.

It didn't stop there. Over one third of fish caught in the world's oceans are taken from 'stocks showing declining yields'. Erosion of agricultural land has left 38 per cent degraded. Perhaps most important of all, the fact that global warming is happening and that people are the cause is now 'uncontroversial'. And climate change, he wrote, will be especially 'tough on the developing countries'. So you have to wonder, if these are the conclusions of a sceptical environmentalist, how bad is the picture coming from average or doom-ladened greens?

This was one of Lomborg's problems. One moment he picked fights with long forgotten ghosts of the environmental movement, such as those who thought that all natural resources would run out next Tuesday. The next, he agreed with negative trends on the planet's health, but came to economic policy conclusions that, in terms of the proof and analytical rigour he demanded of others, fell way below standard.

No environmentalist would disagree with his cursory dismissal of nuclear power as an expensive security risk. Neither would they quibble with his conclusion that solar power and other renewables are the inevitable future for energy, to be adopted as soon as possible. But Lomborg played the role of deliberate contrarian. His hype led you to suspect he would deny the reality of global warming (literal denial). But Lomborg conceded it is happening, it is serious and unpredictable and will impose the greatest costs on those in the world who can least afford to deal with it. He also didn't dispute the possibility of 'catastrophe' scenarios, such as the collapse of the West Antarctic Ice Sheet, causing a 10 metre sea level rise. He wrote that 'we ought to spend more effort' looking into their likelihood because 'it is the extreme occurrences that are truly costly'.

Lomborg then focused on uncertain climatic feedbacks that could swing towards more or less global warming, but emphasised the lower end of future projections. He simply thought things won't be that bad (interpretive denial). He swapped the precautionary principle with the complacency code. Don't waste money on preventing climate change, he said. It would be better to rely on increased aid flows to help poor countries, or trust to the global market place, managed by the World Trade Organisation, where they can earn a living.

Here the sceptical environmentalist became the credulous economist. Because, on one hand, the appalling aid track record of industrialised countries holds little promise. On the other, it is not credible to expect Bangladesh, for example – facing the prospect of an extra 20 million environmental refugees – to fight its way out of poverty by competing with China through the WTO for the world's textile trade. The WTO has been dubbed a nightmare for the poorest countries by the UN and, according to a World Bank trade policy expert, its 'obligations reflect little concern for development'.[21]

Lomborg also wrote about growth and assessed the value of GDP (a measure of national income) as a key indicator without mentioning the widely referenced work of economist Herman Daly on more comprehensive alternatives like the Index of Sustainable Economic Welfare. Daly showed for the United States that growth can be 'uneconomic', i.e.: that as the

economy gets bigger, welfare can decline. The key determinant
to raising welfare, it seems, is not crude growth but policies
that ensure better distribution of wealth.

Lomborg also ascribed a lack of decent property rights
regimes to problems with the global commons, such as the
world's fisheries. But, rightly concerned about the limitations
of the Kyoto Protocol, he failed to even mention the main
contender to solve global warming, which is an approach
based on applying equal per capita property rights to the
atmosphere (see chapter 11), although it would have answered
all his doubts.

Intentionally or not Lomborg wrote the 'business-as-usual'
bible. It would be great to believe the 'crisis what crisis?'
message. We could all retire, climb mountains and write
novels. But Lomborg's assurances felt like those you get from
a barefoot taxi driver with only 20 per cent vision. One who
says everything will be fine, he knows the way, and then,
squinting heavily through the windscreen, speeds down the
motorway at 100 mph. Here is a man in denial.

If we are to move out of denial at a cultural level the media
will have a major role to play. But the structure of reporting,
especially in the broadcast media, often creates spurious balance
(but interestingly only on certain subjects like the environment,
not economics). For years this has meant that whenever climate
change is discussed, for every scientist warning about the
particular impacts of global warming, a contrarian or denier
has been held up against them. To a general viewer or listener
this approach creates the impression that both views are held
equally among the 'expert' community. In fact, where climate
change is concerned, the level of dissent is now similar to the
number of people who deny the process of evolution. In other
words, a small minority. Another problem is that the institutions
of the media can also clearly exhibit the characteristics of denial
– knowing and not knowing simultaneously – just as much as
any individual or government.

The *Independent* is a broadly progressive British daily
newspaper that regularly reports on the threat and reality of

global warming. In the middle of summer on a Saturday in June 2003 almost its entire front page was dominated by a story headlined 'The great rainforest tragedy'. In the previous year, it said, an area the size of Belgium in the Brazilian Amazon was destroyed. In terms of global warming, the Amazon is an important 'sink', soaking up greenhouse gases, but also highly vulnerable to climate change. Several predictions say that warming could cause a massive die-back, leading to the forest emitting more carbon than it soaks up. But at the top of the front page in full colour, there was a bold circulation-boosting newspaper promotion for one of the most climate-unfriendly forms of transport: European short-haul flights. Immediately above the great rainforest tragedy is the encouragement to 'Fly in style'. Another more consistently liberal, progressive daily newspaper is the *Guardian*. After a series of front page news and in-depth companion magazine articles during 2003 and 2004 about the threat of climate change and the uncontrolled expansion of environmentally damaging air travel, it too made an offer on its front page: *2 for 1 flights to America. Fly to New York, LA and 22 other cities in the US. Plus Canada, Mexico and eight other South and Central American destinations.*[22] If one form of travel is more damaging than short-haul flying, it is long-haul. Seemingly unconcerned by this contradiction the same paper produced a series of special magazine supplements in praise of our love affair with the car. The words on the first magazine's cover went like this: 'It costs £103,000. You would need your own oilfield to keep it in petrol. So why would anyone love the Aston Martin DB? Easy: it's very fast, it's very luxurious and it's very, very beautiful'.[23]

Video meliora proboque, deteriora sequor – I see the right, and I approve it too, condemn the wrong, and yet the wrong pursue. To witness these dynamics on a daily basis, look no further than the car parked outside where you live.

8

The Car Park at the End of the World

It frequently happens that an element of the standard of living which set out with being primarily wasteful, ends with becoming a necessary of life.

Thorstein Veblen, *The Theory of the Leisure Class*, 1899

It's no longer a warmth hidden in my veins: it's Venus entire and whole fastening on her prey.

Jean Racine, *Phèdre*, 1677

Transport made of man a new kind of waif: a being constantly absent from a destination he cannot reach on his own but must reach within the day. By now people work a substantial part of every day to earn the money without which they could not even get to work.'

Ivan Illich, *Energy and Equity*, 1974

Beauty, charm and strength of character are enough to drive anyone mad.

Volvo car advertisement, 2003

I don't drive. But my life is dominated by cars. They are around me and inside me, in more ways than one. I breathe their fumes through my mouth and nose every time I walk along a road. As a child I breathed in their glamour and persuaded my parents to buy me countless toy cars. That was in spite of once seeing my dog run over and, on another occasion, seeing a school friend at the age of nine sent cartwheeling through the air by the impact of a late-braking car as he absent mindedly ran across the road (both survived). Card games like Top Trumps

8. The author's childhood indoctrination into the great car economy
is well under way on this ride at Colchester Zoo, Essex, England.

allowed me and my friends to memorise insane amounts of
useless information about automobiles. The first car our family
had even looked like a big toy. It was called a Standard Penant.
Disturbingly I can remember its number plate more easily than
my family's birthdays (it was 540 CJO). When it was sold I
mourned the window stickers from Welsh campsites that I had
lovingly put on the passenger side window. Freudians have a
term for how people invest emotion into inanimate objects.
It's called *cathexis*. It happens a lot with cars.

Now they are everywhere that I look. I dodge between them
going from any one place to any other. I shout over them to
have a conversation walking down the street. I wake up to their
sound systems in the small hours as they park or drive by my
house. Places that I love have been divided and paved over to
make way for cars. Until a new traffic system was introduced
to my home town in Essex I could cross into the town centre

by walking over a road of two lanes. After, I had to cross about 13 lanes.

A car showroom now sits at the corner of that junction. One time, not long ago, I walked past and there were large posters in the window advertising the latest 'retro' model of car produced by the manufacturer Chrysler. As I stood outside, the windows picking up reflections of a bleak landscape – a spaghetti mess of traffic lanes and vulnerable pedestrian islands – the posters nevertheless invited you to 'Buy your soul', by purchasing the PT Cruiser. Dr Faust was at work again.

Cars cover and suffocate our lives like black fly on nasturtiums. But somehow their dominance is also strangely invisible. Our unique adaptability as a species has enabled us to acclimatise to their staggering 'everywhereness', and not see it as odd.

Were the car a disease it would be an epidemic. Were it an insect pest it would be a plague. Were it water, it would be a devastating flood. Yet, spellbound, we embrace the great destroyer and design our lives, communities and countryside around them. We welcome them into our lives when, rationally, we should be emblazoning them with public health warnings in the same style as cigarette packets. 'Driving can seriously damage your health', or 'Driving kills'.

Before even considering the link to global warming, in the century since the first recorded fatal traffic accident the car claimed 30 million lives. Traffic accidents are now predicted by the International Federation of Red Cross and Red Crescent Societies to become the world's third most significant cause of death and disability by 2020.[1] The World Health Organisation estimates that 1.2 million people die on roads each year, similar to total fatalities caused by malaria.[2]

In national elections there is often a crunch moment when votes are being counted that strongly indicates the likely outcome. It usually centres on the result in one particular, carefully balanced constituency. Commentators will say that if the party already in power can hold on to the seat it will keep office, but if the main opposition wins, it could well force the government from office. Basildon in my home county of Essex is such a place. When the Labour Party won the town in

1997 it signalled the end of nearly two decades of Conservative Party rule.

In the case of global warming, a phenomenon that is currently 'holding office' in the atmosphere, the swing constituency in terms of public attitudes is probably how we feel about cars and car ownership. Where the unsustainable use of fossil fuels is concerned, nothing is more symbolic than the car. If attitudes towards the car were to change, in much the same way that attitudes towards smoking already have, we might reasonably conclude grounds for hope. The opposite is also true.

So deeply is the car built into the organisation of society, the running of the economy and the construction of our own identities, that a change in attitudes towards it might signal public readiness for action on climate change. Action that is finally commensurate with the scale of the problem.

The car has not simply stumbled into its current iconic and dominant status. History's biggest red carpet has been rolled out for it. Like a spoilt young prince it was born and brought up with an economic silver spoon in its mouth. Margaret Thatcher, as prime minister when I was growing up, told us we were living in a 'great car economy'. Roads and car parks were built for it at public expense, competition like the railways and trams had already been deliberately run down in its favour. In Britain the Beeching Plan devised by the engineer and chairman of the British Railways Board, Richard Beeching, between 1963 and 1965 paved the way, metaphorically and literally, by shutting down a huge portion of the railway network. His contribution to pulling apart a more environmentally friendly transport system earned him a knighthood. He was made a Lord in 1965.

In the 1920s most significant towns and cities in the United States had their own electric rail systems, the famous streetcar. There were 1,200 separate systems with 44,000 miles of track. The car company General Motors (GM) made a loss in 1921 and feared that the car market had hit a wall. Their answer was to target the street and urban railways with a range of strategies to put them out of business and increase the market for automobiles. A special unit was set up within the company and it was disturbingly successful. Former US Senate Counsel, Bradford Snell, writes, 'GM admitted, in court documents, that by the mid-1950s, its agents had canvassed more than 1,000 electric railways and that, of these, they had motorised 90 percent'.[3]

The good behaviour of the car, such as the ability to get you around (if ever more slowly) was fawned over. Bad behaviour, such as killing and injuring people on an epidemic scale and trashing both the urban and rural environment, was indulged and ignored. Thatcher never mentioned what happened when problems hit the great car economy, and now there is malady in our dependence. Comedian and activist Michael Moore first came to prominence with a film called *Roger and Me* (1989) about the impact on his home town of Flint in the US of the closure of a car manufacturing plant. The town's economy depended almost entirely on it. Across Britain other towns suffered similar fates as car making became increasingly mechanised and shifted to Asia in the 1980s and 1990s. At school one of *the* annual trips was for us to visit the Ford works at Dagenham to the east of London. It once dominated the area, but now barely leaves a trace.

Yet the car's royal protection squad is more active today than ever. And our addiction to an ever more powerful vehicle 'high' is getting stronger. Around 15 million vehicles are sold in western Europe every year. The market is not only big but highly concentrated in the hands of a few giant corporate groups. Just six corporations account for 70 per cent of global car sales.

Potential environmental improvements in car design have been rubbed out by the fact that people want bigger, faster and off-road cars. In the US, overall vehicle fuel economy was lower in 2000 than it was in 1980. According to the Union of Concerned Scientists, 'Two decades of fuel-saving technologies that could have helped curb CO_2 have instead gone into increasing vehicle weight and performance'.[4] In Europe advertisers claim a similar trend. Feeding an 'active car buying audience' on the internet the company Adlink points out that 'Europeans like their cars fast! The average power of car engines has increased by 25 per cent in the last ten years'. Of course the demand for large fast cars doesn't just happen. Around €6 billion was spent on car advertising in the five biggest European markets in 2000. In the US, ad spending to keep cars moving through the show rooms was around $10 billion in 2003 and still rising.[5] The money is not just thrown around. Although car makers keep it quiet, careful psychological research goes into every stage of product development from the design of components through to advertising the final product. Each decision is carefully measured to maintain the apparent indispensability of the car to our lives. The process has been amazingly successful.

In 1950 there were an estimated 70 million cars, trucks and buses on the world's roads. Towards the end of the century there were between 600 and 700 million. By 2025 the figure is expected to pass 1 billion. But the distribution of vehicle ownership is, and will continue to be, highly unequal around the world. In the middle of the 1990s, for every 1,000 people in the United States there were 750 motor vehicles. In China for the equivalent number of people there were eight vehicles, in India seven. Even by the year 2050 with the expected huge growth of car ownership in the majority world, rich countries with only 16 per cent of the world population will still account for 60 per cent of global motor vehicle emissions.[6] Our use of, and dependence on, the private motor car is the badge of membership of the ecological debtors club.

The messages used by the industry exploit our fears with breathtaking hypocrisy, and occupy our dreams like an invading army. They all work to maintain the car in its uniquely privileged and heavily subsidised position. How has the industry been so successful in making the car both physically and psychologically indispensable? 'Of course cars are about sex', wrote Roy Foster reviewing two social histories of the car. 'But they are also about other abstractions that construct consciousness, such as sport and the environment and nationalism'.[7] The investment of identity is so strong, he notes, that Catholic and Protestant communities from Garrison

Keillor's *Lake Wobegon* to Ireland maintained allegiance to different models of car.

Foster indicates the fanaticism which ushered in the automobile age with the tale of Colonel Moore-Brabazon, a man who was to become minister of transport. In 1932 the Colonel dismissed complaints about the rising number of people dying on the roads. 'Over 6,000 people commit suicide every year', he said, 'and nobody makes a fuss about that'. His credentials for ministerial office were clearly impeccable.

Change demands that we 'untell' the stories told every day on behalf of the car in a thousand newspaper and magazine adverts. These adverts are, for the car industry, the equivalent to Stalin's state propaganda posters, news reels and artwork of happy smiling workers. They hide a brutal reality and a naked, dissolute emperor.

MEANING MAKERS – BUILDING MORE THAN CARS

'How to balance your desires with your needs', is the advice from a glossy colour magazine advert. The answer, apparently, is to spend £18,000 on a very powerful and sleek Italian Alfa Romeo sports car. The manufacturer's understanding of how to achieve that most difficult human balancing act, between desire and need (curiously exactly the same challenge facing environmentalists worldwide), is to offer a car that is not only fast, meeting male fantasies of predatory speed, but also practical because it has four doors, unlike other sports cars. If, however, someone on an average income in sub Saharan Africa wanted to balance their desires with their needs by purchasing the car, they would have a problem. First they would somehow have to save an entire lifetime's income. Then they would need to borrow the equivalent of nearly another decade's worth. In 2002 life expectancy in the region had fallen to just 43 years, the lowest level since records began. With an average annual income of £350, saving everything in order to afford the car, and spending nothing on anything else, would take 51 years. With similarly curious values Jeep sell their Cherokee model car with the line, 'The cost of living. £199 a month'. Perhaps they use the same advertising agency. They mean, of course, that more than simply living you can be really 'alive' for what they consider to be a modest amount of money.

From this point of view, cars make the world and its problems harder to understand. English may be a global language, but its words have different meanings in different countries. In one place, where most people's needs for food, clothes, shelter, clean drinking water and a health and education service are largely met, a 'need' usually suggests something beyond these basics. For example, 'I need a new car', or 'I need a bigger house'. The rich world's perceived needs are found in a layer of daily life that floats above actual need. They manifest themselves in the opposite of a 'subsistent' lifestyle. It could be called something clumsy like a 'supersistent' lifestyle, one that pays for itself by borrowing from the environmental bank accounts of the world's low-consuming majority population. Borrowed with, it should be added, no intention of repayment. But this is just the beginning of the distorted lens through which we are forced to look at the central icon of the modern consumer age.

It is helpful to recap on some of the key mechanisms of advertising even if they seem mostly obvious. Adverts both position and mediate our relationship with the car. They both keep us in love and persuade us to buy one type over another. They enable us, through constant repetition of certain images, to imagine that we're coasting on empty country roads when in fact we're stuck in a traffic jam on a smog choked urban freeway. Often we move more slowly than walking pace. Famously, traffic in central London now moves more slowly than the pace of horse drawn carriages in Victorian times. The advertisers, of course, exploit and control our fears and desires. Most of all, they perform wonderful emotional magic. We are persuaded in a variety of ingenious ways to have feelings for cold mechanics.

A minority of, shall we say, enthusiasts will always express unnerving devotion to their machine of choice without needing encouragement. Something more, though, is needed to bring whole societies under the spell of moving metal, plastic and rubber. In this case it is a massive, pervasive, one-sided, highly controlled and constantly reinforced discourse about the car and our relationship to it. It would be better, in fact, to call it a fairy story. In this fairy story, this grand legitimating narrative, we can all, for a price, have our prince

9. Is that a car in your showroom or are you just pleased to see me? It's not only a car you're shopping for, as car manufacturers show how desperate they are to keep us buying.

or princess. For a few thousand pounds we can buy our illusion of a happy ending.

We look at the spells cast by the industry and stitch ourselves into their story. What stops us laughing out loud at the absurdity of their claims, apart from our guilty desire for the claims to be true? Here is a fairly random selection of adverts with a few examined in more detail.

Promises, Promises

Promises of power, speed and sex are among the most common in car adverts. Several secondary promises are also fairly ubiquitous. Depending on which market you fit into, the car will: enhance your individuality (sports car or small get-around), protect what matters to you (saloon or people carrier), make people jealous of you (anything big or, ironically, a bit inadequate and socially ambitious), give you spiritual and emotional fulfilment (any new small to mid-range car that departs from rigidly bland design rules).

You Can Have Power

Car adverts tell us, in the face of daily evidence to the contrary, that we can be powerful. The Jeep Grand Cherokee offers power, a lot of it. So much in fact that Jeep invite you to sit in a force of nature and exert god-like control over the elements. Against a barren prairie-like landscape the Grand Cherokee sucks the air with it, pulling down an old wooden barn in its slipstream. The car, says the advert, has the strength of one of nature's most destructive phenomena. It is on a par with shifts in the earth's crust that can destroy a city, '8 on the Richter Scale', the advert says, 'And we don't mean earthquakes'. Nature, of course, tends to get the last laugh on the copywriters. It's hard to look at the advert and not be reminded of the occasions when real earthquakes have collapsed freeways, squashing even the mightiest four-wheel drives, like bugs. Ironically, given the greenhouse gas emissions pumped out by these gas guzzling monsters, there might be an inadvertent level of truth in their claims. But I suspect it will be a while before a Jeep advert reads, 'Drive the Grand Cherokee and flood Manhattan'.

Look again at the advert and there is something else. The strange schizophrenic, paradoxical relationship emerges that industrial societies have with the natural environment. An anonymous face in silhouette drives the car through the landscape. The car takes you closer to nature but also, shiny and air-conditioned, insulates and isolates you from it. It first appears to put you into a relationship and then holds you back from it. The barren land is both exhilarating and to be feared. Nature is big and powerful but you, in your car, are bigger and more powerful still. Your car not only gives you strength it gives you noble isolation. Under brooding skies and against bare, monochrome brush you are not only a survivor but a conqueror. You have more power than all but the strongest earthquakes.

And all this from a production line car with 'electrically adjustable suede and leather-trimmed seats'. In practice the advert also means that if you, the proud owner, ever actually leave your urban or suburban confines, you'll be able to drive swiftly through the landscape, take whatever romantic notions it has to offer, and then leave nature behind.

This, it should be added, is one of the more bland, less inspiring adverts on offer. Someone should perhaps take Jeep to task over their strapline, 'There's only one', and invoke the Trade Descriptions Act used to prevent the mis-selling of products. If there really was only one Jeep, their environmental impact would be considerably less.

Another promise of power comes from the manufacturer Mitsubishi. It sells a big car whose name pushes you up against the wall and threatens to run you through. The Lancer Evolution VIII. Mounted military spear coupled with *the* force of nature. Not only that, but it has evolved to version VIII. Be afraid, can you handle this much power? It boastfully reaches 'speeds of up to 157 mph' in a country where the speed limit is 70 mph. Why? I once asked a British judge who loved cars why it was legal for cars to be sold with the potential for gratuitously breaking the law. As someone charged with enforcing the law he didn't seem particularly bothered. He admitted being lenient on 'speeders' and could only think that all that extra power was needed for over-taking.

You Can Have Sex

Adverts tell us both that cars can help us have sex, and that cars are as good as sex. It is where advertising comes into its own with the promises it makes. This is just a small choice.

> **Volvo**: 'Lust, envy, jealousy. The dangers of a Volvo'.
> **Alfa Romeo**: 'How about a sexy little number you can feel secure in?'
> **Mazda**: 'Fancy some bedtime exercise?'
> **SEAT**: 'The new Ibiza. Born out of passion and power'.
> **Mitsubishi**: 'You never forget your first time'.
> **Honda**: 'When Soichiro Honda was 8 years old he saw his first motor car ... "It leaked oil", he recalled fondly. "I got down on my hands and knees to smell it. It was like perfume"'.

For many young people there is a practical connection between sex and the car. The car is about the only relatively private, enclosed space where you can have sex when you're young. As the same is not true for adults, the industry needs to spend millions in advertising to continually re-sexualise the car. It goes far beyond the obviousness and cliché of big red sports cars.

From standard production line Asian models to the Swedish solidity of Volvo, we are told that cars are the gateway to sexual gratification and fulfilment. But, just like the paradoxical promises of power, the 'sex messaging' also seems to bestride irresolvable contradictions.

First, for the majority, the actual experience of driving must resemble sex only in the way that teenagers stumble, or fumble, across it. There is a difference between the hype and reality. Expensive, gridlocked, hard to park, road-raged and often broken down, if cars offer anything sensual, it is very bad sex. The real thing falls far short of the words and images.

Alfa Romeo's message offers classic, confused fantasy as well as being mildly pornographic. A padlock hangs on a zip, descending slightly down the spine of a beautiful young woman. Semiologists from the 1970s and 1980s who deconstructed the buried meanings of images would have had a field day. There she is, passive and willing, open to the male gaze, objectified. Her back is to the viewer and her lips are parted in sexual invitation. The intimation is of intercourse from behind. The padlock on the zip suggests that she, like the car, is there for you to lock up, unlock and have sex with at will. The dress is a latter-day chastity belt. Here, on offer for between £13,000 and £18,000, is gratification, exhilaration *and* security. It is quite explicit, it is 'a sexy little number you can feel secure in'. There are no wider obligations, just as there are none in the false promise made by pornography of readily available, uncomplicated sex with unquestioning women. This car, and woman, won't answer back they'll just give you pleasure. Again, like pornography, these are the ingredients of disappointed addiction. An alternative interpretation of the woman as viewer is equally problematic. The dress *can* be locked up, or left open. No means no and yes means yes. Which would be all very good and empowering but the advert is not constructed that way. The woman's posture is not discriminating. Her gaze does not meet the eye and challenge the viewer, it is passive, looking away to the right. Her gradual undressing is offered for everyone to see, it is an open invitation.

Almost all adverts exist and work to separate their product from the actual conditions of the product's manufacturing and consumption. The monotony, mechanisation and pollution from car manufacturing rarely make an appearance in the sleekly seductive glossy advertising for the finished product.

A car like the one in the advert parks outside my house. In a street with cars parked outside every house it doesn't stand out. The young people from next door getting in and out do not look as if they are having, as the strap line suggests, their souls stirred.[8] They look tired, harassed or just blank and indifferent, like most people working in the city. Perhaps the connotation of guaranteed sex and security can be held somewhere in the imagination of the driver. Perhaps it recedes gradually from emotional view, leaving behind that signature, listless malaise of consumer societies. A malaise that dwells in the vacuum of an evaporated promise, a promise that constantly leads us, or misdirects, to believe that having can substitute for being. That collecting a variety of high-end, luxury consumer goods – step forward the car as outstanding example – can, like a cuckoo in the nest, bring fulfilment in place of meaning and purpose.

Put another way, in the context of the current economic system, this perfectly understandable misdirection suggests that you can take a short cut to finding purpose, meaning and wellbeing. Instead of taking a path of questioning and reflecting on how we live, the message is just go out and buy stuff to achieve fulfilment. From the point of view of commerce the former approach is irritatingly free and not available to purchase.

You Can Protect What Matters to You

'Getting the kids safely to their destination is every parent's priority. It's top of our list too'. This is the promise that Ford makes for its Mondeo model. It's fairly typical for cars aimed at the family market. Inadvertently it concedes another element of the way in which cars increase social alienation. Even leading pro-motoring organisations admit that car use is a retreat from the world not an engagement with it.[9] The Ford promise may be genuine and in a very limited sense true. For example, one car may have more safety features than another. In another sense it is rubbish. Why so? The huge increase in childhood asthma of recent years has been linked to the pollution from growing vehicle traffic.

A Working Group on Public Health and Fossil Fuel Combustion looked at the health impacts of fossil fuel pollution, and in particular the ultrafine particles that people breathe in from vehicle emissions. They concluded that a climate friendly policy where developed and developing countries significantly reduced carbon emissions would save a huge number of lives.[10] It would avoid 700,000 premature deaths from reduced particulate pollution, with developing countries getting the best benefit. Over 20 years 8 million deaths including 6.3 million in developing countries could be prevented.

The number of children killed and injured in traffic accidents each year would be the stuff of nationwide panic were it caused by a new strain of the flu virus. As is the case with the bull bars put on sports utility vehicles, very often the safer you make a car for its occupants, the more dangerous it becomes for the outside world.

The 'school run' as it has become known – parents taking children to school and back in the car – is one of the biggest factors in the growing inconvenience of urban congestion, and in Britain is to become the subject of special regulation. Taking the long view, is concern with your child's safety compatible with contributing disproportionately to global warming?

Both in terms of road safety and climate-friendliness, public transport wins every time. But public transport has been sidelined and undermined in favour of the car. It also lacks the advertising budget to win people over. The Ford advert has the type of illustrations you expect to see in a children's book. Fuzzy animals looking after their young. A penguin, a lioness and a kangaroo. Pity the penguin whose frozen home melts with global warming. The car is also portrayed in picture book fashion – 'The Ford Mondeo, one of the safest places to be' – it would have to be considering the havoc that it and its friends are wreaking on the world outside. Just as the car promises us safety it makes us more vulnerable.

You Can Make People Jealous of You

In 1899 Thorstein Veblen published a book called *The Theory of the Leisure Classes.* It was to make his name. In it he coined the term 'conspicuous consumption'. What was shocking and different about Veblen was that he saw human behaviour in the market place as more fit for anthropological study than the analysis of mechanical economics. He observed the age of the robber barons in the United States. America lacked the minute social stratification of Europe's class system so people, using tribe-like behaviour, sought other ways to differentiate themselves. They were not governed by sophisticated economic laws, he thought, but had 'irrational drives' and behaved in 'credulous, untutored, ritualistic' fashion.[11] The successful ones marked themselves out with extravagant displays of wealth and consumption which still holds true today.

Mazda asks: 'What does it take to impress the neighbours these days?' And then offers the solution, 'Why keep up with the Jones's when you could overtake?' And you can do so by buying a Mazda 323 with aluminium interior finish. The manufacturers are merely surfing and encouraging a well-established, if unattractive, behavioural tendency. But, unfortunately, it's like an arms race, never satisfied. Security, or in this case self-satisfaction, is infinitely deferred. There will always be someone else, further down the road or around the corner, to aspire to and surpass. In the meantime Mazda promises that its car will 'get those net curtains twitching'.

You Can Be Different

My favourite, if brief, observation on car adverts is the way that many promise the opportunity to express your individuality by purchasing a mass production car. Go figure.

The car dependent society has been made, and it can be unmade. It was always a chimera, a cloud of mechanical mosquitoes reliant on the finite blood supply of fossil fuels. The great car economy was built on unearned, unrenewable income and false promises. Not so great then, after all.

The last word on unintentional advertising irony goes to the Chrysler sports car that has an average fuel economy of less than 30 mpg. In its advert the strapline invites the potential Chrysler driver to 'Kiss the sky'. If an adequate honesty clause existed for advertisers they would probably have been compelled to change that to, 'Fart in its face'.

Democratic, liberal societies are built on social contracts. Complete individual freedom is constrained by prohibition on behaviour that harms others. At the national level we have recourse to the law if others do us damage. But, at the global level such a contract is largely missing. There is little to prevent the selfish behaviour of one part of the world's population from harming others, inadvertently or not. But with global warming as a motivating factor, that could soon change.

9

Pay Back Time: the Law,
Climate Change and Ecological Debt

The demand that nations act morally and acknowledge their own gross
historical injustices is a novel phenomenon.

Elazar Barkan, *The Guilt of Nations*, 2000[1]

You have undertaken to ruin me. I will not sue you, for law takes too
long. I will ruin you.

Letter from US magnate Cornelius Van Derbilt
to his business associates.[2]

Venice is sinking. Increasingly, raised walkways are brought out
for several hours each day so that tourists can walk with dry feet
across St Mark's square. At first hand it is surprisingly shocking
to see one of Europe's celebrity cities so casually submerged.
Anywhere else, you might expect panic to accompany the
flooding of a city centre, especially one full of architectural
jewels. Tottering along the narrow, criss-crossing walkways,
buildings perfectly mirrored in the flood waters, it feels as
if the view should be a computer generated graphic made
for a disaster movie. But it's a reality that leaves local traders
apparently unperturbed. Panic might, in fact, reasonably follow
any flood where your home is at risk. The reasons for Venice's
situation are complex and as much to do with how the city was
built and the lie of the land as to do with climate change. Sea
level rise, however, hardly helps its already damp prospects.

I was in Venice for the first time early in 2001. I'd been
invited as audience fodder to a conference on the idea of a

global e-parliament. Good conference organisers realise that
'issues', however fascinating, are rarely enough to guarantee
attendance. While the conference was inconclusive it was a
perfect opportunity and appropriate location – St Mark's had
flooded during our first evening – to pursue an idea that had
been itching in my mind for some time. I knew little about
law and the conference had attracted a range of international
legal experts.

One evening, walking along a towpath by the still Venice
Laguna with a quietly burning sky, I put a question to
American professor of international law Andrew Strauss. Could
a country make a claim for damages in the same way that
an individual can? In this case it would be damages against
another country for costs due to global warming. In the face
of ailing international negotiations and inadequate action,
were courts the next home for a deal to stop climate change?
Andrew promised to go away and think about the question.
It seemed a novel idea at the time but a very specific, personal
experience several years earlier planted the thought in me.

Rush hour was over in central London. The remaining
commuters on the evening train leaving Victoria station for the
suburbs had the vaguely desolate, hypnotised glare of dried-out
office workers. Adding to an atmosphere of stupor, the heating
system in the carriage we entered was obviously broken, stuck
on full. It was too hot. People who sat down only minutes
earlier were already allowing their heads to loll, half-eaten
pungent beef burgers still in their hands, beginning to fall. It
was too much. Rachel, my partner, insisted we move to the
next carriage. This one was less womb-like, barely occupied
with perhaps a dozen people dotted around on the nylon blue,
chewing gum encrusted seats. But in the cooler carriage our
fellow travellers' gradual slide into after-work oblivion was
about to be sharply interrupted.

A few minutes outside the station the train was picking
up speed and heaving itself over the points in the track. It
is impossible, thinking back, to tell exactly when I became
suspicious. But I remember grabbing Rachel and to her blank
annoyance dragging her onto the floor of the carriage. It wasn't

passion. As the train was passing over the points it rocked as usual, but then began to slew ever more extremely from side-to-side. Something was wrong. The carriage lurched again and there was a metallic squealing. We were coming off the tracks. The train slowed but as it did so our carriage lifted into the air and twisted sideways. A woman started crying hysterically. A scared young man caught her by the shoulders. An older man, short, stocky and powerful like a retired boxer, raised his voice in a state of near panic and shouted over and over, 'Don't panic, don't panic'. Then, it went dark.

In seconds, everyone in our carriage had made the transition from passive observers of other people's bad luck and joined the family of people whose misfortunes are reported on the evening news. We were lucky, a bit shaken. I injured my back but no one was dead. Within a couple of hours teams of firefighters had secured the precariously leaning carriage and released us.

About three years later I received a small amount of grudgingly conceded compensation for my injury. It took phone calls, doctors' reports, letters, persistence and a lot of time to win a case that, in terms of the 'rights and wrongs', was clear cut. I had a privileged situation in which to pursue my claim. I contacted the railway immediately after the event. And I had access to telephones, fax machines and friends with legal training to give advice.

Against such a fairly trivial experience, I thought that others seeking reconciliation and compensation for great historical injustices, across borders and generations, for disasters like global warming, should surely have the right to use the law? There are, after all, plenty of precedents and parallels and a new readiness by senior politicians to say sorry.

WHEN SORRY IS NOT ENOUGH

Waves of apology have been crashing over international relations in recent years. Memories of slavery, war and the crimes of colonialism now manage to extract degrees of humility from politicians and heads of state unseen in other areas of public life. In 1993 the Clinton administration apologised to Hawaiians on the centenary of the US conquest of the island. Touring Africa in 1998 President Clinton made a 'semi-apology' for slavery. Japanese Americans were apologised to in 1988 when the US congress passed a Civil Liberties Act acknowledging the wrongs done by internship during the Second World War. Alternatively the Japanese government itself has had a harder time saying the word 'sorry'. A high profile campaign to recognise the country's Second World War crimes of forcing women into sexual servitude failed to extract any display of genuine remorse.

In 1995 Queen Elizabeth II on a visit to New Zealand made an apology to the indigenous Maoris for their dispossession and treatment by the British. She gave another postcolonial apology to Sikhs from India. Interestingly in the case of the Maoris, the royal sorry failed to halt future use of the traditional Maori insult of the bared arse during official royal visits.

When in 2003, against the grain of the powerful belatedly apologising to the powerless, villagers from Fiji apologised to descendants of a British missionary eaten 136 years earlier by the Fijians' ancestors, the art of apologising became the subject of satire. British national newspaper *The Times* joked that, in the light of the Fijian example, it was time for Scandinavia to apologise for the Viking attacks on Britain in the millennium before last; that Moses' descendants should apologise to the Egyptians for even earlier plagues he called down on them, and that the manager of defunct but once-popular pop group The Spice Girls should apologise to the whole world for his cultural vandalism.

The message was clear. Saying sorry, it seemed, had gone too far. But the irony is that, as far as the rest of the world is concerned, saying sorry hasn't gone nearly far enough. On top of a rise in the culture of litigation in predominantly Anglo Saxon countries, using the courts to right historical wrongs and settle disputes is increasingly popular between people and countries spread around the globe. More and more, the pursuit of reparations for both the guilt of nations and the crimes of corporations is a matter for the courts.[3]

In the last few years alone a plethora of cases and potential lawsuits have emerged. Swiss banks UBS and Credit Suisse were named in legal actions in US lawsuits brought on behalf of victims of apartheid South Africa.[4] An eight-year-old Iranian boy refugee took out a civil legal action against the Australian government. Life at the Woomera detention centre on Ashmore reef, over 500 miles to the west of Darwin, left him with acute, possibly chronic, post-traumatic stress disorder. The boy's lawyer said, 'Incarcerating a five year old [his age at the time of detention] is an instance of child abuse of an institutional kind'.[5] In October 2003 British auction house Christie's was publicly humiliated and became the subject of legal action for allegedly hiding the past of a painting by a Dutch master, Jacob Duck, which had been looted by the Nazis.

Evidence from the diaries of British officers who occupied parts of East Africa in the late nineteenth century formed the basis of a compensation claim by the King of Bunyoro, whose lands are based in what is now western Uganda. King Iguru sought £2.8 billion compensation from Britain for acts of brutality and exploitation clearly admitted in the diaries dating from the 1890s. An order from Colonel Henry Colville, British consul of Uganda, instructed an officer thus: 'I consider the capture of Kabalega's [Iguru's grandfather] treasure to be your primary objective'. A captain's diary commented, 'I have, and will in the future burn their houses, destroy their crops and cut down the banana plantations'.[6] A similar case was filed in the US in 2003 by descendants of the Herero tribe of Namibia. The tribe was virtually exterminated by German colonial forces during the 'scramble for Africa'. An estimated 65,000 were killed between 1904 and 1907. The £1.2 billion claim was against still-existing German firms accused of complicity in the historical crimes.

The difference between some of these cases and mockery of the fashion for long-range apology is the tangible impacts that these examples have on people alive today. There is a clear colonial fingerprint on much of the trouble, conflict, dependency and hardship that modern Africa experiences. Many of the reasons that drive refugee movements and people to seek asylum are similarly rooted in history. Crimes of Nazi Germany still live in the minds of those who experienced them. And there are still legal disputes over what should happen to looted wealth hidden in the Swiss banks that facilitated Nazi crimes.

In a case that shows how we are still touched by the long shadow of colonial abuses, lawyer Martyn Day recently took on the starched might of the British military establishment to represent a large number of Kenyan women in a case that accused army personnel of the repeated rape and mistreatment of local women dating back decades to the 1950s.

In the theatre of the courtroom, however, one image stands out of the mighty brought low by the law. It changed people's expectations about what can be achieved by using the law to force people to take responsibility for their actions. In 1990 the chief executives of America's largest tobacco companies swore, and were filmed, in front of a congressional committee that the nicotine they put in cigarettes was non-addictive, and as a result, and by implication, they could not be held responsible for the cancer deaths of thousands of addicted smokers. Cutting a very long story short, when evidence was produced to show that they had lied, the case of 'big tobacco' made the little person finally believe that the courts could be used to bring wrong-doers down, no matter how big they were. The moment was so iconic that it led to several books and films. Multi-billion dollar lawsuits followed. Global warming, however, could make big tobacco look like small beer.

CARBON GOES TO COURT

After thinking about the idea for a couple of months, Andrew Strauss agreed that it was not only possible for victims of climate change to turn to the law, but that there were numerous approaches they could take. In the summer of 2001 he presented his thoughts to Britain's first conference on ecological debt, which I organised at London's Institute of Contemporary Arts. Then things started to stir on a larger stage.

As heads of state from around the world prepared to gather in Johannesburg for the disappointment of the tenth anniversary of the Earth Summit, a shock was waiting. In the exhausted world of making global deals a new strategy was emerging. One small vulnerable country was preparing to abandon the negotiating table for the courtroom.

The Prime Minister of Tuvalu at the time, Koloa Talake, surprised the international community by announcing his country's intention to bring legal action against the world's worst polluters over their emissions of greenhouse gases. But it shouldn't have surprised anyone. Rising sea levels, coupled with extreme and unpredictable weather resulting from global warming will devastate Tuvalu and any other low-lying island country. Their small size and marginalisation from world affairs left them few options to seek redress. A lawsuit is an almost inevitable result of the increasing legalisation of international relations to meet perhaps the greatest environmental threat of our times. After war crimes tribunals, Nazi holocaust reparations and now suits for slavery as a crime against humanity, here was further evidence that what was once either ignored or the subject of diplomatic deal-making, was now open to international legal redress.

The trend toward the legalisation of international relations happened for several reasons. One driver is the failure of diplomacy and frustrations with a complex and constantly undermined United Nations. Another, ironically, is the success of economic globalisation. As more and more business deals take place across national borders, a more mature and comprehensive body of international law is needed to protect them. A further irony is that it is also due to the global ambitions of the United States. Wherever it goes it tends to take along its uniquely litigious political culture. Around half of all legal cases in the US are so-called 'tort' claims.[7] These are claims for compensation and punitive damages where injury or harm has resulted from reckless, negligent or improper behaviour.

The US is a country where, as nineteenth-century French historian Alexis de Tocqueville famously observed in 1840, there is 'scarcely any political question ... that is not resolved sooner or later into a judicial question'. As the warming atmosphere is a big and growing political question in which the US plays a large role, it is sooner rather than later that judicial resolution is emerging. Of course things will not be straightforward. The law needs evidence, litigants, appropriate jurisdiction. It needs both the ability to assess compensation commensurate with damages, and to constrain the perpetrators of harm. But there is now a greater scientific consensus about global warming's causes and consequences than on almost any other environmental issue. All industrialised countries consume fossil fuels at a rate per person that is far above a global sustainable threshold. This is their ecological debt. The climatic consequences in terms of floods, storms and droughts are borne by the world's majority in poor countries. So, it is also only logical that the law should be called in to instruct the ecological debt collectors.

At one end of the scale of scientific expectations for the coming decades, Tuvalu and at least four other small island states would become uninhabitable, whole nations ceasing to exist. At the same time, millions more from Asia to Latin America, the Middle East and Africa will be turned into environmental refugees. Immigration is already an explosive political issue in Europe, exploited in such a way that it threatens social stability. Huge new pressures resulting from a problem of the rich world's own making could push things to breaking point, as environmental refugees outnumber their political counterparts, yet lack recognised legal protection.[8]

There are serious unanswered questions about what will happen to the exclusive economic zones of such countries and what status and identity their populations will have. Where whole countries become uninhabitable, should their nations have new sovereign lands carved out for them in other states? Without proper environmental refugee status, will the world have to create lots of new little Israels for the environmentally displaced? Or would they become the first true 'world citizens'? If there is no state left, how can the state protect its citizens? With global warming creating a potential 150 million environmental refugees by 2050, according to Oxford

University academic Norman Myers, it is a huge challenge to international refugee law. Merely ignoring the problem will not make it go away. It seems that the law will have to adapt in the same way that threatened communities will. There will be quibbles but the environment can clearly be used as 'a tool to harm' by the state and to persecute people, which under current legislation is what would have to be proved. Yet also to fit the argument for refugee status, could the harm be called intentional? Yes, if a set of policies is pursued in full knowledge of their damaging consequences, such as flooding a valley where an ethnic minority might live. The causes and consequences of climate change – who is responsible and who gets hurt – are now well understood. Actively disregarding that knowledge is clearly intentional behaviour.

In 2001 the *World Disasters Report*, published by the International Federation of Red Cross and Red Crescent Societies, predicted that an international legal challenge over climate change was inevitable. The following year the same report produced new figures showing a huge increase in the number of people affected by climate-related disasters. For the Oceania region including the South Pacific islands the figure had grown 65 times.

The UN Environment Programme's attempts to assess the economic costs of global warming show the figure could soon reach around $300 billion per year. Technical problems in accurately assessing costs in poor countries – few things get insured for example – means that figure could easily be double, or more. No proper global assessment has been made yet of what it will cost poor countries to adapt physically to climate change. Large amounts of population and infrastructure are typically concentrated in areas that will be most affected, such as coasts and rivers. The best guess of development groups is that climate change could cost developing countries up to £6.5 trillion over the next 20 years, many times anticipated aid flows.[9]

None of these calculations, however, can measure the losses due to nations faced with their own extinction, the loss of their land, history, exclusive economic zones and sacred sites.

A new size of balance sheet will have to be invented. In spite of these problems, though, how can we be so sure that the law will bear fruit?

There are few basic principles in law. One is that if someone does you harm two things should happen. First, they should stop what they're doing, and second, they should compensate you for the harm done. Climate change is doing harm to some people and it is the consequence of what other people are doing.

The climate convention signed by most countries at the Earth Summit in Brazil in 1992 committed the signatories to sharing equally the global commons of the atmosphere. Given the slow progress since, and even backsliding, that it was signed at that time was an amazing success. Any country, consequently, pouring more than its fair share of pollution into the atmosphere could be challenged. The United States, obviously, makes a particularly compelling legal target. Not only does the US with 4.6 per cent of the world's population account for 25 per cent of anthropogenic greenhouse gas emissions, but the Bush administration has refused to submit the international climate agreement, the Kyoto Protocol, for Senate ratification. Figures released by the British government's Environment Secretary, Margaret Beckett, suggested that George Bush's energy plan could leave US emissions 25 per cent higher in 2010, compared to the 7 per cent cut that the US agreed to when negotiating in Kyoto.

Various legal options are being explored by countries like Tuvalu. They range from contentious cases against other countries before international tribunals, to suits against private corporations in domestic courts. The way forward will not be easy. As with any legal action on such a large scale there are, again, many problems ranging from attaining jurisdiction, to attribution, demonstrating legal causation and proving damages.

Another reason why climate change will increasingly end up in court, is because it doesn't only affect people in the majority world. Rich countries get hit too. German interior ministry officials estimated the costs of the great floods that hit

Germany in the summer of 2002, affecting a third of a million people, at €9 billion. Heat waves in France in summer 2003 killed around 15,000 people more than the seasonal average, with the highest fatality rate centred on Paris, leaving countless aggrieved relatives.[10] House prices in increasingly flood prone areas will be depressed by rising insurance premiums and lower buyer confidence. Only the technical problems of attributing blame and therefore proving liability, and setting a price for damages, have put people off looking to the law to seek compensation.

Standing at the front of the queue to solve this problem is the industry most exposed to the fall out from global warming, and likely to pass on its costs – the insurance industry. Myles Allen writing in the science journal *Nature* explained how they might do it.[11] Insurers, for example, on a balance of probabilities will raise the cost of premiums to householders where there is an increased risk of flooding due to climate change. That both represents an immediate direct cost and sends a signal that will also likely lower a house's value. All you have to do, says Allen, is work out a 'mean likelihood-weighted liability by averaging over all possibilities consistent with currently available information'. Unpacked from industry jargon that means that if past greenhouse gas emissions have increased flood risk (or storm damage, or crop loss due to drought) tenfold, 90 per cent of the damage caused by a flood can be attributed to past emissions. Because greenhouse gases mix in the global commons of the atmosphere, 'an equitable settlement would apportion liability according to emissions', according to Allen. Insurance costs are incurred in advance due to changing risks. But similar calculations could possibly be used after the event to help seek compensation for actual damages. From unhappy householders with yuppy flats in London's Thames Gateway development ruined by flooding, to the South Pacific islanders of Tuvalu or Niue, these kinds of calculations could enable many more to seek reparations.

At the time of writing in early 2004 the first trickle of climate-related legal actions have begun. They may well turn into a flood to match what is happening along river banks and coastlines around the warming world. Intriguingly, in the context of trade stand-offs over steel and genetically modified food between the European Union and the United States, there is another, slightly more indirect route that could be more effective than any of the above. The short-term objective is to force US compliance with the international process. Their current opt-out avoids the costs of implementing reductions under Kyoto, which effectively amounts to a subsidy to domestic US businesses. The EU could calculate the value of that subsidy and apply 'border tax' adjustments to a selection of US exports until America started to play ball again. Then the US would have recourse to take a complaint to the dispute mechanism at the World Trade Organisation where it would have to defend its behaviour. Trade sanctions, imposed collectively by a group of countries in defence of a multilateral environmental agreement negotiated in good faith like the Kyoto Protocol, are however, entirely legitimate in international law and the decision would very likely go against the US.[12]

It was probably an awareness of this possible course of action, which had received some international media attention at the annual climate conference in 2003 in Milan following a short report I wrote on the subject,[13] that led to the odd appearance of one of George W. Bush's climate change advisors on British national radio the day after the president's re-election result in November 2004. Myron Ebell of the ultra conservative US Competitive Enterprise Institute, part funded by Exxon, was interviewed on BBC Radio 4's agenda-setting *Today Programme* in the early morning on 4 November. Tellingly his was the first major interview to be given by someone closely associated with the administration. And, it was the first indication of the new 'unifying' tone the administration would take. Global warming, according to Ebell, was a European plot to undermine US economic dominance, and there was no way that the Kyoto Protocol would be signed during a second George W. Bush term of office. The timing, the subject and the aggressive tone of the interview were all clear signs that the issue was being taken seriously, and not just in the US.

After publishing the short report mentioned above, I asked my friend the Green Party Member of the European Parliament, Caroline Lucas, to write officially to the then Trade Commissioner for Europe Pascal Lamy. The question was simple, did he agree that Europe having ratified the Kyoto Protocol could take action against those who hadn't, like the United States, to level the economic playing field. His response was a delicious example for students of the nuance of high government and the political art of the denial, non-denial. Beginning by calling the idea a 'thought provoking contribution' to the debate that has raged since the US refused to ratify Kyoto, he then kept his options wide open.[14] It would be 'counterproductive', he wrote, to contemplate trade action while the EU was persuading Russia to ratify the protocol – but that problem has since been solved. Then he wrote, 'There is a clear case for being aware of any adverse effects on our industry and doing everything in our power to minimise these. In that sense it is relevant also to keep under review the scope for action under WTO rules to "level the playing field"'.

Interestingly something of a precedent has already been set in which the roles were reversed. At the time of the Earth Summit in 1992 the European Commission was considering a climate change tax. To support the idea they cited the US Hazardous Substances Trust Fund, popularly known as Superfund. Superfund is a financial mechanism geared towards the clean up of domestic toxic sites. It is paid for by taxes levied on the petro-chemical industries. Higher rates of tax are levied against imports of petrol and chemicals. This means that a direct trade measure is being used to pursue clear environmental objectives. Superfund was considered by a GATT (General Agreement on Tariffs and Trade) Dispute Settlement Panel following a complaint made by the European Community. The Panel decided that the tax was consistent with GATT rules and that the effective border tax adjustment was not an unacceptable restraint of trade.[15]

If there is a problem with using the law to tackle the slackers over climate change, it is that ad hoc legal processes cannot replace the need for an effective global climate deal. Nothing can replace the need to set a target for safe concentration of greenhouse gases in the atmosphere low enough to prevent runaway climate change, and then shrink emissions to meet it. Nothing, also, can substitute for a proper global constitutional framework within which to do that. The shrinking size of the carbon cake and laws of physics also mean that the framework will have to spell out how the cake will be shared equally among the global population. But as we work painfully towards that end, a litigation laxative might just get things moving. America, in particular, has led the way in showing the world how litigation can be a central mechanism for putting wrongs to right. If the law rebounds on the US over global warming it will simply be that unique American sense of justice coming home to its place of birth.

10

Data for the Doubtful:
the Lessons of War Economies

History teaches nothing, but only punishes for not learning its lessons.

Vassily Kliuchesky[1]

I have been charged with attempting to apply totalitarian methods to a free community. No criticism could be more misdirected. In a totalitarian state the problem of the distribution of sacrifice does not exist ... It is only in a free community that the task of government is complicated by the claims of social justice ... The aim of these pages is, therefore, to devise a means of adapting the distributive system of a free community to the limitations of war.

J.M. Keynes, *How to Pay for the War*, 1940[2]

Decades after the last artillery was fired in anger on the fields of Belgium during the First World War of 1914–18, their shells keep killing people.[3] Farmers who plough the difficult clay soil of the old battlefields still unearth unexploded ordnance. In 1983 a 'muffled explosion' near the village of Loker announced that Jacques Covemeacker's tractor had hit a bomb. It killed him leaving a son and widow. No one knew if the shell was German or Allied. In a 25 km radius around the town of Ypres alone, 350 tonnes of explosives are recovered every year. A specialist bomb disposal squad called the Dovos get called out 15 times every day, another 30 requests for help are logged. Belgian authorities estimate it will take 150 years to clear the rest away.

To misquote a famous speech from the Hollywood film *Gladiator*, we should be careful what we do in life because our actions echo long after we die. Greenhouse gases that we put into the atmosphere today will continue to disrupt the climate causing even greater upheaval than the First World War's unexploded bombs. That is one parallel. But there is a more optimistic lesson from such tragic events that we may be 'punished' for not learning.

When governments really want to, they can do almost anything, including good things. That is the simple point of this chapter. However enormous the task, if a convincing case for necessary action can be made, anything is possible. More recent history demonstrates that whole economies can be re-geared in short periods of time, which is exactly the demand global warming makes of us. The British Prime Minister Tony Blair said, for example, we needed to reduce emissions by 60 per cent by 2050. If not probable, the past says it is possible.

You don't have to be a fan of war to learn from conflict. War focuses the mind of government to a striking and instructive degree. Could it be that the experience of social and military mobilisation in wartime might answer the biggest question to do with global warming: are we capable of changing our lifestyles and economies *enough* and *in time* to stop it?

The enemy is not another country, but a hostile atmosphere that needs to be disarmed of its increasingly violent arsenal of droughts, floods and storms. Can it happen? The greatest challenge of sustainable development is to reduce consumption levels in rich countries. Cynics say it is impossible for the comparatively wealthy to change their lifestyles. Hiding behind one Bush after another, the US appears ready to let the world burn to defend its 'way of life'. Yet action to preserve a habitable atmosphere, like putting enough fuel in a plane to get from A to B, is non-negotiable. And history shows that while not easy, behaviour can be changed by focused leadership, public education and a sense of common cause.

In view of the publicity you have accorded to Mrs Barrow's letter in your edition of to-day, I hope that you will spare me space to say, as an advocate of the consumption of grass-mowings, that I have eaten them regularly for three years, and off many lawns. The sample I am eating at present comes off a golf green on Mitcham Common. (J.R.B. Branson, letter to *The Times*, May 1940)

It's not possible to find out what happened to the health of J.R.B. Branson as a result of his or her grass eating habit, but the pall of austerity that held wartime and postwar Britain is not as miserably straightforward as it can at times seem.

My parents grew up through the Second World War and learned the habits that would stay with them until today. Words from magazines like *Good Housekeeping* in 1942 rang in their ears. 'Learn to regard every type of waste as a crime', wagged the finger, and, 'If you have the will to win, Save your Rubber, Paper, Tin', intoned the rhyming copywriters.

When as a teenager I became an active environmentalist my mother reflected on the new green activism. 'I reckon we were the first greens', she said. From a time when most resources were in short supply she listed the myriad ways they developed for saving fuel, conserving food and recycling objects. I think she was perplexed that a new generation had re-invented values that were second nature to her own. She was amused that they preached with the enthusiasm of explorers believing they had discovered a new continent, while she knew people had been living there for years.

Grow fit not fat on your war diet! Make full use of the fruit and vegetables in season. Cut out 'extras', cut out waste; don't eat more than you need. You'll save yourself money, ... and you'll feel fitter than you ever felt before. (Food Facts No 1, Ministry of Food, 1940)

The upbeat and hopeful tone of the government was part of a double strategy, persuade and legislate. It proved to be more than self-serving rhetoric. The combination of moral leadership and rationing had two significant results. People did, indeed, become fitter and healthier, and consumption of resources was drastically cut. The awareness that each had a personal role to play spread through the population. Lady Reading's comments to the Women's Voluntary Service in July 1940 take on an unintended paradoxical flavour in the context of global warming: 'Very few of us can be heroines on the battlefront, but we can all have the tiny thrill of thinking as we hear the news of an epic battle in the air, "Perhaps it was my saucepan that made a part of that Hurricane"'.

Every aspect of people's lives came to be scrutinised. The Board of Trade issued an advisory leaflet in 1943, *Getting Ready for Baby*, that urged the population to, 'Never buy more napkins than you really need. Remember fair shares for others, too'. Non-government groups also took part in the refashioning of people's behaviour. In *Feeding Dogs and Cats in Wartime* the RSPCA in 1941 advised people that, 'Potatoes are plentiful and if you put in extra tubers when digging for victory you will not have it on you conscience that shipping space is being taken for food for your animals'.

There was nowhere to hide from the message that the defeat of an external threat depended on how you carried out the tiniest of acts in your daily life. Then, as now, one of the greatest challenges was fuel conservation. The government dubbed it the 'Battle for Fuel'. If you stayed in a hotel in late 1942 and decided to wash away the anxiety of wartime Britain you would have been confronted with this sign from the Ministry of Fuel: 'As part of your personal share in the Battle for Fuel you are asked NOT to exceed five inches of water in this bath. Make it a point of honour not to fill the bath above this level'. The Ministry of Fuel and Power would let no one forget that, 'Britain's 12,000,000 households are 12,000,000 battle fronts in this great drive to save fuel'. People were told to lag their hot water tanks properly, save milk bottle tops and recycle tyres and inner tubes.

Good Housekeeping magazine strictly reminded its readers in 1943 that, 'Few books bear second reading – comb your bookcase for salvage'. Would any of today's overworked book reviewers disagree? The National Savings Committee reminded people that: 'The "Squander-bug" causes that fatal itch to buy for buying's sake – the symptom of shopper's disease'. For Joanna Chase writing in *Sew and Save* the cause was taken to evangelical lengths as she told readers, 'Gone are the days when any of us have either the money or the space to possess six of everything in our undies drawer. But you should try to have three of everything, one set on your back, one in the wash, and one clean and ready for any emergency that may crop up'. So, even the classic English reserve was sacrificed to the war effort.

The barrage of information was a success. A combination of emergency powers brought in during the war and a concerted public campaign on changing attitudes dramatically cut waste. By April 1943, for example, 31,000 tonnes of kitchen waste were being saved every week, enough to feed 210,000 pigs. Food consumption fell 11 per cent by 1944 from before the war. Scrap metal was being saved at the rate of 110,000 tonnes per week.[4]

> At this most important time
> Needless travel is a 'crime'.
> Rail companies' advertisement, 1942

Between 1938 and 1944 there was an enormous 95 per cent drop in the use of motor vehicles in the UK. Even in the United States fuel was strictly and successfully rationed to eliminate unnecessary travel. Such a drop exceeds even the deepest cuts in consumption that the most pessimistic climate watchers say is needed in wealthy countries today. In a similar period, 1938–1943, the use of public transport increased by 13 per cent.

Across all goods and services consumption fell 16 per cent but with much higher drops at the household level.[5] In just six years from 1938 British homes cut their use of electrical appliances by 82 per cent. At the same time spending on 'amusements' went up by 10 per cent.[6] In case anyone might question the massive conservation drive, the Ministry for Information produced a manual, *Data for the Doubtful*.

History also judged kindly the overall effect on people's health of the new ways of living. The period from 1937 to 1944 saw a dramatic fall in infant mortality, a clear indicator of more general improvements in the nation's health. At the start of the period around 58 children per 1,000 died before their first birthday. By 1944 that figure had fallen to 45 per 1,000.[7] Experience shows that the shift to a low energy economy could create more convivial lifestyles. On its current course of growth transport, mostly vehicular, as shown in the earlier investigation of the car, is predicted to become the third most common cause of death and disability by 2020.

It is easy to imagine the cry that will go up today when people realise the degree of cuts in consumption necessary to preserve and share a habitable planet. To many it will seem a sacrifice too far. And most decision-makers live far removed from the murderous reality of climate change. For people in industrialised countries the threat of global warming still seems too distant to justify significant disturbance to their private lives and consumption habits, especially for those whose houses have not been flooded. Action will seem rather more urgent for Bangladeshis and Mozambicans living in flood zones than for Londoners living on Primrose Hill. But the situation in the global environmental war economy is not so different from the dilemma that faced individuals in Britain's Second World War economy. As Hugh Dalton, head of the Board of Trade, put it in 1943, 'There can be no equality of sacrifice in this war. Some must lose their lives and limbs, others only the turn-ups on their trousers'.

Today's major industrial powers all have relatively recent experience of war economies. In 1942 the US limited gasoline to 3 gallons per week for 'nonessential' vehicles. Germany had rationing throughout the war and Japan introduced forms of rationing in 1941. Rationing in the US was motivated by a patriotic desire to ensure that both citizens and soldiers received a fair distribution of goods. Gasoline entitlement was set by how necessary a person's vehicle was to them. When the US implemented energy rationing at the time of the first OPEC oil crisis in the early 1970s a similar logic was used. A Congressional Declaration of Purpose announced that 'positive and effective action' was needed to protect 'general welfare ... conserve scarce energy supplies' and *'insure fair and efficient distribution*' (my emphasis).[8] Apply the same principles more generally today and you have a plan for tackling global warming.

MAKING THE CASE

At every turn though, even in the face of Nazi aggression, the case for major government action to conserve resources during war-time had to be argued. The big question then was how to find the resources to fight industrially resurgent Germany. Just as in reverse today, the case is made by politicians from the United States to Russia, without investigating the costs of inaction, that halting global warming will be too expensive. At the outset of the Second World War fiscally conservative magazine *The Economist* argued that government expenditure should be raised to more than three times the contemporary level of revenue to finance the war. J.M. Keynes also lobbied the Treasury through a series of articles in *The Times* newspaper and a pamphlet called 'How to Pay for the War'. According to the official war history Keynes set out to 'bring home the true nature of the war-time problems' and pointed out that even a 'moderate development of the war effort necessitated a very large cut in general consumption'.[9] If taxes, rationing and scarcity were inadequate to lower consumption, Keynes foresaw the danger of an out-of-control inflationary spiral of wages and prices. In that case the 'spirit and efficiency' of the nation would be at risk. To avoid it Keynes proposed a plan of compulsory saving, backed with the promise of a payback at the end of the war.

Although it may seem astonishing with the benefit of hindsight about the Second World War – because surely no measure was too great to fight Hitler – Keynes' medicine was thought too strong. Opinion was not ready. It's a lesson for governments too tentative to act affirmatively in the face of climatic catastrophe. Keynes lamented, 'My discomfort comes from the fact, now made obvious, that the general public are not in favour of any plan'.[10]

Keynes faced problems that haunt modern officials tasked with re-gearing the economy to be climate-friendly and climate-proof. Measures that were simple to promote were also understood to cause 'troublesome complaints of hardship and inequity when their detailed enforcement hit individuals'. Even then Keynes, the friend of redistribution, thought this was no reason for inaction. And he had found a key to unlock official intransigence – agitation. His 'great service', wrote *The Economist* in 1939, 'has been to impel the so-called 'leaders of opinion' to reveal the state of their ignorance on the central economic problem of the war'.[11]

Sir John Simon was Chancellor of the Exchequer at the time and certainly became aware of the trouble he was in. Think of his words marked down in Latin in a memo at the time, echoing through a modern day government, aware of global warming yet committed to a pattern of conventional economic growth with its unavoidable, related greenhouse gas emissions. 'Video meliora proboque, deteriora sequor', translated in the official history it reads: 'I see the right, and I approve it too, Condemn the wrong, and yet the wrong pursue'.

As the war progressed purchase taxes were introduced as an attack on luxury spending. As more time passed the taxes became more sophisticated. Real luxuries like fur coats, silk dresses and jewellery were hit with the top rate. Essentials such as towels, bed-linen and utility clothing were exempt. Still, even these measures were a struggle. The fur trade lobbied government emphasising its economic importance. It would be wrong to leave the industry crippled at the war's end, it said. As a result, a special tax exempt category of 'utility furs' made of rabbit and sheepskin was introduced.

From now on governments will struggle with how to reduce consumption of the many things whose manufacture and use relies on burning fossil fuels. They will struggle to convince a sceptical public, and in rich countries a largely comfortable one, that take many things for granted. As Thorstein Veblen pointed out more than a century ago, once luxuries become generally available they cease to be seen as luxuries, instead taking on the character of essentials.[12] Famously in Britain during the Second World War there were collections of pots and pans and the railings from outside houses to provide extra metal to help the war effort. Some believe that the more important purpose of the collections was to convince the public of the seriousness of the war situation, and that the metal itself was secondary. Today agitation like Keynes' will be needed before governments are prepared to go to the public with similar confidence of purpose.

I was invited with others to a dinner in the run up to the tenth anniversary of the Rio Earth Summit organised by several government departments. We met around an intimate dinner table in a private hotel dining room. The civil servants were looking for ideas. They wanted a big idea to take with them to Johannesburg in 2002 where the summit was to happen. I first suggested we should approach a conference in Africa with humility, and acknowledge our ecological debts. The official from the Department of Trade and Industry scoffed. By the time dessert came round I made another suggestion. Why weren't they honest with the British public and tell them what life would be like if necessary emissions cuts were made. Why not prepare public opinion now, by admitting the scale of required action, so it would be possible to sell the appropriate policies later? There was the sound of choking. Unlike the forthrightness of public communications during the war, the most the civil servants felt able to do now was 'suggest' that people might like to make one less car journey a month.

Of course, the contemporary general public is far less credulous about what the government tells it than it was in the 1940s. The impact on lifestyles of real constraints on the use of fossil fuels will also make many feel uncomfortable about changes they will have to make. We have become accustomed to the only restraint on our consumption being how much money we have to spend. The idea of fuel rationing will be seen as intolerable and cause outrage. But it is rationing only in the sense that our take-home pay is a ration of wealth. We can no more live beyond our environmental budget than we can our financial budget, without running into problems. And, it will be rather harder to come back from a bankrupt climate than bank account. The other big difference in this analogy, which affects how we work out a solution, is that the atmosphere is a global commons bounded by physical limits of environmental tolerance. Financial budgets, at least in theory, display far more flexible limits. There is no reason, because of that, why anyone should, either by right or accident of place of birth, have more of that global commons than anyone else.

Climate change is not considered as imminent as a potentially invading army, or as threatening. Yet, in terms of the balance of modern civilisation it threatens greater global upheaval, drawn out over a much longer time than the Second World War.

There should still be some small comfort in the knowledge that all these problems have been wrestled with before and, to a degree, have been overcome. But they have been overcome only *when* the urgency and necessity is generally understood. Our current dilemma, compared to 1940s Britain, will be managed differently. Modern communications methods are more sophisticated. And many people have already thought hard about how on earth you can protect the global commons of the atmosphere on the one hand, and balance the world's competing claims to use it as a dustbin for our economic waste on the other.

11

The New Adjustment

Venus favours the bold.

Ovid, *Metamorphoses*

The per capita wattage that is critical for social well-being lies within an order of magnitude which is far above the horsepower known to four-fifths of humanity and far below the power commanded by any Volkswagen driver.

Ivan Illich, *Energy and Equity*, 1974

THE MAN WHO OWNS THE SOLAR SYSTEM ...

You can buy a one acre plot of land on the moon for £19.95. Slightly cheaper is Venus, which can be had for £14.25 per acre, plus registration fee. You can do this because on 22 November 1980 Dennis M. Hope went into the offices of San Francisco County and filed a declaration of ownership for both.[1] Just to be sure he then also filed with the Federal Government, in the USSR, and at the General Assembly of the United Nations. You get a copy of the declaration with every property purchased. Dennis Hope was nothing if not, well, hopeful. He also declared ownership of the planets Mars, Mercury, Jupiter, Saturn, Uranus, Neptune, Pluto and all their respective moons. Soon plots of land on Jupiter's moon, Io, will be available. He set up the Lunar Embassy in Rio Vista, California and started to license others to sell plots. One such, MoonEstates.com, describes itself as the United Kingdom's 'only extraterrestrial land agents'.

They can't be serious, can they? In 1967 the Outer Space Treaty was signed by the international community, expressly forbidding any government from claiming any celestial bodies as their property. But there was a loophole. The committee responsible for the Treaty's wording forgot to include private firms or individuals in their draft. The mistake was spotted and in 1984 the Moon Treaty was agreed. It would have prevented the exploitation of space for private profit. But only six countries signed.

Those eager today to sell you a space ranch see this as a good thing. In their eyes the Moon Treaty, 'would outlaw property rights in the rest of the universe and indefinitely bog down space settlement in a "common heritage of all mankind" morass'. Thousands of people are buying plots. Look no further for evidence that the prospect of great wealth linked to property rights can loosen your grip on reality. Condemning the evil of the Moon Treaty, the sellers point out, 'If it had been ratified and oil was found on the Moon; any company would by law be prohibited from mining it. Surely, that is not in the public's interest. (and if you find it on your property ... well, congratulations ... you could be very rich!)'.[2] No thought here of the scenario's unlikeliness, or even the few problems inherent in extraction and transport or, indeed, the climate change that results from burning oil. The sellers go to great lengths to establish their seriousness. For Mars, a careful Bill of Rights has been written to mediate in the event of land disputes arising between you and a 'native creature'. They deny that their product is a novelty item.

Property regimes are a balancing act. The wrong sort can cause misery. Restrictive patents applied to medicine, for example, can kill. Charities such as Oxfam working on health issues estimate that 37,000 people die every day as a consequence of patents making drugs too expensive for people living in poverty to buy. These are avoidable deaths that follow from the way that a property right, by another name, is also a right to exclude. However, the absence of property rights can also be lethal. Global warming is a text book example of the tragedy of the commons. The concept entered popular debate before consensus emerged on climate change, but the atmosphere slips into the notion like a too-well fitting shoe.

Taking the idea from a pamphlet written by William Forster Lloyd in 1833 (the year before Robert Malthus died leaving European imaginations gripped by the dangers of population growth), Garrett Hardin published in a technical journal his own famous essay 'The Tragedy of the Commons' in 1968.[3]

Hardin, too, saw problems with the psychology of denial. Using the example of over-grazing and the resulting destruction of common pasture land by herders on whom no restrictions were placed, he saw individuals prepared to pursue their own short-term gain at the expense not only of the wider community but also, importantly, their own longer term interests. But he was hopeful too, believing that 'education can counteract the natural tendency to do the wrong thing', but that it was also necessary to 'constantly refresh' the required knowledge.

The reason for the United States' refusal to act meaningfully on global warming was given with remarkable consistency by Presidents George Bush senior and junior. It is the reluctance to accept any restraint on the freedom of US citizens to pursue their way of life. According to Hardin this is the attitude at the heart of the tragedy of the commons:

> Every new enclosure of the commons involves the infringement of somebody's personal liberty. Infringements made in the distant past are accepted because no contemporary complains of a loss. It is the newly proposed infringements that we vigorously oppose; cries of 'rights' and 'freedom' fill the air. But what does 'freedom' mean? When men mutually agreed to pass laws against robbing, mankind became more free, not less so. Individuals locked into the logic of the commons are free only to bring on universal ruin; once they see the necessity of mutual coercion, they become free to pursue other goals.

There is a lobby group in Britain called Freedom to Fly. They oppose environmental restraints on the aviation industry. It is a signature of the tragedy of the commons that individuals pursue their own interests in denial of responsibilities to the wider community. When reckless pollution, in full knowledge of its likely consequences, actually results in death, economic damage and great physical harm in the case of climate change, how different is it from drunk driving?[4] If your nation's lifestyle actually requires you to go to war in order to ensure a continued supply of cheap fossil fuels, how different is that from mugging or armed robbery? In which case, why not have lobby groups called Freedom to Drive Drunk and Freedom to Mug? They would amount to much the same thing. Could it be so simple? Could it be that we allow crises like climate change to occur only because we do not perceive them to represent criminal damage and injury, when we have no problem seeing other, far more petty crimes in that way? The challenge, then, would be to have a constitutional, legal framework for the management of the atmosphere which would force us to change our perception of the atmosphere – a framework which would determine both our rights and responsibilities.

Received wisdom among government circles in places like Britain and the US is that radical lifestyle changes are politically impossible to promote. Ironically those same governments have, for decades, been demanding that many of the world's poorest countries tighten their belts, cut spending and completely reshape their economies to pay their foreign financial debts. Eminent Indian academic M.S. Swaminathan wrote:

> The World Bank and IMF talk about structural adjustment in monetary terms. My own feeling is what we really need is adjustment to sustainable life styles [that] the Bank would not recommend. Because their structural adjustment is in money terms, not value. But if developing countries have to undergo such an adjustment in terms of financial problems ... industrialised countries will also have to go through a structural adjustment process.[5]

Conventional economic adjustment in poor countries is a two-stage process. Stabilisation comes first, followed by a root and branch re-gearing of the economy. How might this apply to tackling ecological debt and establishing environmentally sustainable economies?

The first task would be to remove major distortions. Currently standard economic measurements do not include social and environmental costs. This means two things. The economy free rides for example, on the way that families provide free upbringing, care and maintenance for the workforce and the way that natural resources like fossil fuels get used up, treated like free income to the economy and spent like a one-off family inheritance. The second effect is a hugely over-valued economy, one that doesn't count either depreciation or expenditure. It is reminiscent of the sort of accounting that brings Enron-like corporations to ruin.

Full cost accounting on the other hand would create the proper feedback of information to the economy, helping return balance to the nation's accounts for more prudential economic planning. Adjustment though will be a much longer, negotiated process. First, a broad range of reforms is needed to develop greater economic democracy. Second, all economic planning needs to be set within known or precautionary environmental limits, primarily in this case climatic tolerance. These changes are about restoring what might be called the balance of environmental payments – after the common economic term that refers to the flow of imports and exports – but in this case a balance that results from the trade between human economic activity and the natural environment. The primary objective would be to eliminate the ecological deficit, manifest in the damaging accumulation of CO_2 in the atmosphere. But what orderly procedure and framework could guide and shape such a process?

THE MAN WHO THINKS THE ATMOSPHERE SHOULD BE OWNED EQUALLY BY US ALL

Einstein famously observed that a problem cannot be solved from within the mindset that created it. He would have been happy, in that case, to see an extraordinary musician stepping into the world of international climate negotiations. Even more so for two other reasons: one, the instrument he played, and two, for the particular direction that theoretical physics took following Einstein in its quest for a universal theory of matter and creation.

I first met Aubrey Meyer in the late 1980s when we were both involved with the British Green Party. I'd been inspired as a teenager by Petra Kelly of the German greens and got involved with my local party before drifting after college into the party's crummy-but-eager national office, on the equally crummy Balham High Street in south London. I ran around working on campaigns, being the party's youth speaker and sitting on its council. At the time all anybody knew of Balham came from a mocking travelogue by the late comedian Peter Sellers. Mention the place and anyone of a certain generation would smile and say, 'Ah, gateway to the South'. But history is full of extra-ordinary things beginning in ordinary places.

The latest attempt to describe the fundamental make-up of our universe is called string theory. In its basic form it suggests that all matter at a sub-atomic level is made up of 'strings' that vibrate differently to lay the foundations of the elements. It is oddly appropriate, then, that the future of our climate should fall into the hands of a former professional viola player and composer.

Getting to know Aubrey was like getting to know a city that reveals itself only slowly. I'd known him on-and-off for several years before first visiting his house. We were meant to be talking about work but I saw a violin leaning against a wall. I mentioned that I liked the Max Bruch Violin concerto. Casually saying that the piece wasn't in his repertoire he nevertheless picked up the violin and began to play, note perfect, a passage from the concerto. But to understand the depths of his passion about climate change a glossy concert programme held the key. Aubrey is a composer as well as a musician. A piece of his music had recently been performed by a major British orchestra. As composer the concert programme duly had space for his photograph and a short biography. Aubrey had insisted that instead of the details of his life, beneath the standard photograph of him in the musician's bow-tie uniform, and for the benefit of otherwise oblivious concert goers, was an explanation of the constitutional solution to global warming that he called contraction and convergence and which he set up the London-based Global Commons Institute to promote.[6]

Through the greens in the late 1980s and early 1990s Aubrey met a group of people interested in the problems of energy, natural resource depletion and climate change. What came out of those conversations was a genuine plan to save the world. What Aubrey understood was that, unlike Dennis Hope's planetary land grab, if we were to save the climate, everyone would have to have an equal entitlement to its life support system. Opposite to the centuries-long process of expansion and divergence between rich and poor in the global economy, both global warming and considerations of human equity meant a process of contraction and convergence had to be the next step.

WHAT IS CONTRACTION AND CONVERGENCE?

If you set out on a journey without the right destination, you are unlikely to get there. That is what international negotiations on climate change are like. They have set an arbitrary target to reduce greenhouse gas emissions by an average of 5.2 per cent among rich countries below 1990 levels by the period 2008–12, a target that has nothing to do with the science of what is actually necessary. And, so far, the community of nations has even failed to hit that random goal. While it is good that countries talk together, the journey plan is clearly wrong. How should we understand the arcane workings of such environmental diplomacy?

It is as if a group of people discover that in order to receive a life-saving medical treatment they have to travel to the city of Barcelona, as it is the only place the particular treatment is available. But disagreements emerge, some don't like Spanish food, others don't speak the language and for others the weather is not right. So they compromise and instead decide to travel to Berlin. There are, after all, similarities. It too is a major European city, and its name begins with a 'B'. No one is entirely happy, but all agree that progress has been made. The journey has begun. Unfortunately, however, the life-saving treatment is not available in Berlin. All the group are aware of this, though a silent agreement prevents it being mentioned too openly. They still need to get to Barcelona, and time is running out. To complete the analogy with international climate negotiations, the story would unfold something like this. The group then fail to reach even Berlin. There is an argument on the plane about who is going to sit where, which leads to several group members refusing to travel. Others then say they can't afford the time to travel. As all their luggage needs removing from the hold, the plane misses its take-off slot. Airport staff get suspicious about what is going on and under new security regulations the flight is cancelled until the following day.

The destination in climate change negotiations will be the concentration of greenhouse gases in the atmosphere at a precautionary level considered to be safe. Such an agreement won't be easy. Some low-lying South Pacific Islands consider existing levels of greenhouse gases to be already too high. In the very long term it might be possible to lower concentrations below what they are today, back towards the levels that existed before the industrial revolution.[7] Increasingly, however, agreement is emerging that the atmosphere should not be allowed to warm on average by more than 2 degrees centigrade. Any more could trigger a series of irreversible environmental processes like the break-up of the great Antarctic ice sheets and the death of forests, in turn causing uncontrollable global warming. Working out what accumulation of greenhouse gases in the atmosphere would push us towards such a maximum temperature rise would create a target for climate policy. That is the first step to halting climate change and in the process of contraction and convergence.

In effect, it sets the maximum allowable size of the carbon cake of fossil fuels to be eaten by the global economy. When governments agree to be bound by such a target, the diminishing amount of carbon dioxide and the other greenhouse gases that the world can release could be calculated for each year in the coming century. This target sets the initial parameters for contraction. Convergence describes how each year's slice of this global emissions cake gets shared out among the nations of the world.

It is never likely that everyone in the world will use identical amounts of fossil fuels. Our circumstances are too different. However, it is highly likely that any deal to manage the global commons of the atmosphere will have to be based on the principle that, in a carbon-constrained world, everyone should have equal entitlements to their share of the atmosphere's ability to safely absorb greenhouse gas emissions. Up to the point that the world converts to clean, renewable energy, this roughly equates to access to economic opportunity. However, the process couldn't happen overnight without the world going into the economic equivalent of toxic shock. It would need to happen over an agreed timeframe, or convergence period.

To summarise the process so far: first it is necessary to cap total greenhouse gas emissions, then progressively to reduce them; entitlements to emit then get allocated, or 'pre-distributed', in a pattern of international convergence that moves in a set timeframe towards being equal per person. Under an emerging plan like this, people and nations that take economic benefits by emitting more than their fair share – eating more carbon cake than their allocated slice – will somehow have to pay compensation to the 'under-polluters' by purchasing their spare entitlements, or carbon cake. Otherwise they run up a huge ecological debt.[8]

Anything less than a global deal cannot solve climate change. There will always be the problem of uncontrollable greenhouse gas emissions from free-riding countries. Probably, the only way to begin negotiations on how to cut the world's carbon cake is to start with the principle that we all have equal rights to it. What we do with them is another matter.

This has enormous and, from a development perspective, very positive consequences. It can liberate vast resources to finance development. But, if action to combat global warming is delayed, emissions grow and populations rise, the size of an acceptable carbon cake slice will get smaller and smaller. In other words, the sooner we act the better. The only weakness of contraction and convergence is that it will take time to negotiate and many poor countries desperately need the resources to adapt to climate change now. All that means, though, is that this cannot be the only international mechanism relied upon to transfer resources from rich to poor.

The notion, though, that there are limits, even if unpredictable and flexible, that we must work within is still difficult for many to grasp. This can be demonstrated by how easily even senior civil servants can completely misunderstand the challenge. Take this graph from the UK government's environment department Defra (see Figure 11.1).[9] Even for those who react allergically to the sight of graphs it is worth looking at one particular, monumental oversight. Their projection for cutting emissions to 'stabilise' greenhouse gases at a certain level shows that by around 2070 there will be no fossil fuels left at all for countries outside the rich countries' club – not a barrel of oil, heap of coal or canister of gas to burn. Quite how Britain's famously smooth civil servants will explain their logic to delegations from India, China, Brazil or Ethiopia will make for an interesting ministerial meeting. They have shown the necessary contraction of emissions, but not the convergence. Yet the two must occur together.

The other great doubt, of course, is what to do about the most reluctant nation, the United States? When the US pulled out of climate talks in early 2001 there was uproar. But even before that it was negotiating in bad faith. At international talks in The Hague in late 2000 it proposed a form of 'carbon laundering', claiming domestic forests and farmland as carbon 'sinks' and credits against necessary emissions reductions. I call it laundering because it replaces one reliable and stable store of carbon in the form of coal and oil for an unstable storehouse in the form of trees and plants which die and re-release their carbon. US proposals then could have led to an overall 14 per cent increase in CO_2 emissions rather than any real cuts.[11]

Under the first George W. Bush administration (1999–2004) the US used two arguments to defend its withdrawal from international negotiations. One was flippant and can be dismissed, the other was interesting and creates a small opening

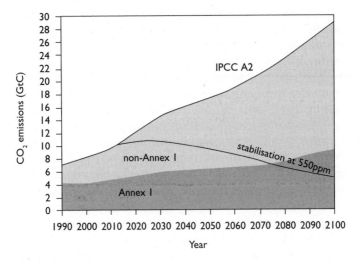

Figure 11.1   Projected global emissions under one business-as-usual scenario and a possible pathway to stabilisation at 550ppm as visualised by government department Defra, but which leaves non-industrialised countries with no allowable emissions

Notes:
Annex 1 – the first major 'first world' industrialised nations – includes some 'transition' economies
non-Annex 1 – all other nations not included in Annex 1
A2 – is one of the scenarios used by the IPCC to project likely future climate change; it is more conservative than others that assume faster economic growth.[10]

of opportunity. First, they say that they cannot 'afford' to act. But, if the wealthiest and most resource hungry country in the world can't afford to act, who else can? Certainly not India where the average citizen emits around 20 times less CO_2 than their US counterpart, or Mozambique where the average citizen is responsible for nearly 300 times fewer similar emissions.

The second position stems from the so-called Byrd-Hagel resolution adopted in 1997 by the US Senate. It committed America to only 'limit' or 'reduce' emissions if poor countries were also involved in the deal. The Byrd-Hagel resolution accepted the logic of both controlling and cutting global emissions. This means that a total global emissions budget must be agreed on, capping greenhouse gas concentration levels in the atmosphere. It also means that the US, committed by its own declaration of independence to human equality, can embrace the contraction and convergence model.

There are several, subtly differing, equity-based proposals for global frameworks to tackle climate change that could supersede the current agreement, the Kyoto Protocol, when it has run its course by 2012. Only contraction and convergence, though, passes the tests for both environmental integrity – working within secure environmental limits, and political feasibility – offering real entitlements to majority world countries.

But is there any chance at all that the advanced industrial economies could make the kind of resources cuts necessary to fit into such a model? First, the historical experience of war economies described above suggests that they can if politicians are willing.[12] Second, to turn our back on the challenge would be the deepest hypocrisy. Why? Because the world's poorest countries have been reshaping their economies for decades and for a much worse reason. If they can do it to pay service on dubious foreign debts (that they are only partly responsible for), under the strict gaze of the World Bank and IMF, I see no reason why rich countries can't do it to pay off their more real ecological debts.

Majority world countries, lacking the systems of health, education and social support that the north enjoys, have tolerated badly designed 'structural adjustment programmes' intended to solve the orthodox debt crisis. But even the conservative *Financial Times* commented that the IMF through promoting these programmes under the so-called Washington Consensus 'probably ruined as many economies as they have saved'.[13] This thought is echoed by the Nobel Prize winning economist James Tobin who said, 'Their standard remedies, fiscal stringency and punitive interest rates, are devastating to economic life'.[14] It would be a shameless double-standard now to suggest that we in the rich world, using the targets that contraction and convergence will give us, can't work within the framework of 'sustainability adjustment programmes' to balance our ecological budgets. Is it asking too much, are we too soft to take the medicine?

Yet it is possible that neither the contraction and convergence framework, nor the approach of an environmental war economy, will succeed alone. Reform of our monetary system to re-connect the abstract world of finance and the supply of money to the physical world of natural resources may also be needed. Coming full circle, there once was a link between the money supply and gold and silver. Its availability was, to a degree, a limiting factor on what economies did, how big they grew.

If trade in emissions permits were to be conducted in dollars, for example, there would still be an in-built bias in favour of the dominant 'hard currency' countries. The US could further exploit its position as the world's key currency holder and print money to meet its needs. This would mean that it could escape pressure to reform, and entrench existing imbalances in the world economy.

The point is not to reduce the amount of energy that people use *per se*, but to reduce the amount used that comes from fossil fuels. A proposal for how this could be done comes from Richard Douthwaite. He says spare emissions permits from under-consuming countries in the contraction and convergence framework could be traded in a special currency the 'ebcu' (energy-backed currency unit). The ebcu issue to governments would be a one-off, and on the same per person basis as the emission permits. Spare permits, under a given ceiling, would be made available upon payment in ebcus. Thereafter, when 'spent', the ebcus get withdrawn from circulation and used permits are destroyed. This strictly controls the volume of spare emissions permits or 'special emissions rights' in the market. Such an approach creates a parallel monetary system, with built-in incentives, to ease the managed withdrawal from a fossil fuel economy. The complexity of implementation is reduced by the fact that, according to Douthwaite, '80 percent of the fossil carbon that ends up as man-made CO_2 in the earth's atmosphere comes from only 122 producers of carbon-based fuels'.[15]

How Contraction and Convergence (C&C) Works to Reconcile the Ecological Debt of Climate Change[16]

All countries collectively agree a target for a stable atmospheric concentration of carbon dioxide in the atmosphere. A 'global emissions budget' is then calculated, taken from the concentration figure. The target is reviewed annually so that it can be revised along with new scientific findings. Once the 'contraction budget' has been decided, the next question is how to distribute the entitlements between countries. Under contraction and convergence, the allocations of emissions entitlements between countries would converge to be equal, per person, by a specific date. Then entitlements would be allocated in proportion to national population, at the level it was in a specified baseline year to avoid perverse incentives to increase population. Emissions trading is a feature of the model.

C&C would reduce the complexity of climate negotiations to two simple variables that would need to be agreed:

- the target atmospheric concentration of CO_2, and
- the date when entitlements converge to being equal per capita

The approach offers the best chance of solving a great, and immensely destructive, international paradox. Majority world countries stand to be hit first and worst by global warming. For example, as mentioned above, all the internationally agreed targets for reducing poverty to emerge out of the 1990s decade-long series of UN conferences – collectively known as the Millennium Development Goals – will be tragically undermined by climate change.

Yet majority world countries have been reluctant to play along with the climate negotiations in the way they've been run to-date. They see no reason why, if rich countries have had a free-ride on the earth's finite fossil fuel resources for the whole of their economic development, they should jeopardise their own development through accepting any perceived restraints on economic activity. But C&C deals with this seemingly inescapable trap. Developing countries have consistently refused to take part in a framework that pre-allocates the property rights to a finite carbon budget in a manifestly inequitable way – so-called 'grandfathering' – in which the starting point is one where countries 'inherit' their past emission levels. That approach creates, in effect, a carbon aristocracy.

By specifying a set date for convergence at equal per capita rights, the C&C approach would give developing countries surplus emission allocations that they could then sell to countries that need extra permits – most of them developed. The revenue from the sale of surplus permits would give developing countries an income, which would encourage participation in a global climate deal. It would also create an added incentive to invest in clean technologies. Majority world countries also stand to benefit more, the sooner such an agreement is made. Because, as time passes, the cuts needed to prevent runaway global warming get

▶

bigger and so tradable emissions get fewer. In the pre-deal intervening period, it also means that rich over-polluting countries are abusing the global commons of the atmosphere without having to pay.

C&C and the US

Interestingly, C&C would also fit the stated position of the otherwise recalcitrant United States. In his statements on climate change, President George W. Bush set out specific criteria for what sort of treaty the US would be willing to sign. They included: a truly global deal including emissions targets for developing countries (or, from another perspective, entitlements), and the need for a science-based approach. Contraction and convergence, with its global participation design and formal greenhouse gas concentration target, is exactly such an approach.

12

Minerva's Owl

Over his shoulder I saw a star fall. It was me.

Tracy Chevalier, *Falling Angels*, 2001[1]

The owl of Minerva spreads its wings only with the falling of the dusk.

G.W.F. Hegel, *Elements of the Philosophy of Right*, 1821

'I reckon about a third of the town is gone', said Terry Murray, one of the damage survey crew. On a weekend in early November 2002 a 'swarm of tornadoes and powerful thunderstorms' hit during the night and flattened the US town of Carbon Hill, Alabama. Bodies were found by the roadside, and the smell of fallen pine and oak trees filled the air.[2] Less than two weeks earlier, the oil giant and Europe's biggest company, BP, lowered its forecast for producing oil and gas for the third time in a year.[3] As a result, the price of its shares fell and profits slumped. The reason? BP blamed tropical storm Isidore and Hurricane Lili for disrupting production at its offshore rig in the Gulf of Mexico.

If god in whatever form dropped hints, I think this is how he or she would do it. A town called Carbon Hill in the country most reluctant to act on climate change is destroyed by an extreme weather event of the sort to become more common due to global warming. A company that makes 80 per cent of its profits from oil and gas, the fossil fuels that pour greenhouse gases into the atmosphere, is similarly brought low by another extreme weather event.

I began with a reference to Venus the planet and the goddess of love. Now it is time to invoke another god, the most popular in classical Greece, Minerva the goddess of wisdom. Minerva was also known as Athena. The owl was the sacred bird of Athens and through its connection with Minerva became a symbol of wisdom. As in Hegel's famous phrase above, dusk is gathering quickly on our young civilisation. If wisdom is to take flight, it has little time.

There is growing evidence that civilisations throughout history have collapsed due to climate change. Classic Maya society collapsed in the ninth century at the time of the worst drought experienced during that millennium. And, when drought and cooling struck around 4,300 years ago societies ranging from Egypt to Mesopotamia, Palestine, Greece and Crete fell on hard times and declined.[4]

Today, with sophisticated weather forecasting techniques and technology to adapt we may feel more secure. But there are reasons to doubt. In many ways we grow increasingly vulnerable. More of the world's population crowd into mega cities of 10 million people or more. Most of those are in locations, on rivers or by the coast, that are on the front line of global warming. Many of the people are in poor or slum housing that barely can stand heavy rain let alone hurricane force winds or flooding. Access to clean drinking water and fertile ground to grow food can only become harder.

Both the scientific warnings and energy alternatives needed to trigger our lifestyle changes have been available for decades. Yet we have moved further in the opposite direction and continue to do so, consuming more of what harms us.

Back on the planet Venus where we started, some scientists speculate that life survived the runaway greenhouse effect, retreating in microbial form to survive in the higher atmosphere's sulphurous acidic clouds.[5] Even if true, it's a little way short of a survival strategy for us.

In my mind I have an image of a global grid of history – a great mass of complex interwoven wires, alive and humming with the current of events that power the modern world. They appear explosive, dysfunctional, diverse, rich, poor, smug, scheming, deluded, caring and hopeful. If some historian-psychologist-electrician could just figure out the wiring I feel we could improve things. It's a rational and benign view. Because I believe that people are, mostly, good. But there is another problem. In modern life the world's historical wiring has been largely hidden away, buried in the political walls, under the school floors and behind the commercial furniture. Worse, it seems as if someone has found the mains switch and closed the circuit down. It can seem as if we live in an island of the present, unshaped by anything that went before and with no responsibility for what will follow.

To progress means reconnecting to our history, to understand the traces it leaves upon our time. It means thinking in terms of the long-now as do those pioneers of the mental landscape who devised the clock of the long-now which ticks not according to the enclosed moment of a human day, but the life span of a species existing over thousands of years.

At the fifth anniversary of the Earth Summit in 1997, the United Nations said that without radical change in the way that we produce and consume things, 'The next quarter century is likely to be characterised by declining standards of living, [and] rising levels of conflict and environmental stress'.[6] At the same time a special session of the UN General Assembly noted only 'marginal progress' since the original Earth Summit in 1992.

WE CAN'T HAVE THE PLANET AND EAT IT

As we munch away at our finite fossil fuel inheritance, we munch away too at our life supporting atmosphere. Business-as-usual is at best a form of reckless environmental speculation and at worst a submission to our own fear that we cannot change. But change is necessary and possible. The world's very poor live with austerity measures imposed under the aegis of often dubious conventional external debts. They also lose their loves, lives and limbs, and their farms and families when global warming strikes. These are things to keep in mind when we worry about giving up that second car or long-haul flight to paradise.

In the recent past the US conserved energy to protect 'general welfare' and 'ensure fair and efficient distribution'. In wartime they called it rationing. Today it would be a form of issuing equity and living within our environmental budget. Majority world countries could for the first time receive their fair entitlements. The health of the planet would be protected using a formula that gave people equal rights to key elements of its natural wealth. Contrary to many fears, prudent management to balance the environmental budget wouldn't mean the death of business, but it would set new parameters.

Maturing is partly a process of learning which behaviour is seriously anti-social. If it wasn't we would sit and scream on the office floor if we did not get our way, pour paint over our colleagues' heads and throw food at them. Teenagers learn painfully that they are not the centre of the universe, just as employers learn that exploiting child labour is bad, and societies learn that slavery is wrong. Climate change merely introduces a new, but significant parameter on anti-social behaviour. Throughout history people and businesses adapted to new regulatory environments. To get even close to the necessary cuts in fossil fuel consumption requires governments first to make and then win the argument for action in public. Not to do so now in the rich world could leave countries ungovernable when necessary measures have to be taken later.

Ecological debt suggests a fundamental realignment of who owes whom in the international economy. A new mood of humility on the part of rich countries needs to characterise their relations with less developed countries.

THE ECONOMIC POSSIBILITIES FOR OUR GRANDCHILDREN

So what are the economic possibilities for our grandchildren? When Keynes asked that question in 1930 the prognosis seemed miserable. Reckless speculation on shares had led to spectacular stock market crashes. A long depression had begun. But Keynes was optimistic. He saw in the long-term growth of capital – remember Drake's pound – and dramatic advances in technical efficiency, a great prize looming within 100 years of his writing.

He considered the end of what he called 'the economic problem' in sight. 'The struggle for subsistence' – meeting those needs which are absolute not preferential – characterised not just the human race but the whole 'biological kingdom'. All that had to be avoided were any 'important wars' and any important increases in population. Keynes could have known neither the immensity of the conflicts to come, nor the precise dynamics of population growth. But to balance that, he could not have known of the coming breathtaking technological acceleration. It is fair to say then, that on his terms, it is still the case that the economic problem is not, or does not have to be, 'the permanent problem of the human race'.[7] But Keynes was also writing in ignorance of global warming. His sense that deep economic trends bade well for human society today faces a tougher obstacle.

Now everything we take for granted in the global economy will have to change. Opportunities for development built on the fossil fuel economy have, by definition, to be shared. Enter, stage right, the unquestionable assumption driving the global economy – the growth imperative, with its beating heart of capital accumulation. If the causes and consequences of climate change are accepted, there is one enormous, inescapable and, for many, shattering conclusion. How cautious must we be before making bold predictions?

In the language of economists Robert Heilbroner dares point out the elephant in the room. Climate change generates 'externalities' that are so huge they put obstacles in the way of 'the accumulation process on which the system's life force depends'.[8] Can that be put more simply? I think so. The problem is that the appropriate language is so tainted with old political struggles, so heavy with history, that its meaning can become lost amid the inevitable bluster of reactions. But global warming probably means the death of capitalism as the dominant organising framework for the global economy. If that sounds dramatic, remember it's already the case in Britain, for example, that one third of the economy is taken up by government spending which marches to the beat of different ideas.

If the demise of capitalism really is likely, what will replace it? What we recognise today as markets were once a tiny proportion of the stuff of economic life. A wheel may now have turned full circle. Facing greater environmental, economic and political volatility, the notion that the struggle for private gain can provide the glue to hold societies together suddenly seems absurd. What were we thinking? The economy we have now is the result of countless minute decisions made by individuals supposedly maximising their 'utility'. But, measured mostly by money or status, this ultimately results in an unsatisfying and ever increasing consumption of goods and services. People in market economies, it seems, are very bad at predicting their own utility. As one analyst put it, you may think that having a big red Ferrari will make you happy, but it doesn't, then you think a private jet might do it, but that doesn't either.[9] Because all those short-term decisions are not informed by their long-term consequences, there is no feedback. Each decision is apparently innocuous, and unsatisfying, but gathered together over time, they become devastating in their environmental consequences.

Measuring and managing for ecological debt would create the necessary information flow. We would no longer be trapped in the moment but live in the long-now. But is there a human emotion that can overcome the pursuit of maximum short-term gratification? The answer, I believe, is an economy driven not in practice by individual wealth accumulation, but by an even stronger emotion, the collective desire for survival, and the protection of family and loved ones.

Like Keynes, the scientists of the IPCC also like to look 100 years into the future. Their scenarios for global temperature increase and sea level rise imply enormous upheaval, in all cases. In moderate to bad scenarios they suggest pressures that could lead to the opposite of Keynes' optimism – a great reversal of human progress. It is not merely a prognosis for countries least able to adapt. In the summer of 2002 the German election was affected by extreme flooding across Europe. In August 2003, French high government officials resigned after a lethal heat wave left thousands dead. Direct one-to-one causal relationships can rarely be proven. But climate change will lead to more extreme weather events of this sort. And even to hold climatic instability at its current level implies cuts in carbon emissions that no government privately believes are possible.

Nauru, visited briefly earlier, is a remote South Pacific island. Guns, booze and venereal disease signalled its earliest encounters with the development brought by Europeans. Then, in 1899, progress really took off when a visitor, Albert Ellis, saw a lump of high-grade phosphate being used as a doorstop. It was bird guano (shit) accumulated over thousands of years. The whole interior of the island was made of it. Over the following century the island was dug out leaving the indigenous population clinging to a rim of land around the island's edge, almost entirely dependent on imports for their needs.[10]

When environmental limits are transgressed on an island, it is just possible, notwithstanding restrictive immigration laws, that people can move. But when the limits are crossed on an island in space, like earth, the problems presented are a little more difficult, regardless of immigration laws.

How will a growing, increasingly unequal world population fit into the shrinking environmental space of a carbon constrained economy? In the rich world we know the answer, even if we are unprepared to accept the consequences. We have to use less, much less, of the things that come from burning fossil fuels. The academics who studied the history of Nauru boiled it down to this in their conclusion:

In the long run, a lavish existence – whose attributes include big cars and vans for transportation; goods originating thousands of miles away; large homes, second homes, yachts, and recreational vehicles; and resort-style vacations in faraway places – has huge environmental effects that result in a much smaller carrying capacity for an area than a lifestyle with a quite different consumption pattern that includes travel by bicycle and mass transit; a diet of locally grown grains, fruits, vegetables and other foods; simple but adequate homes; and local vacations.[11]

This seems obvious. But how many of us who have the luxury of being able to make the choice are actually prepared to take it?

We have looming atmospheric chaos and a global economy hopelessly addicted to fossil fuels. What does the future hold for a world riven with widening inequality, and the conflict, unhappiness and instability that it ushers in? Not much, unless we have the imagination and logic to begin a process of reversing several hundred years of economic history, and to find a way to reconcile life-threatening ecological debts.

A great problem, still, is the profession of economics. Robert Heilbroner characterised the early nineteenth century as a world that was 'not only harsh and cruel but that rationalised its cruelty under the guise of economic law'.[12] The laws dressed in the costume of natural forces and could apparently be no more defied than the law of gravity. With choking irony, today immature economic assumptions that treat natural resources as free income to the economy are usurping a natural order that took millions of years to establish. Keynes called on economists to think of themselves humbly, on a 'level with dentists'.[13] Now would be a good moment for them to get back into the dentist's chair.

The roll-call of supporters for contraction and convergence to tackle climate change gets longer every day. Governments of rich and poor countries alike, commissions, industry and, belatedly, academics and environmental campaign groups. Importantly, just because we need to contract those parts of the economy that rely on the exploitation of non-renewable natural resources, does not mean that other, beneficial parts of the economy cannot expand.

Research shows that people's happiness rises along with conventional wealth only up to the point that our needs for basics like adequate warmth, food, clothing, and shelter are met. After that our well-being depends on other things like friendships, opportunities for creativity and the quality of our family relationships. This means that with better awareness of what really gives us a sense of wellbeing, by ignoring the adverts, we could actually consume less and be happier.

We can expand the informal, social economy, for example, recognising the often unpaid work of carers. In an increasingly bland and uniform retail economy, dominated by a handful of brands and chains, we can expand diversity by encouraging micro and small businesses. We can expand human wellbeing with an economics that redefines wealth, and measures the losses to social and environmental welfare that occur in the current system. The economic ghost towns that grow alongside the rise of retail giants like Walmart in the US and Tesco in Britain are not inevitable. They are the result of particular choices and how we run the economy.

Local currencies and innovations like Time Banks, where the medium of exchange for goods and services is equal units of people's time, can help marginalised and officially unemployed people to make useful social contributions. They can create new economic space in the vacuums left by orthodox 'free' markets in poor communities and housing estates around the world. There can be expanding economies based upon a cycle of economic re-use, recycling and innovation, rather than one of throughput and the waste of materials.

Keynes saw the wealthy classes of his day as the 'advance guard ... spying out the promised land' of a world liberated from striving for its basic needs. Based on his observation he looked forward with dread. The wealthy had 'failed disastrously' to put their freedom from want to good use. Ironically this could be a message of hope. If better distributed, there is already enough wealth to meet the basic needs of all. All we would need to do then, is follow Keynes' advice to free ourselves from the ephemeral satisfactions of conspicuous consumption and become those people who 'can keep alive, and cultivate into a fuller perfection, the art of life itself and ... not sell themselves for the means of life'.[14] Evolutionary biologist Richard Dawkins posed the big question of why are we here? He came to the conclusion that it was to seek, to strive, to have foresight, and to communicate, make things and search for meaning.[15]

But now, if we look over each other's shoulders, we can see a star falling. It is ours. The brief ascendance of modern human civilisation is set to fall. We have been a highly unlikely species

in the universal scheme of things and, therefore, you would think, worth doing everything to protect. But unless we can stop global warming, on the best evidence currently available, little else will shortly matter. Because the stake at play – a habitable planet – means that all other economic concerns, however important, become secondary. In January 2004 US president George Bush announced a plan to put a man on Mars as part of the search for life in space. He said once before in a speech to NASA that it was time for humankind to join the solar system. But I rather like it here. Why don't we leave Mars and Venus and all the other planets for the little robots and space probes, and keep the best, earth, for ourselves and the plants and animals. After all, we already know that there is life here. For now, at least.

13

In the Footsteps of Stanley

The conquest of the earth ... is not a pretty thing when you look into it too much.

Joseph Conrad, *Heart of Darkness*

You already know enough. So do I. It is not knowledge we lack. What is missing is the courage to understand what we know and draw conclusions.

Sven Lindqvist, *Exterminate all the Brutes*

There is a walk you can take that leaves opposite the Museum of Central Africa in Brussels. A sign pointing into the woods invites the interested visitor to head off 'in the footsteps of Stanley'. It's an interesting invitation. As mentioned, Stanley once boasted of throwing himself down the Congo, 'shooting down terrified natives left and right'. Yet there appears to be no shortage of people and organisations still prepared to take up the offer and walk in his footsteps, whether metaphorically, economically or otherwise.

For example, in the Congo, in late 2006, the World Bank became embroiled in revelations concerning 'opaque mining deals and the mishandling of reconstruction funds'.[1] An internal World Bank memo said the bank risked 'perceived complicity and/or tacit approval' in corruption linked to bank-funded 'reforms' of the mining sector. It wasn't the first time such revelations had faced the bank, but considering its lecturing of poor countries on the theme of 'good governance', it was one of the worst. Previously, when Mobutu Sese Seko ran his kleptocracy in former Zaire, loans worth billions of dollars,

10. In the footsteps of Stanley at the Museum of Central Africa, Brussels.

that created enormous, unserviceable sovereign debts, were still given to Mobutu for up to a decade after warnings were given from the international financial institutions' own staff.

The Congo's rainforests are the world's second largest after those of the Amazon. Expected deforestation up to the year 2050 is set to release over 34 billion tonnes of CO_2 – somewhere close to the UK's entire emissions over the course of 60 years. Overall, up to a quarter of greenhouse gas emissions are thought to come from the clearance of tropical forests. But the forests are valuable for many reasons: in their own right, as home to rare primates and other species, as a bulwark against further global warming and, in the case of the Democratic Republic of Congo (DRC), they provide livelihoods including food and medicines to 40 million people, two thirds of the population. Once again the World Bank is compromised in the threat to the area's natural resources. Following a period of conflict, the bank began lending to the DRC in 2001 and had channelled over $4 billion to the country by 2006.

In spite of its leverage as a creditor, things have gone badly. That is in spite of a moratorium on new logging 'titles' or the expansion of existing ones since 2002, and the introduction of forestry codes. In four years from 2002, 107 new contracts to log a total of 15 million hectares of forest were signed. Promised benefits to local people from the trade have also failed to materialise. Tax avoidance and timber smuggling are reportedly rife. One assessment concluded that 'the World Bank maintains the illusion that logging companies will be largely beneficial to local communities', and 'has so far failed in its objectives of controlling the expansion of industrial logging'. Instead, it helped introduce a moratorium that has been 'a cover for behind-the-scenes jostling for valuable forest resources'.[2]

China's rise and rise as the factory for the western world is startling. Homes and businesses across the UK, the rest of Europe and the US have developed a 'China dependence'.[3] It's not a wholly new phenomenon. I grew up surrounded by plastic toys stamped 'Made in Taiwan'. But China is different to the emergence of other developing countries. It doesn't just enjoy 'comparative advantage', as economists like to say, in certain sectors. It seems to have potentially *absolute advantage* in all economic areas. Even China can't achieve global economic dominance alone, however. Considering its size, as a relatively resource-poor country, it can only meet the insatiable demand of wealthy global consumers for its products by sucking in natural resources from elsewhere., Once again, Africa is a key target. Nearly half of the UK's estimated £500 million worth of imported illegal timber products come from China.[4] And China sources a good share of that timber from Africa.

With China now in more obvious competition with Europe and America, there is talk of a new 'scramble for Africa'. Over half of the money flowing into Africa as foreign investment goes straight to the oil sector, according to the UN's *World Investment Report*. The line-up of countries may be slightly changed: US, China, Britain, France and, potentially India. In April 2008 the first 'India–Africa' summit was held with 14 heads of state. Already importing 11 per cent of its oil needs from Nigeria, India hoped that with the promise of billions of dollars worth of credit and other financial help, its 'resource diplomacy' would open up the continent to meet its rising demand for commodities.

Minerals, forests and fossil fuels are all up for grabs, but so it seems is Africa's soil. Also in 2008, a South Korean firm, Daewoo Logistics, announced plans to buy a century-long lease on over 1 million hectares of farmland in Madagascar. The purpose is to grow a combination of crops for food and biofuels for export to South Korea. Speculation on similar deals in which wealthier countries buy up the productive soil of poorer countries touched Laos, Sudan and Cambodia. China, again, was one of the countries looking to borrow the soil of economically weaker countries, as it faced the threat of domestic soil erosion in the country's north east, reducing harvests from its breadbasket area by 40 per cent over five decades.

The consequence of the new scramble may well be the same as the last time, when at the end of the nineteenth century foreign powers carved up the continent. Jacques Diouf, head of the otherwise conservative UN Food and Agriculture Organisation, described land deals like the one in Madagascar as creating a form of 'neo-colonialism'.[5]

Oil and gas play a role in bloodshed from Angola, to Nigeria, Sudan and potentially on the borders of Somalia and Ethiopia. Chad, Algeria, Egypt, Libya and Equatorial Guinea are also key producers. In a report published in 2001, the development agency Christian Aid reported on Sudan that 'Troops are terrorising civilians, burning homes and attacking villages from the air in a war for oil.'[6] 'Oil has brought death. When the pumping began the war began', said Malony Kolang, a chief of the southern Sudanese Nuer people.

Sometimes the bloodshed is the geopolitical oil-equivalent of collateral damage in warfare. In Lagos in December 2006, hundreds of people died because of a paradox. Nigeria is one of the world's largest oil producers. But fuel shortages in its own towns and cities are common. So is poverty. As a result, when a fuel pipe leaks or is left ruptured by organised gangs who siphon off fuel by night, villagers come with any container they can carry to collect the precious liquid. But on this occasion the punctured, underground pipe exploded. Many of the hundreds of bodies were burned beyond recognition.

By 2015 the US is expected to get one quarter of its crude oil imports from West Africa, and in 2007 established a continent-wide military command called Africom. 'This century's scramble for Africa could be as undignified, and as deadly, as the last', warned Mary Turner, a research fellow in peace studies at Bradford University.[7]

And the continent should be worried if Iraq's experience following its second US-led invasion is indicative. It is perhaps the crudest example of historical continuity concerning the exploitation of a region's resources, and the one in which the gap between the rhetoric and reality of Pax Americana is revealed most clearly. Against the wishes of Iraqi trade union federations and civil society groups, intense pressure was placed on the country's government (at the time of writing) to adopt an oil law that would grant abnormally generous terms to foreign oil companies.[8]

Global oil politics intensified still further over the course of 2006 and 2007 as Venezuela progressively took back control of foreign-owned sectors of the oil industry within its boundaries. Following the move by President Hugo Chavez, thousands of workers moved overnight into oil fields in the Orinoco basin, and foreign companies including BP, Chevron, ExxonMobil, ConocoPhillips, Statoil and Total conceded operational control to Petroleos de Venezuela.

In every direction, seemingly, ecological debt walks hand in hand with global warming and poverty, like a world-weary grandparent to whom a sad child on either side looks up to for answers.

THE SHORT ARM OF THE LAW

In line with a nascent trend highlighted in the first edition, there has been a huge rise in redress to national and international law in relation to fossil fuel use and global warming. But, as in the rest of life, the law is an unpredictable and imprecise weapon in the fight against climate change.

The people of the Niger Delta also endure day-to-day environmental degradation linked to the oil industry. Gas flaring in the area is a lazy by-product of the oil industry, estimated to cost the country $2.5 billion each year. The annual CO_2 emissions that result are estimated to match those of the whole of Sweden. In spite of ample time to comply with legal orders to stop gas flaring in Nigeria, the Anglo-Dutch oil company Shell continued beyond the deadline imposed by the court order at the end of April 2007.[9]

The Achuar people, an indigenous tribe from the Peruvian Amazon, sued the giant oil company Occidental in 2007 for activities spanning three decades that included 'irresponsible, reckless, immoral and illegal practices' that were part of an 'unchecked plan to profit from Amazonian oil'. The Achuar people wanted compensation for harm to their health and the local environment, and money to clean up the messy legacy.[10]

Earlier, in Chapter 6, there was a short trip into the history of British oil company BP. More recently, BP advertised itself to meet the mood of a time coloured by increasing environmental concern. The company launched a campaign in which the 'B' in its initials represented 'Beyond' rather than 'British' Petroleum. Adverts targeted at the general public easily could have left the impression that BP was an energy company predominantly dealing in clean, renewable sources. Yet even a cursory reading of the information that the company made available to potential investors showed that for BP, its search beyond petroleum was, in fact, to find a lot more petroleum. 'Our main activities are the exploration and production of crude oil and natural gas; refining, marketing, supply and transportation; and the manufacture and marketing of petrochemicals', it said in 2006.[11] Over 70 per cent of its capital investment still went towards finding more oil and gas.

So focused, in fact, is that search to secure the 'fix' it needs to supply an oil-addicted economy that things like safety, the environment and other people's livelihoods are not allowed to stand in the way. A single month in summer 2006 stands to demonstrate. BP has strong links in Colombia, for example, in exploiting the Cusiana-Cupiagua oil field. Oil revenues in Colombia funded the country's internal conflict and, in turn, companies have had to pay to protect their commercial operations.[12]

Against this background, in July 2006 BP was forced to pay a reported £3 million in compensation and legal costs to Colombian farmers left destitute by the building of a major oil pipeline through their land. The lawyers representing the farmers, Leigh Day & Co., accused BP of failing to compensate farmers for damage reaching back to 1995 and of gaining advantage from terror tactics employed by others to guard the pipeline.

Shortly after that embarrassment BP faced more fines and legal repercussions after having to shut its huge Alaska Prudhoe Bay oil field. A corroded pipe had led to a massive oil spill. The news caused world oil prices to hit another record high and the Chief Executive of BP America, Bob Malone, to grovel. 'We regret that it is necessary to take this action and we apologize to the nation and the State of Alaska for the adverse impacts it will cause', he said in a public statement.[13]

According to an International Climate Change Taskforce set up with the support of the former UK Prime Minister, Tony Blair, on current emission trends, the point at which runaway climate change becomes a serious possibility could be reached as soon as 2015. Still others, like NASA scientist James Hansen, say we have already gone too far and need to hit reverse. Yet, when Lord Browne, still then a leading 'progressive' corporate chief executive, made BP engage in the climate debate, he operated on a target date that was more than half a century later, giving his company fatally large room for manoeuvre.[14] BP's most recent ruse is to suggest that motorists have the chance to become 'carbon neutral' by offsetting their emissions from driving.

Unfortunately, climate science gives little credibility to the whole idea of offsetting. Kevin Anderson, a senior scientist at the Manchester Tyndall Centre for Climate Change Research, believes the approach is both uncertain and ineffective, describing it as 'a dangerous delaying technique'.[15] And even as awareness of global warming has gone up, that greater understanding has been matched in financial centres like the City of London by ever more money flowing as investment into the fossil fuel industry.

Around the world, courts are increasingly busy with litigation related to climate change. The Australian government were challenged by conservation groups for not considering the impact of global warming on the environment, while elsewhere in the same country a judge ruled that the consideration of greenhouse gas emissions should be a factor in the planning decision over a proposed new coal mine. In Germany a legal action was launched to compel the government to disclose the effect on climate change of projects given official taxpayer support through the German export credit agency. In the US, campaigners are using the Clean Air Act legislation against the Environmental Protection Agency to force legally binding cuts of greenhouse gases.[16]

Elsewhere, the Inuit peoples of Arctic regions of Canada and the US filed a petition to the Inter-American Commission on Human Rights 'seeking relief from human rights violations resulting from global warming caused by acts and omissions of the United States'.[17]

But in spite of the growth of legal action against polluters and officials, the limitations of litigation remain painfully obvious. Emissions are still rising, along with investment in fossil fuel industries. This has led some to look for more fundamental solutions. One outcome that we'll return to in the last chapter is the idea that, in line with the latest climate science, substantial fossil fuel reserves should be declared 'unburnable', and that companies should be prevented from presenting these as assets when they declare the scale of their reserves. Separate accounts would have to be prepared for burnable and unburnable carbon.

THE RISE OF ECOLOGICAL DEBT AS AN IDEA

On 9 October 2006, the British national newspaper, the *Independent*, ran a front-page headline for World Ecological Debt Day (see picture). It came from a report in which I and my colleagues had coined a way of looking at the calendar year using the well-established measure of humanity's ecological footprint.

11. Ecological debt arrives on the front page.

We worked out the day when, in effect, the world began consuming at a level that overshot its available biocapacity.

For ideas and the people who support them, more used to dwelling in the shade rather than the glare of public attention, it was an extraordinary moment. But it showed how, in a short time, a once perplexing notion was slipping with relative ease into the general imagination. The words 'ecological debt' are now commonly found in speeches from senior politicians, UN figures and the reports of international agencies. Conferences are being held, academic papers are being written and international networks are growing that campaign on the issue.

With its rising profile, there exists a powerful temptation to put a price on the ecological debt (a temptation I have failed to resist myself). Since producing a few illustrative figures over the years, and in this book's first edition, others have been produced. For example, the Jubilee Debt Campaign[18] estimated that rich countries' annual 'carbon debt' was in the region of $1 trillion. Low-income countries, on the other hand, had a notional carbon credit of $93 billion, as their fossil fuel use was well within a safe, per capita global share.[19] Such numbers highlight, for them, the continuing absurdity of a global system of daily usury in which around $100 million passes in financial debt payments from poor countries to the governments of the rich world, and their private companies and international institutions, amounting to around $40 billion a year.

The figures are arrived at by applying the same UK Treasury estimate of the environmental damage cost per tonne of carbon, used in this book's first edition, to the amount by which nations are, on a per-person basis, over-consuming (or not) coal, oil and gas.

Still more recently, an academic study examined the impact of six key types of environmental damage. It looked across a range of pressures on natural resources driven by the lifestyles and levels of consumption in rich countries and set out to put a price on them. From the intensification and expansion of farming, to deforestation, over-fishing, loss of mangrove swamps, ozone depletion and climate change, the researchers drew the same conclusion as others before them: that environmental damage disproportionately harms poorer nations. The price of the damage caused to them was put at $1.8 trillion[20] worth of lost output, and was more than their total foreign debt.[21]

Like a bidding war in a game of mutually assured destruction, another study on the economics of ecosystems, funded by the European Commission and the German government, estimated that annual forest loss had a price tag of $2–5 trillion.[22]

These are useful illustrations. Without a price, things pass either undervalued or completely unvalued in a market economy. Environmental cost accounting goes some way to redress that imbalance. Some even suggest that all environmental problems could be solved if only we had an accurate system that included in the price of things the full cost of the damage their production caused. This would make life much easier for governments and policy makers. The business of saving the world could then be left to businesses operating in the lightly regulated markets of neo-liberal dreams.

But there is a problem that no pricing system, however clever, can solve. It means there can be no simple, price-based market solution to ecological debt. In the custom of 'doing what it says on the tin', I'll call it the paradox of environmental economics, and pose it as a question: *'How do you put a price on the tonne of carbon that, once burned, tips the balance, triggering catastrophic, runaway climate change?'*

A climate that is habitable, even comfortable, for humankind is like the greatest work of art imaginable; literally priceless. It is without price in the sense that accounting for the full consequences of its loss is, in any meaningful sense, both impossible and pointless. It is also priceless in the sense that runaway global warming is just that – something which will have escaped our wit to control. We almost certainly could not 'buy' it back, even if we wanted to and were prepared to make any kind of sacrifice to do so. In seeking solutions to our ecological debts, then, we should remember both the limits of market mechanisms that rely on price and the importance of collective political initiatives (however insufferable and intensely frustrating they prove to be). That is not to say that markets cannot be useful, when used as our slaves rather than our masters, and when equity has been designed-in from the outset; for example, by pre-distributing to all an entitlement to share equally in the planet's substantial biocapacity.

New areas of interest rapidly spawn disciplines that demand their own specialised language. My original definition of ecological debt was simple, namely: if you take more than your fair share of available biocapacity you run up an ecological debt. There is now carefully codified language to circumscribe the meanings of 'ecological debt', 'deficit', 'overshoot' and 'footprint'. While they need not detain us here, the eager can pursue them.[23]

And nothing will happen without major cultural shifts, the kind of which the first shoots are beginning to appear.

Car makers like General Motors (GM) in the US saw sales drop in a single quarter by nearly one fifth. Recession was a large factor but, at that point, petrol prices had also fallen. And, more interestingly, GM was hit in particular by a 'slump' in demand for large SUVs.[24] Opening any colour supplement magazine reveals car makers performing amusing mental gymnastics to stress the environmental credibility of lunking off-road vehicles (most destined, of course, never to leave the road except by accident).

Similarly, a shift in consciousness has begun to afflict the short- and long-haul flight industry. Laboured, and mostly implausible, promises to offset carbon emissions now accompany travel sections of newspapers and many airline offerings. Belatedly, an emboldened railway network now markets itself as climate-friendly. From local communities to campaigners like Plane Stupid and numerous Members of Parliament, the future, for example, of plans to build a new runway at Heathrow airport get questioned like never before. We are witnessing a significant backlash against the unthinking use of other high-polluting transport such as long-haul flights, and for good reason.

We already know enough. We know it from the brittle demeanours of SUV drivers pulling out of urban supermarket car parks, to the defensive bluster of politicians who claim, on one hand, to be as concerned as anyone about climate change, while on the other, promote new airport runways and coal-fired power stations. What we need is the courage to understand, draw conclusions and step out of Stanley's footsteps.

It turns out that we have, after all, known enough for several decades. In 1972 when scientists at MIT published the *Limits to Growth* report it was widely denounced. Folk memory says they got it wrong, exaggerating the planetary predicament and discrediting the wider environmental movement.

Dismissed and criticised for 'crying wolf', it now seems that there was after all a wild and hungry carnivore at the door. A detailed study compared the original projections of *Limits to Growth* with 30 years of subsequent observed trends and actual data. It found a solid correlation between projection and reality; in fact, they 'compared favourably'.[25]

Matthew Simmons, founder of the world's largest energy investment banking firm, commented that its message was more relevant than ever and that 'we wasted 30 valuable years of action by misreading the message of the first book'. Time, then, to move swiftly on.[26]

14

Tick Tock Climate Clock

The first law says you can't win, the second law says you can't even break even.

C.P. Snow, on the laws of thermodynamics

If humanity wishes to preserve a planet similar to that on which civilisation developed and to which life on Earth is adapted ... CO_2 will need to be reduced from its current 385 ppm to at most 350 ppm CO_2 but likely much less than that ... If the present overshoot of this target CO_2 is not brief, there is a possibility of seeding irreversible catastrophic effects.

James Hansen, NASA/Goddard Institute for Space Studies[1]

There is a moment in the classic comedy film *Monty Python and the Holy Grail* when a group of rather pathetic knights, pretending to be on horseback with the accompaniment of clattering coconut shells, come face to face with a frightening adversary. Instead of engaging in battle with a command such as 'Attack!' or 'Charge!', the cry goes out, 'Runaway!' It distils, perhaps, how many feel when confronted by the reality of climate change.

With global warming, however, ultimately there is nowhere to run to. And it is the idea of *runaway climate change* that has gained ground in the scientific community in the very recent past. In his book *The Last Generation*, Fred Pearce, a long-term writer with *New Scientist* magazine, collated a range of peer-reviewed research into nature's complex atmospheric feedback mechanisms, and looked at how they are responding to climate change. From ice cover to permafrost; forests, oceans, and even, more controversially, the behaviour of clouds, almost every feature seemed to wobble like a badly balanced domino – each threatening to fall and knock the other in a catastrophic chain reaction. Other dynamics include the decreasing ability of oceans to absorb CO_2 due to higher wind strengths linked to climate change. This has already been observed in the Southern Ocean and the North Atlantic, increasing the amount of CO_2 in the atmosphere and adding to climate change.

A rough consensus has emerged that an average global temperature rise of more than 2 °C above pre-industrial levels is the threshold that should not be crossed. Beyond that, the likelihood of major, irreversible climate change becomes unacceptably high. But there are problems even with this ambitious target, which means that we might not be able to consider it 'safe'. This is because an 'average' temperature rise masks significant regional variation. Collapse of the Greenland ice sheet, for example, which could trigger a sea-level rise of seven metres over the course of the next millennium, becomes likely with a local warming of 2.7 °C, and this corresponds to a global mean increase of 2 °C or *less*.[2] Others believe that a global rise of just 1 °C, to which we are already almost certainly committed, is enough to condemn the Greenland ice, and that it could disappear over three times as quickly, in as short a time as 300 years.[3]

Ice loss is one of the oddly termed 'positive feedbacks'. Odd because, where climate change is concerned, positive feedbacks tend to have negative consequences. Ice loss leads to less heat being reflected. Darker land and water surfaces are then revealed that absorb still more heat – the cycle of warming intensifies. Even so, keeping to a target of 2 °C implies much more realistic and deeper cuts in greenhouse gas emissions – to the extent that concentration levels in the atmosphere should cease rising now. When the UN's group of scientists known as the Intergovernmental Panel on Climate Change (IPCC) published their *Fourth Assessment Report* in 2007, it confirmed and strengthened the consensus on the fact of human-driven warming, but was criticised for having projections that were too conservative and failing to give sufficient weight to the impact of environmental feedbacks.[4]

The prospect of *not* avoiding runaway change for billions of people whose livelihoods come directly from the land is unthinkable.

Recent research that modelled future patterns of drought around the world truly deserves the epithet 'terrifying'. The UK's Hadley Centre for Climate Prediction and Research, part of the government's Meteorological Office, looked at the share of the earth's land surface that is prone to extreme, severe and moderate drought. They concluded that the percentage of land surface suffering extreme drought had already trebled from just 1 per cent to 3 per cent in less than a decade. Then, using a medium scenario for climate change, the Centre projected that this trend will continue until extreme drought conditions affect more than 30 per cent of the globe by 2090.[5]

Drought will hit the great grain-growing areas of Europe, North America and Russia, as well as the Middle East and Central Asia, North Africa and Southern Africa, Amazonia in Brazil, and Central America. Change is already a reality for some. There are an estimated 3 million pastoralists in northern Kenya. According to one agency, drought increased fourfold in the Mandera region in the last quarter of a century. These changes in the climate forced approximately half a million people, one third of the herders living there, to abandon their nomadic way of life.[6]

Although the models forecast a severe, overall drying pattern, certain areas will get much wetter. More rain is forecast for Central Africa, the Horn and East Africa and parts of coastal West Africa, China and Eastern Asia, and high Northern latitudes. But higher rainfall could come in the destructive form of great deluges as easily as beneficial rains. Devastating floods hit a swathe of African countries in September 2007, for example, killing livestock, destroying crops, bursting dams and leaving hundreds of thousands homeless.[7]

Historically, a total of 20 per cent of the earth's land surface has been in drought at any one time, be it extreme, severe or moderate. This has now risen to 28 per cent and is predicted to reach 35 per cent by 2020 and cover 50 per cent – half the earth's land surface and still rising – by 2090. Droughts will also be much longer in duration.[8]

And it isn't just the land we need to worry about. An ocean famine is being created by global warming in tropical and sub-tropical seas. Warmer seas in these regions mean that phytoplankton, microscopic green plants upon which the food chain depends, grow less. To have conditions for them to grow, water at the surface needs to mix with deeper nutrient-rich water. But higher temperatures at the surface prevent it.[9] Vast amounts of carbon dioxide in the atmosphere get absorbed into the oceans. As that happens the oceans acidify. Past periods of acidification have coincided with mass extinction events of oceanic species. Having occurred, it can take tens of thousands of years for a balance to be restored. But the last word on nightmare scenarios belongs not to the predictions of computer models that peer into the future, or to the overheated imaginations of Hollywood film-makers, but to the evidence of the past. Paleo-climate research is beginning to reveal that the biosphere is both more sensitive than we thought and capable of changing much, much quicker than the relatively smooth curves on the graphs of the IPCC would suggest. Imagine yourself walking through a wood fearing that the worst that could fall on your head is a large pine cone, when suddenly a Gothic cathederal falls from nowhere. The IPCC's worst case warned of a 6 °C rise over a century. But the paleo-climate record indicates the planet has previously experienced a 10 °C temperature shift in only a decade, and possibly 'as quickly as in a single year'.[10] And going into and coming out of the last ice age, there were 'local warmings as large as 16 °C' that happened repeatedly.[11] The fact that such huge natural variation can occur means that humanity is toying with a system far more prone to sudden change than previously thought.

If meetings of important men are a useful indicator, the sheer weight of evidence accumulating finally seems to be having an effect.

Since the first edition of *Ecological Debt*, climate change finally moved from the political margins to the mainstream at a single stroke in central London. On the panel sat the (then) future Prime Minister, Gordon Brown, the then Prime Minister, Tony Blair, the Secretary of State for the Environment, the soon to be Foreign Secretary, David Miliband, and the slightly overawed-looking lead author of a new report on the economic impacts of climate change, Nicholas Stern. It was his work they had come to launch.[12] But it was more than just another show of high-level Westminster political theatre. It was the moment that the establishment more widely finally came to believe in the reality of climate change. And it wasn't just in Britain; it helped to tip opinion much more broadly in the western world.

But just as the report woke many from a trance of mundane denial, it simultaneously administered a sedative to dull the pain of awareness and avert the course of necessary action. Although a very long report, its headline messages were few and simple. Above all, Stern concluded that it would cost the equivalent of only 1 per cent of GDP to tackle climate change. It was the good news that many wanted to hear. But there were two fundamental problems with his approach. First, it relied on the fact that you could buy adequate amounts of carbon out of the atmosphere using a range of technological fixes. Second, its conclusions were based on stabilising greenhouse gas concentrations in the atmosphere at a level that science increasingly sees as dangerous and far too high.

At the time, Stern, in line with public statements from David King, who was then the government's chief scientific advisor, entertained the idea of aiming to stabilise the concentration of carbon dioxide (CO_2) in the atmosphere at 550 parts per million (ppm) CO_2.[13] By way of introduction, in 2007, CO_2 concentration climbed to a new high of 383.6 ppm, and, according to NASA's Goddard Institute for Space Studies, that year tied with 1998 as the second warmest year on record.[14] Commentators like King, however, suggested that 550 ppm was the lowest politically pragmatic level to aim for.

But NASA scientist James Hansen, widely credited as one of the first to bring the threat of climate change to the attention of governments, went on record in early 2008 to say that, rather than debating over a future, higher level at which to stabilise the amount of CO_2 in the atmosphere, there was already too much and we would need to cut back. To prevent many of the nasty 'positive feedbacks' listed above, he said, we need to get back down to 350 ppm CO_2. At present, though, we are fast heading in the wrong direction.[15] Those hoping that technology alone will engineer a path out of climate change, leaving lifestyles unchanged, also had bad news from Hansen. To 'geo-engineer' just 50 ppm CO_2 out of the atmosphere would cost, he estimated $20 trillion.[16] That is, not 1 per cent of global income, but between a third and a half of the value of the world economy in 2007.

The global growth rate of carbon dioxide emissions is spiking upwards. Findings from the Global Carbon Project in 2008 showed that the global average percentage rise since the year 2000 was over three times higher than the previous decade, rising again significantly in the previous year.[17] These growth rates are now worse than the worse-case scenario used by the IPCC to model potential global warming. Levels of carbon in the energy mix for both rich and poor countries are also going up.

An emerging consensus suggests that, at best, we have less than a decade to stabilise global greenhouse gas concentrations before potentially irreversible changes to our climate begin to happen.

100 MONTHS, AND COUNTING ...

If you shout 'Fire!' in a crowded theatre when there is none, don't be surprised if you get arrested for irresponsible behaviour and a breach of the peace. But statistics on climate change are like smoke billowing beneath the door.

What constitutes a 'dangerous' level of warming depends to an important degree on two things: where and how you are living in the world, and the probability of certain events happening. Scientists like Hansen think we have already gone too far. But even if you take the parameters set by the more cautious majority of the scientific community, things look bad. Based on a very conservative estimate, from August 2008, there were only 100 months left before the world enters a new, more perilous phase of global warming.[18] Approximately 1,000 tonnes of CO_2 are released into the earth's atmosphere every second, due to human activity. And when these gases accumulate beyond a certain level – often termed a 'tipping point' – global warming will accelerate, potentially beyond control. Faced with circumstances that clearly threaten human civilisation, scientists at least have the sense of humour to term what drives this process as 'positive feedback' (see above). Once a critical greenhouse concentration threshold is passed, global warming will continue even if we stop releasing additional greenhouse gases into the atmosphere. If that happens, the earth's climate will shift into another, more volatile state, with different ocean circulation, wind and rainfall patterns.

It's possible to estimate the length of time it will take to reach a tipping point. To do so you combine current greenhouse gas concentrations with the best estimates for the rates at which emissions are growing, the maximum concentration of greenhouse gases allowable to forestall potentially irreversible changes to the climate system, and the effect of those environmental feedbacks.

The 100-month timeframe comes from following the latest trends for carbon emissions, and making allowances for all human interferences that influence temperatures, both those with warming and cooling effects, then comparing that with what the IPCC suggests it will take to retain a good chance of not crossing the critical threshold of the earth's average surface temperature rising by 2 °C above pre-industrial levels. This calculation is cautious in several ways, optimistic even, and perhaps too much so. A rise of 2 °C may mask big problems that begin at a lower level of warming. For example, collapse of the Greenland ice sheet is more than likely to be triggered by a local warming of 2.7 °C, which could correspond to a global mean temperature increase of 2 °C or less (the disintegration of the Greenland ice sheet could correspond to a sea-level rise of up to seven metres).

This timescale also uses the lower end of threats in assessing the impact of vanishing ice cover and other carbon cycle feedbacks. But the result is worrying enough.

One hundred months from August 2008 we will reach a concentration of greenhouse gases at which it is no longer 'likely' that we will stay below the 2 °C temperature rise threshold. 'Likely' is a definition of risk used by the IPCC. But even just before that point, there is still a one third chance of crossing the line.

The difficulties with the Stern report mentioned above resulted, perhaps, from the fact that anyone addressing economics and climate change walks straight into the final economic heresy – questioning growth.

IMPOSSIBILITY THEOREM

After the panel gave their presentations it was time for a handful of questions, most of which were planted in the audience. The whole event bugged me. What was the point, I thought, of arriving at a correct diagnosis of the illness, and then offering a palpably wrong prescription for treatment? The outcome would be the same as having no diagnosis at all. So I threw my hand up to ask a question, more in hope than expectation. Certain unavoidable dynamics were obscured in the analysis. These were, in fact, the laws of thermodynamics. In an infinitely growing and materially heavy global economy, as C.P. Snow put it, *'The first law says you can't win, the second law says you can't even break even.'* Even in the most optimistic scenarios for the uptake of renewable energy and energy efficiency used by the IPCC, continued overall global economic growth,[19] even at low levels, carries the world beyond the point of potential no-return toward runaway change.[20]

The problem is a fairly simple, if intractable one. Economic growth is predominantly fuelled by oil, coal and gas. But we need to reduce the greenhouse gas emissions that come from burning fossil fuels (we shouldn't forget that growth also creates a burden by extracting many more natural resources from, and dumping more waste into, our life-supporting ecosystems). The only way to reduce emissions, then, would be to reduce the carbon content of growth (or 'intensity' as it is called) *faster* than the rate of growth itself. It would also have to happen *fast enough* to avoid getting to the point of no return (and this point, as mentioned, could arrive all too soon).

What does that look like in a real world example? Here are a few very important numbers. The International Energy Agency projects global economic growth to rise at about 3.4 per cent per year. So, in order to get real reductions in carbon emissions by just 1 per cent per year, the carbon 'intensity' of the economy would need to improve by 4.4 per cent. Unfortunately, even this modest target appears to be well-beyond the technological efficiency of an advanced, wealthy economy like the United States. And CO_2 emissions from fossil fuels globally have been doing exactly the opposite, accelerating at a rate of 1.1 per cent per year during 1990s, and by more than 3 per cent per year for the first half of the following decade.[21]

The sharp-eyed will have spotted yet another logical flaw with the credo of 'infinite economic growth'. To survive within the flexible, but real, natural resource limits of our planet, reductions in the overall *material* intensity of growth would also have to continue forever, and at a rate greater than the growth itself. And, on this score, the news is not good. The first edition of this book (included now in Chapter 2) are some rough calculations on the problem of exponential growth by an astro-physicist who became interested in the clash between conventional economics and climate change.

While it remains a heresy punishable by career suicide for economists to question growth, other disciplines seem able to view the issue more logically, their views less obstructed by doctrine. At a guest lecture in May 2007, given by Prof. Roderick Smith from the Royal Academy of Engineering at Imperial College, he again made the point that is so difficult for economists to grasp. The physical view of the economy, he said, 'is governed by the laws of thermodynamics and continuity', and so 'The question of how much natural resource we have to fuel the economy, and how much energy we have to extract, process and manufacture is central to our existence'.[22]

Engineers must deal every day with the stuff, the material, the 'thingyness' of the world around them, the stresses and strains that makes things stand up, fall down, last or wear out. Because of this, they are perhaps more in tune with the real world of resources than the economist working with abstract mathematical simplifications of life. Hence Smith honed in on one of the economy's most important characteristics – its 'doubling period', by which its bulk multiplies in proportion to its current size. Even low growth rates of around 3 per cent, he points out, lead to 'surprisingly short doubling times'. Hence 'A 3 per cent growth rate, which is typical of the rate of a developed economy, leads to a doubling time of just over 23 years. The 10 per cent rates of rapidly developing economies double the size of the economy in just under 7 years'.[23]

But then, if you are concerned about humanity's ecological debt, comes what Smith quaintly calls the 'real surprise'. Because, according to Smith, 'each successive doubling period consumes as much resource as all the previous doubling periods combined'; adding, almost redundantly as jaws in the room fall open: 'This little appreciated fact lies at the heart of why our current economic model is unsustainable.'[24]

Although awareness of climate change leads to a focus on energy issues, it is as important to monitor whether we are denuding our fields, forests and oceans faster than they can regenerate, *and* whether we are creating more waste than ecosystems can safely absorb. First, even with all the sophistication of modern information technology, in respect of living within our environmental means, we are very far away from dematerialising the economy faster than we are growing it. And we are moving in the wrong direction. But even if we could do better, the problem is that growth economics suffers a headlong crash with those laws of thermodynamics. Efficiency simply *cannot* increase endlessly alongside continuous economic growth. Or, as C.P. Snow put it, in terms of the conservation of energy, you cannot win, and you cannot break even.

As Seth Lloyd, a professor of Mechanical Engineering at MIT, wrote in the journal *Nature* in 2004:

Nothing in life is certain except death, taxes and the second law of thermodynamics. All three are processes in which useful or accessible forms of some quantity, such as energy or money, are transformed into useless, inaccessible forms of the same quantity. That is not to say that these three processes don't have fringe benefits: taxes pay for roads and schools; the second law of thermodynamics drives cars, computers and metabolism; and death, at the very least, opens up tenured faculty positions.[25]

The reason that we are in our current environmental predicament appears to be that we have become hooked on the fringe benefits while deliberately forgetting the potentially catastrophic consequences of the ecological debts they ring up. Recent trends also suggest that where the world's biggest economy, the US, is concerned, many of the low-hanging fruits of efficiency may already have been plucked.

Now, back to that glittering panel. Somehow, being sandwiched between men in suits created an illusion of respectability for our row of seats, and I was able to ask one of only a couple of non-stage-managed questions. 'Assuming the best-case scenario for clean energy and technology,' I asked, 'had Stern looked at what level of economic growth, globally, was compatible with keeping under a safe threshold of greenhouse gases in the atmosphere?' Silence falls. Muttering. Stuttering, and nervous faces. Not a single attempt follows from any speaker at a cogent response. Why? Because, first, they hadn't looked. And second, if they had, they would instantly be cast out of the circle of respectable opinion. Their crime? Making inadmissible observations and questioning growth. That is in spite of the fact that several decades have passed since a very respectable economist pointed out this clash between economics and physics (and, one might add, even longer since the clash between fossil-fuelled economic growth and atmospheric chemistry was noted; see Chapter 2).

This is how the economist Herman Daly put it, himself drawing on older work by another economist, Nicholas Georgescu-Roegen, concerning entropy and economics. 'The notion that we can save the "growth forever" paradigm by dematerialising the economy, or "decoupling" it from resources, or substituting information for resources, is fantasy. We can surely eat lower down the food chain,' he wrote, 'but we cannot eat recipes ... I admit that if the ecosystem can grow indefinitely then so can the aggregate economy'.[26]

Depletion, waste and pollution are inevitable consequences of an economy based on the throughput of material resources. The consumption of fossil fuels is but one, very serious, example of the flaw in the system. It takes a low entropy raw material and turns it into a high entropy waste. Apart from the waste, the additional consequence is, of course, climate change. Daly's famous phrase (which I quote far too often) is that our economic system treats the planet as if it were a 'business in liquidation'. Any system based, in this fashion, on the throughput of resources is headed towards insolvency.

The important caveat is that there is nothing to stop unending qualitative improvements, which Daly calls 'development', but there are physical laws (not to be confused with ideologies) to prevent infinite 'growth' in the way measured by economists. 'The market cannot by itself', he writes, 'register the cost of its own increasing scale relative to the ecosystem.' Worse than that, to have the growth of GDP, as both the principal policy goal and measure of economic success is 'not only a passive mismeasure but ... an actively distorting influence' that has the effect of 'maximising depletion and pollution'.[27] As an indicator it is so wrong-headed that even when we spend 'defensively' to clear up costs of growth like pollution, this, too, is counted positively as growth.

A global economy based upon growth, by definition, recognises no biophysical limits. But these limits, fuzzy and unavoidably real, have been there for decades for all of us to see. Ever since space exploration yielded the first photographs of the earth from space, a life-supporting planet floating against the void in glorious isolation, we've known that we have no near neighbours to turn to should things go horribly wrong.

Increasingly sophisticated measures of humanity's ecological footprint suggest that, on very conservative estimates, the human population as a whole has been exceeding its available biocapacity since the early 1980s. We've been taking more from our fields, forests and oceans to consume than ecosystems can replace, leading to a net run-down of the natural assets upon which the real economy ultimately depends. And, it appears, we are heading further in the wrong direction each year.

A world going deeper into ecological debt can be seen, for example, in the collapse of ocean fish stocks. One estimate suggests that, at current rates of depletion, most fish stocks internationally will collapse by 2048.[28] A clear overall demonstration comes from looking at the day in a typical calendar year when the world, in effect, starts eating into its stock of natural resources and goes into ecological debt. The date has been creeping ever earlier in the year since the world entered deficit in the 1980s. By over-consuming, in 2008 for example, the human population collectively went into ecological debt on 23 September.[29] And things are much more extreme where many wealthy countries are concerned. If everyone in the world wanted to live like people in the UK, for example, on a very conservative estimate, we would need over three planets like the earth, and head into deficit in early April.

The ecological footprint is a measure of human consumption compared to available biocapacity. Trying to run the world without using a measure like this as a basic tool for policy makers is like trying to run a business with no knowledge at all of your cashflow or assets. Anyone trying to run a company like that should not be surprised if they became bankrupt. Why do we suppose it will be any different in the way we treat the environment?

THE LAST DEFENCE OF THE ECONOMIC COWARD

As patriotism was once derided as the last defence of the coward, so the last defence of global growth is that it is necessary to tackle poverty. But other recent evidence has shown this notion to be flawed, inefficient and disingenuous. At a national level, conventional economic growth will happen in poor countries as a consequence of effectively reducing poverty. But at a global level, the policies designed to pursue growth have become a mask for making the rich richer, while leaving the poor with few benefits and abandoned to deal with the consequences.[30]

During the 1980s, the so-called lost decade for tackling poverty, from every $100 worth of global economic growth, around $2.20 found its way to people living below the absolute poverty line. Bad enough, but a decade later that had shrunk to just 60 cents – the slice of the growth cake going to the poorest has been getting smaller. Meanwhile, the actual mean income of those living under the absolute poverty line of $1 per day in Africa also fell, from 64 cents per person per day in 1981, to just 61 cents in 2001.[31]

There has been, in effect, a sort of 'flood up' of wealth from poor to rich, rather than a 'trickle down'. Perversely, it means that for the poor to get slightly less poor, the rich have to get very much richer. It now takes around $166 worth of global growth (made up of all those giant flat screen TVs and SUVs) to generate a single dollar of poverty reduction for people living below $1 a day, compared with around just $45 dollars in the 1980s.[32] Earnings of between $3 and $4 per day is the rough level at which the strong link between your income and your life expectancy breaks down. So what would happen if we agreed $3 per day as the absolute minimum acceptable level of income to escape absolute poverty?

As mentioned, if the whole world wished to consume at the level of the United States, we would need, conservatively, more than five planets like earth to support them. The figure for Britain would be slightly more than three planets. But because of the skewed distribution of benefits in the global economy between rich and poor, and because for the poor to become slightly less poor the rich have to get much richer, and because all this uses up a lot of resources, this simple exercise demonstrates that without radical changes in distribution, we will tip over the ecological edge. Under the current system and pattern of economic growth, to lift everyone in the world onto a modest income of $3 per day would require the resources of around 15 planets like ours. So, where, you might ask, will the other 14 come from?

Ecological debt can be seen ever more clearly as a by-product of growth, of expansion and of divergence in the global economy. Growth as a measure of a nation's overall virility and success is an anomaly. Its survival is a testament to the power of economic doctrine triumphing over logic, evidence and repeated exposure as the emperor with no clothes. It is an astonishing 40 years since Robert Kennedy demolished the idea with these words in a speech given in 1968:

Gross National Product counts air pollution and cigarette advertising, and ambulances to clear our highways or carnage. It counts special locks for our doors, and jails for those who break them. It counts the destruction of our redwoods and the loss of our natural wonder in chaotic sprawl. It counts napalm and the cost of a nuclear warhead …

Yet the GNP does not allow for the health of our children, the quality of their education, or the joy of their play. It does not include the beauty of our poetry or the strength of our marriages, the intelligence of our public debate or the integrity of our public officials. It measures neither our wit nor our courage, neither our wisdom nor our learning, neither our compassion nor our devotion to our country; it measures everything, in short, except that which makes life worthwhile.[33]

For years we lacked a decent alternative. Then several new ways of measuring came along that sought to 'adjust' growth downwards to take account of social and environmental costs. Generally, though, they took the flawed growth measure as a starting point. Until, only recently, a novel approach was proposed that brought together a measure of fundamental economic purpose – so called 'happy life years', a combination of life expectancy and levels of life satisfaction – with the ecological footprint. The result was something quietly revolutionary – a measure of the ecological efficiency with which we can deliver relatively long and happy lives, dubbed the Happy Planet Index.[34] It's findings revealed that mostly middle-income Latin American countries and small island states were the most ecologically efficient at producing human longevity and wellbeing.

Yet in spite of these innovations, and after decades of non-debate on the subject, no amount of rational exhortation seems capable of getting the issue addressed seriously in the mainstream. So how about this less-rational illustration conjured up out of sheer frustration to make the point by myself and a colleague at work?

> From birth to puberty a hamster doubles its weight each week. If, then, instead of levelling-off in maturity as animals do, the hamster continued to double its weight each week, on its first birthday we would be facing a nine billion tonne hamster. If it kept eating at the same ratio of food to body weight, by then its intake would be greater than the total, annual amount of corn produced worldwide.[35]

There is a reason that in nature things do not grow indefinitely.

BREAKING THE BANK: FINANCIAL DEBT AND ECOLOGICAL DEBT

In her book *The Coming First World Debt Crisis*,[36] Ann Pettifor, the woman who led the headline-grabbing Jubilee 2000 international debt relief campaign in the late 1990s, subsequently turned her attention to other financial misdemeanours perpetrated by rich countries. The steady inflation of a massive bubble of credit (or debt, depending on which label you prefer) is the most striking feature of both the US and UK economies in recent years.

And a clear link emerges between the over-consumption that is creating ecological debt and the easy provision of the reckless credit that pays for it by the banking system. 'I see a strong contradiction between what Herman Daly calls, "the sickness of unlimited wants," or in other words, consumption financed by debt,' she writes, 'and the absolute scarcity of already depleted resources such as oil and the ability of the atmosphere to absorb our wastes'.[37] While money to pay for consuming goods can be lent into existence by banks, unfortunately we are yet to uncover a benign creator who can lend matter into existence to replace what we use and turn into waste.

The year 2007 saw serious debt-fuelled crises in both the US and UK that grew progressively worse in 2008. Both were linked to credit made available for house-buying in inflated property markets at a time when interest rates were low. When trouble hit the UK, there were long queues of worried customers waiting to withdraw their savings from high street banks, scenes reminiscent of Argentina during its economic collapse. The question in every commentator's mind as the financial system teetered was, 'Is this a crisis of liquidity, or of solvency?' Even if it was only the former, many were aware that, depending on people's reactions, it could easily lead to the latter. The speed and depth of the government's response – ensuring that tens of billions of pounds were immediately made available to underwrite the system – showed how seriously the threat was taken.

Sadly, still no such concern is evident for the financial system's parent company, the biosphere. In an ecological timeframe, our life support systems also may be teetering between a crisis of liquidity and irrecoverable insolvency. Yet this deeper, more threatening problem is met instead with the equivalent in advice of telling worried savers not to worry, and to go a little easier on their purse during their next shopping trip. But is it possible that such timidity might finally be about to change? There are some tentative signs.

AN 'ENVIRONMENTAL WAR ECONOMY'

Of all the themes in the first edition of this book, one provoked more disbelieving scoffs than others. I'd taken several steps too far, it seemed, in suggesting that we needed to re-engineer the economy at a scale and speed only previously seen during wartime. To tackle the problems facing us, I argued, we needed the equivalent of an environmental war effort. To say this, I was told, was out of touch, wildly disproportionate and historically irrelevant. But since then, something strange has happened.

Strolling into a mainstream bookshop in late 2007 I am confronted by a table heaving with books on the theme of 'life during wartime'. All of them cast back to the 1940s. They are a mixture of facsimile reproductions of the government information leaflets mentioned in Chapter 10, such as *Make Do and Mend* and *Sew and Save,* and some that are pure nostalgia; some interesting contrary accounts that look more on the dark side, puncturing simplistic myths of social cohesion amid a blitz spirit, and there are moving personal diaries of daily life on the home front. Elsewhere in a picture-framing shop I fall into conversation with the owner. She mentions in passing that the current surprise poster 'hit' for which she finds herself making endless frames is a reproduction of a public information poster printed, but barely distributed, in anticipation of the outbreak of the war in the late 1930s. In simple white lettering against a red background the colour of London buses, it carries the words *'Keep Calm and Carry On'.*

In a cultural atmosphere buffeted by the warm and cold fronts of many other issues, at some level people are, apparently, registering that we face a deep crisis. In response, we seem to be culturally self-medicating, half-consciously bracing ourselves for the changes to come. It could be that we are preparing to adapt by reminding ourselves that we *can,* while seeking some comfort in the fact that we have done so before. Whatever the exact interpretation, the deluge of coverage of climate change in the media appears to be affecting a wide range of shifts in attitude.

That shift has invaded the political sphere, where debate (if not action) on climate change now moves at the speed of a receding glacier – in other words, very fast.

First came the surprising comment of former UN weapons inspector for Iraq, Hans Blix – the man whose pleas were ignored by the US and UK for more time to establish the truth concerning the presence of 'weapons of mass destruction' in the country. Contradicting the media and political narrative dominant at the time, Blix said that climate change was a greater threat to humanity than international terrorism. His sentiments were echoed first by Sir John Houghton, the climate scientist and former senior figure at the IPCC, and then Sir David King, chief scientific advisor to the UK government, and even Prof. Stephen Hawking, who said: 'The West should have a war on global warming rather than a war on terror.'[38]

When the same UK government produced its first report on the economic impacts of climate change, its principal author, Sir Nicholas Stern, carefully and deliberately drew parallels with the Great Depression, precursor to the Second World War.

Soon the parallels drawn were becoming even more official and explicit. Climate change increasingly came to be seen less as a technical and scientific problem and much more as a security concern. The high politics of government normally demands nuances of language whose meanings are lost to all but small, inner circles. This was not the case when UK Foreign Secretary, the Rt. Hon. Margaret Beckett MP, gave the Annual Winston Churchill Memorial Lecture in April 2007 to a meeting in New York of the wonderfully dubious-sounding 'British American Business Inc.'[39]

Invoking one of the most iconic and resonant political phrases of the last century, and a touchstone of the US–UK 'special relationship', the theme and title she chose was 'Climate Change: "The Gathering Storm"'.

'It was a time when Churchill, perceiving the dangers that lay ahead, struggled to mobilise the political will and industrial energy of the British empire to meet those dangers. He did so often in the face of strong opposition and not always with success: wasted opportunities that he subsequently referred to as "The Locust Years"', Beckett said, recalling the atmosphere in the approach to war with Germany. And in case there was any residual ambiguity, she continued:

> But in the end it was his foresight and his determination to prepare for a threat which – to many – was still seemingly distant and uncertain that in the end guaranteed the liberty and indeed survival of my country and that of many others.
>
> Today politicians and business leaders alike once again face an increasing danger to our security and prosperity, and growing calls for early and resolute measures. Climate change is the gathering storm of our generation. And the implications – should we fail to act – could be no less dire: and perhaps even more so.[40]

The shift of perception is by no means limited to the British political scene. When Stavros Dimas became European Commissioner for the Environment, green hearts sank. He had a reputation as an advocate of unregulated market economics. Exposed to the realities of climate change, however, it wasn't long before he was calling for the effort of a 'war economy' – a notion imbued with all the political parameter-setting and intervention in the working of the market that such a project entails.

'Damaged economies, refugees, political instability, and the loss of life are typically the results of war. But they will also be the results of unchecked climate change', said Dimas in January 2007, elaborating that 'It is clear that the fight against climate change is much more than a battle. It is a world war that will last for many years … It is like a war because to reduce emissions something very like a war economy is needed.' Such an effort, he said, could bring public health benefits, just as it did in Britain in the 1940s. Plans to reduce emissions by 20 per cent by the year 2020 and increase the share of renewable energy in the EU to 20 per cent by the same year, were called part of a new 'industrial revolution'.[41]

So there is a growing consensus that climate change demands an economic mobilisation on a wartime scale. But another security threat due to global warming must now be conceded. Environmental change could itself become the cause of conflicts. Returning to the theme of climate change, British Foreign Secretary Margaret Beckett, no doubt influenced by her time as Environment Secretary, said that climate-related competition for declining resources fuelled the conflict in Darfur and that Ghana was prone to similar unrest. Already unstable, lower rainfall in the Middle East would cause even greater instability. Saudi Arabia, Iran and Iraq were particularly vulnerable. 'The threat to our climate security', she said, drawing powerful links between personal behaviour and global consequences, 'comes not from outside but from within: we are all our own enemies.'[42]

The Ministry of Defence, taking an opportunity to justify its call on the public purse, and scanning the horizon for new threats and enemies, also entered the climate debate. The ministry commissioned a multimillion-pound research contract in 2007 from the UK Met Office.[43] Its task was to highlight where in the world conflicts could begin or worsen due to climate-related scarcities of food or water. As the UK plays a prominent role in instigating conflicts in which the control of oil – a climate 'push' factor – is a central theme, it's logical also to keep an eye on the subsequent climate-related 'pull' factors of conflict.

In the final chapter we'll come back to what the analogy of a war economy might mean in practice.

But the much more recent experience of one country, very much and long maligned, provides a glimpse of what the near future may hold for others. Cuba has already lived through the economic and environmental shocks that climate change and the peak and decline of global oil production hold in store for the rest of the world. In 1990 at the end of the Cold War it suddenly lost access to cheap oil imports and continued to suffer from the economic isolation imposed by a tight US embargo. At the same time, Cuba sat in the flight path of the annual hurricane season, regularly contending with extreme weather events. Yet Cuba demonstrated that, in the face of a sudden and unpredictable shock, it is possible to feed a nation with very little or even no fossil fuel inputs, and to tackle extreme weather events with little harm to human life.

The final chapter of this book looks at where Cuba went right and had its success enviously dubbed the 'anti-model' by officials in Washington, DC.

CASSANDRA COMPLEX

Already I prophesied to my countrymen all their disasters.
Cassandra, in Aeschylus, *Agamemnon*.[44]

Folk memory has been cruel to Cassandra, mythical royal daughter of Troy. Now her name is a gentle term of abuse used to dismiss anyone whose outlook seems negative. Cruel irony, as her god-given curse was to have the power of prophesy and yet be disbelieved. She saw tragedies coming, including her own, but could do nothing to stop them.

For decades, the mainstream has dismissed the environmental movement as a 'bunch of Cassandras', unaware of the lethal paradox.

That we might escape terrible fates what else should be noted, before I inadvertently write a whole new book, when all that was intended was a short update? As all these things can be read about in more detail elsewhere, it's enough to provide a few references. Many things warned of are indeed now believed. Whether it has happened in time to forestall tragedy is another matter.

For years a Cassandra complex surrounded those who warned that the global peak and decline of oil production was imminent. But in a dry publication called the *Medium-Term Oil Market Report* published in 2008 by the International Energy Agency, an official advisor to most of the major economic powers, its words were cautious to avoid panic, but unequivocal.

About world oil production there will be, it stated, 'a narrowing of spare capacity to minimal levels by 2013'. Since the previous year alone it had made 'significant downward revisions' on 'both non-OPEC supplies and OPEC capacity forecasts'.[45] The fuel price rises of the last year look to be a foretaste of a far more massive crunch that will follow as the graph lines for global oil demand and supply head in opposite directions.[46] The Agency's motto, 'Energy security, growth and sustainability', is very nice, except that there doesn't appear to be any.

Similarly, in 2003 when I wrote a pamphlet with Molly Conisbee on environmental refugees, they were something that the UN's specialist refugee body wanted nothing to do with. Partly, they were afraid that their existing responsibilities with political refugees would be overwhelmed.[47] Now, several parts of the UN see this problem as being a fundamental challenge to human security.[48] Estimates for the number that will be displaced by climate change range from tens of millions to hundreds of millions.

The true, mournful spirit of Cassandra envelops the second great financial crash starting in 2007 and rapidly accelerating throughout 2008. Five years earlier, **nef** published a book called *Real World Economic Outlook* edited by Ann Pettifor.[49] It said that 'Removing controls over the finance sector paved the way for ... increased instability.' The consequences of which for the global economy were grave, including: 'An enormous increase (or "bubble") in the stock of financial assets in relation to the real economy ... [and] an explosion in the level of indebtedness amongst households, corporations, and governments ...' It then predicted a very troubled outlook for the world economy: 'There will be a collapse in the credit system in the rich world, led by the United States, leading to soaring personal and corporate bankruptcies ... The risks of a debt-deflationary spiral in the rich world are significant.'

This is not intended as an unattractive and self-satisfied 'We told them so.' The point is that systematic marginalisation of non-orthodox voices weakens politics, the economy and society. Without this crucial informational feedback loop, we are all left more vulnerable to system failures – the worst of which might be runaway climate change.

It's now two decades since the Berlin Wall came down, drawing the line under the old Eastern bloc. For all its brashness, triumphalism and smug self-satisfaction, finance-driven capitalism managed to reign supreme for fewer than another two decades before it, too, fell apart.

No one is more synonymous with the era of financial liberalisation than Alan Greenspan, former Chairman of the US Federal Reserve. Under cross-examination by the US House Oversight Committee, his words were heavy with the pathos and bombast of the fallen emperor: 'I discovered a flaw', he said, 'in the model that I perceived is the critical functioning structure that defines how the world works.'[50]

But in the aftermath, in Britain and the US, there are intriguing possibilities. Following nationalisation of much of the finance sector, two governments formerly wedded to light touch, and sometimes absent, regulation find themselves owning, in effect, great swathes of their countries' economies – banks, homes, buildings, infrastructure and much else besides. Both are now in positions to direct investment and revolutionise the energy use and efficiency of much of the economy.

It may be that governments still entangled in the habitual rhetoric of free markets are embarrassed by their new, unaccustomed role. It could be that, having outsourced the exercising of power to the marketplace, they feel unpractised and not sure what to do. But the climate clock is still ticking – even speeding up. And they now have an enormous opportunity to do what democratically elected governments are meant to do – take responsibility and protect their people from disaster. This opportunity is discussed in more detail in the closing chapter of this edition. To borrow terms from the world of finance, the challenge is to prevent the current ecological liquidity crisis from turning into a solvency crisis.

15

The Ducks' Choice ...

You never change things by fighting the existing reality. To change something,
build a new model that makes the existing model obsolete.

Richard Buckminster Fuller

The great Latin American writer Eduardo Galeano tells the story
of a flock of domesticated farmyard ducks who are presented
one morning with two options. I heard it something like this.
The day is sunny and the farmer smiles, bearing news as he
approaches the ducks' favourite pond. 'I have the enormous
pleasure to tell you', he says, 'that this evening there is to be a
great feast.' To the ducks' delight, he adds: 'You are all central
to its success and I have come to offer you a choice of dish.'
The farm was not wealthy and treats were rare. A quacking
excitement spread around the pond.

Then they listen in anticipation. 'For the enjoyment of our
guests I am able to offer you the option of being cooked either
in an exquisite orange sauce, or being roasted with herbs and
stuffing.' The ducks' stunned silence quickly breaks into ruffled
confusion. Shock and consternation ripples over the water.
'But to be cooked and eaten in one of two different ways is
no choice at all', they complain. 'We want the option of not
being cooked at all!' 'Ah,' explains the farmer, 'but that choice
is not available.'

Now, we humans are the ducks. The farmer is giving us the
range of economic options available in the face of climate
change. In spite of all we know about how global warming is
linked to our economic behaviour, not one option officially
on offer is remotely capable of keeping the heat at bay. Each

ends in us being cooked. But fortunately, compared to the ducks, we have a useful mixture of complex language, human consciousness and opposable thumbs. We are far more equipped to increase our range of choices and change apparently pre-determined outcomes.

Some say we even have democratic systems that can be used to insist on us not being roasted or marinated. Such confidence, however, requires further study. But let's pretend, for now, that we can muster our impressive range of skills and human ingenuity and focus them all on resolving the ecological debt crisis and preventing catastrophic climate change. What would be the key ingredients of a plan to keep us out of the oven, one that we could start work on ourselves and take to convince the farmer?

Here is a sketch. It is neither comprehensive nor exclusive and each point could alone expand to become a chapter on its own, or even a book. Of course, half of the first edition of this book was an assessment of different ways forward, but there's no substitute for a little mildly disciplined boiling-down. Keeping it short is, after all, much harder than making it long. Noam Chomsky once politely refused a request to summarise his thoughts on an issue in 500 words: 'If they'd asked for 5000,' he commented, 'I could have done it.'

GETTING OUT OF DEBT: HOW TO THRIVE ON AN ISLAND PLANET

Two fascinations recently descended upon me. One is for Roman history – quite acceptable in Victorian Britain but incongruous today. The other is for the deep past of humanity's evolution in Africa and its subsequent diaspora around the globe. This is being recalibrated constantly as new research flows from the work of archeo-anthropologists. The history of humans in Britain alone was recently pushed back a further 200,000 years.

Slightly random distractions perhaps, but in pursuing them I stumbled over two further reasons to readjust our priorities. The first concerns questioning the nature of progress: what justifies the name, at what human or environmental cost is it bought, and can something be called 'progress' if it contains the seeds of its own, and our, ultimate downfall? The second modest insight – obvious to decent historians but often challenging otherwise – is that progress does not march forward through history in a straight line, like some immortal, unstoppable Roman legion, as, even in the case of Rome, not only were many of its gifts to civilisation ultimately lost for centuries, they were also, in the first place, predicated on a vast slave-based economy.

The course of settlement by humans in Britain should, by itself, be enough for us to realise how fragile is civilisation's hold on the stable climate that supports it. The first humans are now thought to have arrived in Britain 700,000 years ago, when the climate was warm enough for hippos to lumber around East Anglia. But there has been continuous settlement only for the last 11,500 years. In response to severe changes in climate, time after time, Britain was entirely emptied of people, needing to be repeatedly recolonised.[1] Vast periods passed, sometimes lasting over 100,000 years, when you wouldn't have heard so much as a pebble drop in a pond. There was no one to drop the pebble, and no one to hear it plop.

Living in one of the most stable climatic periods of the last half a million years has lulled us into a very false sense of security. Now, even if we avert runaway global warming, climate change locked in by the ecological debts we have already racked up means that our grip on ordered, reasonably benign societies will be heavily shaken.

All this points at a necessary reorientation away from the current economic obsessions with growth and international competitiveness, and toward principles that will help us, at least, to maintain our grip.

The new focus will be on maximising local resilience to external economic and environmental shocks, on the capacity to adapt, and on shifting our consumption patterns into a state of '*dynamic equilibrium*' with the world of natural resources – the target of one-planet living. (See below: I prefer the term 'dynamic equilibrium' in favour of Herman Daly's 'steady state economy'. It seems to capture better the relationship between two things that, while needing to achieve balance, will never be static – namely, our consumption patterns and the biocapacity available to feed them.)

So how will we build *resilience*, the *capacity to adapt*, and move toward a *dynamic equilibrium* between society and the natural world, while ensuring both *equity* and *sufficiency*?

First, we should get real.

Face Reality

If the claims of advertising alone could save the world, we would by now be home and dry. When BP launched an advertising campaign in which the meaning of its 'BP' initials were changed from 'British Petroleum' to 'Beyond Petroleum', it seemed to herald a new age of corporate action on climate change. But as we saw above, what lay 'beyond petroleum' turned out to be more petroleum. BP's initiative was, however, significant for another reason.

It signalled a confident new advertising trend, using green images and captions diametrically opposed to the core business of the company it was promoting. Another oil company, Shell, went so far that its creative efforts earned it a rebuke from the Advertising Standards Authority (ASA). Much of the company's advertising could fool you that Shell was, in fact, principally a renewable energy company. Their adverts invoked flower power, literally.

The ASA condemned Shell for creating the impression that all its carbon dioxide emissions were cosily recycled to help grow plants in greenhouses. In fact, that was true for only a fraction of 1 per cent of the emissions from its direct plant operations. Later, the ASA again ruled against a Shell advert. In this one Shell claimed that its exploitation of Canadian oil sands, one of the most polluting and least efficient forms of fossil fuel, was part of its 'sustainable' approach to meeting energy demands. The ASA was not alone in thinking otherwise. Both BP and Shell dropped involvement in key renewable energy projects as their advertising continued to emphasise a commitment to green energy.

Land Rover makes big, heavy, fuel-inefficient cars, but contrives to promise guilt-free motoring through the miracle of carbon offsetting. But their claim to offer 45,000 miles worth of carbon-neutralised motoring with every new car is both illogical and fallacious. The cars do, however, look great in adverts, shot in splendid wild surroundings, compared to their more natural habitat, blocking traffic on the North London school run.

E.ON, the German company that bought Powergen, is another interesting case. It promotes itself with the tagline 'The power of nature'. The firm's adverts – a combination of strong winds blowing and wildlife appearing unexpectedly – again create the impression of a company mainly selling renewable energy (either that, or as an organiser of safaris).

But E.ON's main business is generating electricity from a combination of coal-fired power plants – it is the company pushing for a new coal-fired power station at Kingsnorth in the UK – natural gas and nuclear power stations. In fact, according to the environmental group Greenpeace, as a company, it is the country's single large emitter of greenhouse gases. E.ON's advertising strategy is better understood in the context of trying to maintain a positive public image while planning, and hoping, to profit from any government decision to allow a combination of new coal-fired and nuclear power plants to be built in the UK.

As E.ON said itself in its advertising, it is 'one of a number of companies that have announced that they plan to pursue nuclear development opportunities in the UK'.

The irony, and the problem, is that as green-tinged advertising spreads and awareness of climate change increases, the amount of money being poured into fossil fuel industries through the City of London rises, inconveniently, along with greenhouse gas emissions.

'London has become a global centre for financing the expansion of the fossil fuel industry', says Mark Campanale, a specialist in clean technology with London Bridge Capital, adding that 'Inaction on this point by either the Treasury or its subsidiary, the Financial Services Authority (FSA), serves to undermine any positive policies brought to bear elsewhere, for example, through carbon trading or voluntary action by the public.'[2]

In spite of rich countries' technological advancement, their total greenhouse gas emissions continue to rise. Pushed by economic growth in highly industrialised countries and resurgent Central and Eastern Europe, their emissions hit an 'all time high' in 2005, continuing the rise of the previous year. Pollution from the transport sector rose the quickest.[3]

The point is this: all around us are familiar names, companies and politicians acting as if no fundamental change is needed. It sets a tone, feeding something called the 'bystander effect', coined by psychologists John Darley and Bibb Latané following an infamous, protracted murder which was heard and witnessed by many people who failed to intervene. It suggests that people are more likely to react to an emergency situation when alone than in groups.[4] Darley and Latané tested their hypothesis by having volunteers fill out forms in a room that, after a while, began to fill with smoke. Unknown to them, some volunteers were placed in rooms filled with actors who had been briefed to ignore the smoke. While those left alone were quick to report the smoke, those in rooms surrounded by other people who continued calmly to write did not. The 'astonishing finding' is, as one journalist put it, 'that the inaction of other people can make us underestimate threats to our own safety'.[5]

Now, in relation to climate change, we are surrounded by the active promotion of inaction. With so many soothing, misleading voices speaking over a creeping disaster, it is not surprising that many feel like worried yet passive bystanders.

A lot of guff has emanated from the automobile and airline industries about taking the car and the plane 'out of the environmental equation'. This is usually code for the marginal introduction of new fuel sources such as biofuels, hydrogen fuel cells and electric power. The growth of biofuels has been problematic for several reasons. Variously they stand accused of displacing essential food crops from precious, productive farmland, driving up the price of food to people in poverty leading to food riots, and in some circumstances being significantly less carbon efficient that fossil fuels. This is the case, for example, when peatlands are drained for the production of palm oil.[6] More generally, however, until all these industries proferring substitutes write a new law of physics to break the limits on the conservation of energy, let them remain silent in arguing that energy substitutes alone will be sufficient to resolve our global predicament.

So the challenge facing business, government and the general public is to close the widening gap between rhetoric and reality.

Instead of telling the wood from the trees, we need to see the wind turbine for the oil rig, and the solar panel for the nuclear power station. The advertising of all companies engaged in fossil fuel intensive activities, whether government or privately owned, should carry cigarette-style advertising warning of the threats to public and environmental health from burning coal, oil and gas. That should be coupled with full environmental disclosure of carbon emissions and liabilities, and acceptance of year-on-year emission reductions targets in line with the best science on averting dangerous climate change. In the meantime, to avoid confusion, perhaps we could follow the example of São Paulo in Brazil which simply banned advertising in public places.

Then, Ditch the Great Offsetting Myth

We need a meaningful measure against which to judge progress. According to Kevin Anderson of the respected Tyndall Centre for Climate Change Research, the UK needs to achieve year-on-year cuts in its greenhouse gas emissions over the coming decades in the region of 7–11 per cent, if it is to play its part in preventing potentially irreversible global warming.[7]

In practice, new technology and energy efficiency alone, simply are not capable of delivering savings on that scale. Assuming modest economic growth of between 2 per cent and 3 per cent, he implies the need to reduce the carbon intensity of the economy by up to 13 per cent a year. But the most that has been achieved in the United States, a country with perhaps the biggest room for improvement, is 2.7 per cent. Today, annual improvements languish around 1.6 per cent.[8]

What about carbon offsetting? It's often the first thought of businesses wanting to do something. Directing the money that comes from such schemes into clean technology clearly can be a good thing. But, as a defence against warming, 'offsetting' is seriously and scientifically flawed.

It's not just because of difficulties with accounting for emissions (although it is notoriously difficult, if not often impossible, to match up a tonne of carbon burnt in one place with a tonne recaptured or 'sequestered' elsewhere), or because there are bad projects, or because to swap carbon stored in the stable form of a fossil fuel, for something unstable like forestry, which can easily die or burn, is tantamount to 'carbon laundering' – replacing carbon safely locked away in deep geological structures with carbon that can re-enter the atmosphere at the drop of a match in the dry season.

Offsetting works by seeking to compensate for emissions that have already occurred. It does so in a variety of ways, such as forestry projects, designed to absorb and store carbon. Others initiatives seek to replace carbon intensive activities with lower carbon ones – for example, by encouraging more efficient factories or domestic stoves for cooking in poor countries. Notably, the vast majority of schemes also shift the onus of responsibility from wealthy Northern consumers to poor countries, where, for cost reasons, most offset projects are based. Some have made the comparison that offsetting is like paying someone else to be faithful so that you can have an affair.

Offsetting's basic logic is at fault, and for several reasons. A tonne of carbon released from deep geological storage by burning coal, oil or gas will persist in the atmosphere for decades, possibly centuries, where it will continue to have a warming effect. Once there, it weakens the ability of so-called natural sinks in the biosphere to absorb carbon dioxide by triggering feedback mechanisms such as ice melt and warming of the oceans. Neither of the two basic approaches to offsetting can fully compensate for the carbon already released.

First, schemes based on recapturing the carbon through plant growth do so unreliably and in a warming world in which the plants, soils or forests take time to absorb the carbon and can just as easily re-release it. Second, schemes that offset by encouraging less polluting behaviour do nothing at all to actually remove the carbon already emitted. In both cases the damage remains done, and the cure, while well-meaning, is useless to the patient. It is like taking away a scuba diver's air tank in the middle of the ocean, and promising to replace it in 50 years' time by dropping another oxygen tank in a different ocean on the other side of the world.

Whatever is done, once carbon dioxide from the initial pollution enters the atmosphere it will stay there, causing a warming effect for decades to come.

What matters, once again, is to prevent greenhouse gases accumulating, in the first place, to the point where the 'environmental domino' effect of positive feedback means that global warming potentially runs out of control.

Beware Magic Technological Bullets

Taking a lead from NASA's James Hansen, the global economy needs to go beyond 'carbon neutral' to become 'carbon negative' in order for the concentration of carbon dioxide in the atmosphere to get back down to 350 ppm CO_2.[9]

Beyond the point at which the ecological dominoes start to tumble, it will become an uncontrollable game of climate roulette to attempt to stabilise concentration levels at any given higher level. Suggesting otherwise has been a persistent and crucial oversight in the climate change debate and in the international negotiations. Everyone from the oil company BP to Sir David King, the government's former chief scientific advisor, have suggested that it is not 'pragmatic' to aim lower than 550 ppm. But once uncontrollable environmental feedbacks have been triggered, nobody can guarantee stabilising greenhouse gas concentrations at any given level. The biosphere will be dancing like a climate cat on a hot atmospheric roof, moving to its own beat and dynamics, and deaf to our pleas and exhortations.

There is a tipping point that we must either avoid or go over and face the catastrophic consequences. Any course of action advanced that does not meet that test is a counsel of defeat.

In the first edition of this book, I ignored nuclear power as a quietly glowing, radioactive red herring in the climate debate. Unfortunately, and obviously, that didn't stop the industry itself from co-opting the debate to promote its own interests. Now we stand on the verge of the UK committing itself to an expensive and ineffective programme of building new nuclear generating capacity. Leave aside that some analysts believe current nuclear technologies to be ultimately 'energy bankrupt'. That is to say, it will take more than all the energy generated by the nuclear sector just to manage their own fuel cycle, waste management and decommissioning – adding nothing to the sustainability or security of our energy supply.[10]

Even if that assessment is only remotely accurate, it still renders the current government enthusiasm for new nuclear as one of the most dangerous policy deceptions on record, most threatening because of the more effective action in favour of renewable energy and efficiency and conservation that it substitutes for and steals funding, priority and political focus from. Oh dear. The nuclear horse falls at every fence, a sorry sight described in more detail in a report I wrote with colleagues for **nef**.[11]

Put briefly, in spite of what nuclear power companies say, as a response to global warming, nuclear solutions are too slow, too expensive and limited. In an age of terrorist threats, they are more of a security risk than a solution, while answers to the unsolved problem of waste and decommissioning are nowhere in sight. In terms of the relative costs of lowering carbon emissions, nuclear power comes at the end of a long list of more efficient alternatives. Contrary to myth, nuclear power is not itself a carbon-free energy source, as fossil fuel energy is needed at various stages of its production. As higher-grade uranium ores get used up, nuclear becomes progressively more expensive and carbon-polluting.

Remember that Good Lives Don't Have to Cost the Earth

Now, can you hear the rustle of green handcuffs fastening around your freedom to fuel a patio heater, burn the rubber of a brace of 4x4s, or fly on a long weekend from London to Los Angeles? Calls to change radically consumer behaviour in response to climate change tend to be denigrated as authoritarian.

Just as appreciation of the need to save civilisation from runaway climate change finally seems to be achieving consensus, a sharp and monstrously ironic reaction accuses the environmental movement of being a threat to freedom. In part this represents an opportunistic ideological land grab by a vocal cabal of anti-environmentalists, latching onto genuine concern about rising fuel and food prices.

It ranges from the bewildered outrage of television motoring personality Jeremy Clarkson, like a child caught and told no, he cannot keep torturing the cat, to the sophistry of far left and far right political agitation. Odder still is the free market Czech president, Vaclav Klaus (NB: not Havel), whose book on 'green shackles' was published by the ferociously conservative Competitive Enterprise Institute. He suggested, in effect, that combating climate change is a threat to liberty on the scale of Soviet communism. Somehow, however, the cause of freedom to fry or drown ourselves in a warming world lacks the moral oomph of those other freedoms of religion and association, democracy and universal suffrage.[12]

But the backlash is only likely to grow, driven by the volatility in oil prices, the reality of global warming and the policy responses to both. As the scale and depth of necessary change becomes more obvious, voices become louder calling for there to be less, not more, parameters set around individual consumption. They rally beneath an appeal to 'freedom'.

But, talking of 'green shackles' is like talking about 'anti-child labour' shackles, or the shackles of laws that prevent us burning down each other's houses. We need to set goals for sufficient levels of consumption in order to prevent the footprint of our lifestyles outgrowing the shoe of the planet.

The awareness that one person's freedom to unlimited luxury might deny another's freedom to survive is neither new nor owned exclusively by the left or environmentalists. It was the conservative philosopher Karl Popper, who pointed out that 'proponents of complete freedom … are in actuality, whatever their intentions, enemies of Freedom'. In *The Open Society and its Enemies*, Popper reasoned that unrestrained individual behaviour

> is not only self-destructive but bound to produce its opposite, for if all restraints were removed there would be nothing whatever to stop the strong enslaving the weak. So complete freedom would bring about the end of freedom.[13]

The mantra of consumer choice underpins our individualistic economic system. But now it is the absence of action to curb individual excess that is the biggest threat to our freedoms. It is a depressingly unnecessary threat, grown from chasing the retreating shadows of our own wellbeing down the blind alleys of conspicuous consumption.

It is consumerism that has enslaved us, we should now argue, not the environmentalism that seeks to end its worst excesses. In its cause we have become chained to the workplace, turning our backs on friends, family and the things that bring real contentment. We work longer hours to earn, to buy the consumer clutter that promises happiness but delivers only listlessness and dissatisfaction. Why?

One extraordinary study of people's shopping habits breaks an enduring myth about the importance of unlimited consumer choice. In separate cases, shoppers were offered samples to taste from displays of either 6 or 24 varieties of jam. The bigger range attracted more people but, on average, at either display individuals tasted about the same number of samples. At the checkout, however, a real difference emerged. People who were offered the smaller range were ten times more likely actually to make a purchase.[14]

The other shoppers had been paralysed by too much choice. Major psychological costs also emerge in making choices, and the more you are offered, the higher the cost. So a society that worships consumer choice above more important things (like a habitable planet and caring for those who need it), is a society that is committing itself to high and lasting levels of dissatisfaction (not to mention problems with the planet and wider society). Too much choice really can be a bad thing. Of course, if the choice is only between shallow difference – for example, between a number of equally tasteless mass-produced year-round 'global' apple varieties, rather than several local seasonal varieties – it is not much choice at all.

Barry Schwarz quotes a classic example about lottery winners in his book *The Paradox of Choice*. The winners reported levels of happiness that were no different from the general population. Schwarz explains that

first, people just get used to good or bad fortune. Second, the new standard of what's a good experience (winning the lottery) may make many of the ordinary pleasures of daily life (the smell of freshly brewed coffee, the new blooms and refreshing breezes of a lovely spring day) rather tame by comparison.[15]

Yet action to rescue civilisation from an increasingly hostile environment, it is and will be said, represents an unacceptable and oppressive barrier to owning TV screens the size of football pitches. In response we must argue that if we do, now, manage to balance human need, wellbeing and social justice with the available resources of our parent planet, we will not be left cursing 'green shackles' but breaking our carbon chains. Some might even call it 'liberation ecology'.

Use the Right Road Signs

Our problem is that the conflation of a growing economy with rising wellbeing in wealthy countries like Britain is hard-wired, both in conventional economic theory and in the minds of policy makers. But the theory is wrong. In the UK alone, while our economy has grown continuously over the last few decades, study after study shows that our sense of satisfaction with life has flatlined. Similar trends can be found in a wide variety of other industrialised countries.

In the face of this seeming contradiction, what sort of indicator could better point the way ahead for policy? Basically, we need to assess the efficiency with which we turn fundamental inputs, in this case fossil fuels, into desirable and meaningful human outcomes, such as relatively long and satisfied lives. Standard, comparable data exist for all these factors and for most countries. Interestingly, for those who doubt the robustness of life satisfaction measures, they correlate closely with a wide range of quantitative data on health, depression and suicide. In other words, when asked in the right way, people do have a good idea of their overall wellbeing. Combining life expectancy and satisfaction produces perhaps the most fundamental indicator of human wellbeing, what academics refer to as 'happy life years'. By then adding resource inputs, either carbon alone or all resources measured by the ecological footprint, a measure emerges of the relative environmental efficiency with which societies deliver long and happy lives.

Apply this analysis to Europe using carbon, and a surprising and worrying picture emerges. For all the talk of successful knowledge driven, resource-light service economies, the core European nations have as a whole become less, not more, carbon efficient at delivering wellbeing for their citizens in terms of life expectancy and satisfaction. Europe is less carbon efficient now than it was in 1961.[16]

Better news comes from findings that across Europe, and even more so within the UK, where people report comparable levels of wellbeing, whether their lifestyles are high-consuming and very resource-intensive or low-consuming and leave a much smaller ecological footprint. The range of levels is enormous, from lifestyles that if followed by the whole world's population would imply the need for the resources of six and a half planets like earth, down to just the one that we actually have.

More interesting still is the snapshot of what lies behind different lifestyles found in Britain and across Europe. In a unique survey carried out by **nef**, more than 35,000 people reported both their general, everyday levels of consumption and their levels of wellbeing.[17]

When consumption was compared to different levels of life satisfaction, there was virtually no connection at all (see Figure 15.1). You were just as likely to have a good life if you were thrifty than if your ecological footprint stomped its way around the globe all year courtesy of a 747 jumbo jet, or left its tread courtesy of the wheels of a luxury Bentley.

This is because at most European stages of economic development, when most of basic material needs are met, other things determine the rise or fall of wellbeing. These include the quality of family life, friendships, and the opportunities we have to do things that give lasting satisfaction, such as learning, being engaged in creative pastimes and meaningful work. Typically, these are also the things most likely to be crushed on the hedonic treadmill in the obsessive rush for riches.

Research by colleagues at **nef** identified five key dynamics based on a large academic literature that maximise human wellbeing, and the absence of which, conversely, is likely to be similarly undermining. They are, in effect, the psychological equivalent of the nutritionists advised consumption of five portions of fruit and vegetables per day. All happen to be conveniently low-carbon in nature. They include: being active, continuing to learn, taking notice of the world around you, giving, and connecting with friends, neighbours and colleagues. Although they sound simple, when practised they have been shown to increase wellbeing significantly. If you want to be happy, it is definitely counter-productive to sacrifice the time needed to pursue these five dynamics to chase higher earnings in order to feed materialistic gratification.[18]

The big, difficult message to government and business is that we need absolute reductions in consumption, not just improvements in efficiency and technological fixes.

The good news, of course, is that new, more fulfilling ways of living can be substituted for the old that will be less

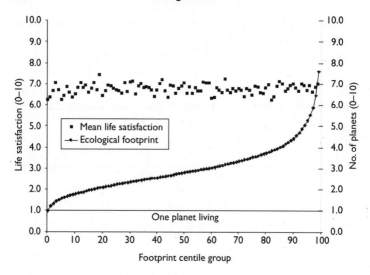

Figure 15.1   Ecological footprint and subjective life satisfaction in the UK

Source: European Happy Planet Index.

dependent on what is often, anyway, misery-making mass consumption.

Take, for example, the supermarkets who fall over themselves to promote their green credentials. Shopping in the big supermarkets provokes significantly more negative than positive emotions in people.[19] But not only do those lonely aisles make us depressed (not to mention eroding the fabric of the food economy and undermining the conviviality of communities), they also lead to an awful lot of waste. WRAP, a government-funded group focused on cutting waste, reported that we throw away one bag of perfectly good groceries in every three that we buy.[20]

To encourage sustainability, then, logically supermarkets should encourage customers to buy one third fewer groceries. Instead of a 'Buy one get one free' promotion (famously known as *Bogof*), the suggestion would be 'Pick up three, put one back' (*Putpob?*) Like it or not, consuming less in rich countries is what sustainability looks like.

In the crucial energy markets a couple of neat initiatives could deliver similar results. One proposal is for a 'demand reduction obligation' that government could place on the utilities. This could work in tandem with the Climate Change Bill to bring the necessary, deep annual emissions cuts. Another idea involves a Copernican shift in how investors and regulators view the big fossil fuel companies.

At the moment, the reserves of oil and coal companies are viewed as assets. But burning all those 'assets' would lead to catastrophic warming. So one suggestion, made by Mark Campanale and a former colleague from Henderson Global Investors, Nick Robins, now head of HSBC's climate change centre, is that some reserves should be listed as 'unburnable' alongside the usual categories of 'proven' and 'probable', and not be given a financial value. We could then also apply the Treasury's estimate for the damage cost of carbon, up to £140 per tonne, thus turning 'assets' into 'liabilities'. In the meantime, a windfall tax on oil companies could help to pay for the transition.

The challenge is to take all the supposed official prudence and market discipline meant to characterise the UK economy and use it to learn to live within our environmental budget. In addition to cutting carbon, that would mean, for example, taking the ecological footprint as an official measure, with a timetable, policies and resources so that we all move to live within our fair, per capita share of available global biocapacity – so-called 'one planet living'.

But let's be direct and not kid ourselves. The scale of change is comparable only to the economic re-engineering that happens in times of international conflict. We are talking about an environmental war economy. But it is one that could bring real human benefits in addition to averting runaway climate change. In rich countries, cutting consumption and getting off the treadmill is likely to improve health and wellbeing.

Remember, We've Done it Before – Learn the Lessons, Good and Bad, of War Mobilisation

> It is no use saying, 'We are doing our best.' You have got to succeed in doing what is necessary.
>
> Winston Churchill

As mentioned, there is a growing consensus that climate change demands an economic mobilisation on the scale of wartime. To be clear, war is bad. It shatters lives and whole societies, often lasting for generations. But, as we've seen, it's not that simple. Some unintended consequences of war, and how society reacts to it, can be good. In Britain in the 1940s, war led to the empowerment of women, rapid technological advancement and a healthier nation. Infant mortality fell and life expectancy increased against a background of rapid cuts in consumption. The use of private vehicles almost ceased entirely, use of domestic electrical appliances fell significantly, as did overall household consumption. On the down side, there was also profiteering, defeatism, bigotry, paranoia and bureaucratic incompetence (for example, more government effort seemed to go into planning the protection of national art treasures than the defence of the civilian population).[21] Our opportunity today is to learn the good lessons and try to avoid repeating the mistakes.

During the Second World War, when my mother was a child, at 8.15 a.m. as she prepared to go to school she listened to the 'fruity voice' of the Radio Doctor, Dr Charles Hill, broadcasting advice on 'Wise Eating in Wartime'. It was part of the Ministry of Food's series of Kitchen Front Broadcasts backed by pamphlets like *Your Baby's Food in Wartime* and *Wartime Food for Growing Children*.[22]

Chapter 1 of *Wise Eating* is titled 'A Little of What you Fancy'. It gives tips on how to 'keep our bodies tuned up to concert pitch by eating sensible, balanced meals', and shows the role simple food can play in 'strengthening, warming and refreshing the inner man'. OK, it's haughty, but it's less patronising than much daytime TV, and you can see what they were trying and succeeding in doing.

The approach to curbing consumption during the Second World War was influenced by the experience of inflation and scarcity during the First World War of 1914–18.[23] The task was identified as how to ensure 'a fair distribution of supplies' and to 'foresee, and obviate, future difficulties', often requiring 'swift action'. Ultimately, the public assented largely because they understood the need for action and that the restrictions 'ensured the fairest possible distribution of the necessities and comforts of daily life'.

But it wasn't straightforward. Working at the height of his powers, J.M. Keynes struggled to find ways to cut consumption and increase savings. Luxury taxes were only introduced slowly and cautiously. Accused of applying 'totalitarian methods', Keynes countered that 'In a totalitarian state the problem of the distribution of sacrifice does not exist.' He saw his challenge, not wildly different from our own as 'adapting the distributive system of a free community to the limitations of war'.[24]

Oddly, given the eclipsing severity of war, at home there were the deceptive characteristics of good times. Wages were rising and employment was growing. Consequently, overall income was up substantially. How, then, to cut consumption of particular commodities?

The government responded with higher taxes, softened by the promise of postwar credits. In effect, a form of compulsory saving was introduced, eased with the prospect of greater future security.

A National Savings Movement held marches, processions and displays in every city, town and village in the country. Propaganda was widely used – especially where rationing was difficult or impossible – such as with certain public utilities. There was also a huge focus on having low-consumption good times. There were campaigns to 'Holiday at Home', and endless festivities like dances, concerts, boxing displays, swimming galas, and open air theatre – all organised by local authorities with the express purpose of saving fuel by discouraging unnecessary travel. Over the course of the war, spending on relatively 'weightless' entertainment went up as classic consumption went down.

Fuel Economy and Petrol Rationing

Initially the 'rationing' of coal was held back in favour of a high-profile campaign promoting fuel economy. To lead by example, very public energy restrictions were introduced in government and local authority buildings, shops and railway stations. The result was successful and the drop in domestic coal deliveries by early 1943 was greater than the cuts previously planned in an over-complex rationing scheme. Petrol rationing, by contrast, was introduced early on and tightened to the point where rations were only made available for 'business and other essential purposes'. The private car 'almost disappeared from the roads'.[25]

Rationing was organised in accordance with need and sometimes bizarrely specific. Clocks and watches, for example, were scarce, except for some imported American alarm clocks. But to get one, you'd have to demonstrate that your job demanded an early hour of rising.

It's vital to remember that adapting was difficult even then. In the 1930s people led sophisticated lives. A range of foreign food and other luxuries were taken for granted as much then as they are now (even if the selection was smaller). It was an *issue* when imported food disappeared almost entirely from the shelves.

Behind all the schemes to manage demand, the objective was to

secure the fairest possible distribution of whatever supplies are available and to ensure ... that as far as possible the things that everybody needs shall be within the reach of all.[26]

And rationing wasn't one-size-fits-all. There were special allowances for mothers and children, agricultural workers and miners who lacked work canteens, vegetarians who didn't take up a meat ration, people with illnesses, and others whose diet was conditioned by their religion.

Even outside the workplace, 'communal feeding' was a big issue. So-called 'British Restaurants' became a national institution. By the end of the war there were over 2,000 nationwide, run by a combination of voluntary organisations and local authorities, serving 600,000 meals per day.

Generally, the government deliberately chose rationing over taxation for reasons that were rational and progressive. Taxation alone, they concluded, apart from disproportionately and unfairly placing a burden on the poor, would be too slow to change behaviour. Rationing was considered quicker and more equitable. Tradable rations were rejected through fear of encouraging fraud and inflation and 'undermining the moral basis of rationing'.[27] Historian Mark Roodhouse derives specific lessons for policy making. If transferred to now, government, he writes, would need to 'convince the public that rationing levels are fair; that the system is administered transparently and fairly; and that evaders are few in number, likely to be detected and liable to stiff penalties if found guilty'.[28]

Agree an Effective Global Climate Deal

The struggle to negotiate an inclusive, effective global climate treaty continues to founder on the large, unresolved and mounting ecological debts of an over-consuming global minority. To pervert Winston Churchill's more famous observation praising the Royal Air Force after its successful struggle with Germany for domination of the skies over Britain, never before in the history of the world has so much been owed by so few, to so many.

As described above, any effective deal will need to deliver reductions in global emissions, and in the process, unavoidably, share out what is left more equally among the world's people. In other words, any solution will follow the curve of an emission's path that contracts and converges. There is, though, one important change to note since writing the first edition of this book.

In the classic model described in Chapter 11, the economic benefits of emissions trading between high and low polluters bring in themselves large hoped-for development gains to poor countries. Increasingly, though, the depth and speed of necessary emissions cuts, plus the need for immediate financial support to help poor countries adapt to global warming, suggests that an additional mechanism is essential to meet the needs of the majority world.

However described, any lasting and effective global deal will have to possess certain key characteristics. Basically, they need to work to stop runaway climate change; in other words, to have 'environmental integrity'. And they need to work politically to win the support at least of the major populous countries of the global South and the wealthy countries who are home to the major per capita polluters. Touched on above, these will include:

- *Setting a formal greenhouse gas atmospheric concentration target likely to keep global average temperature rises below 2 °C.* Paradoxically, while many governments including the European Union have accepted the temperature target, they have not agreed on a concentration level likely to meet it. They have, in effect, decided collectively to travel from Kyoto to Copenhagen, but refused to set off from their base because they cannot agree on what route to take. Now, though, more people are arguing that even a 2 °C rise represents a level of warming that is unacceptably dangerous for many of the world's people. And NASA scientist James Hansen believes that, to be safe, no further rises should be allowed, and carbon dioxide levels should be significantly reduced from current levels to at least 350ppm.[29]

- *The delivery of a global, effective and equitable agreement beyond 2012* that deepens reduction targets in industrialised countries. Wealthy industrialised countries should be setting legally binding and constantly contracting 'carbon budgets' that plot a course, year by year, towards an emissions cut of well over 80 per cent against 1990 levels. In agreeing the price for full participation by developing countries in a global deal, industrialised countries need to be aware that, to the global South, even equal per capita rights to the global commons of the atmosphere appears a compromise in the face of historically grossly unequal emissions.

- *Re-engineering the global economy to allow real poverty reduction in the context of serious carbon constraints.* This means far greater flexibility over economic policy, and plugging the leakage from the poor to the rich of the assets and wealth that they do possess. It also means a shift from hoping, with fingers firmly crossed, that a dwindling trickle down of wealth will end poverty as a side-effect of the rich getting richer, towards a more targeted and guaranteed approach of redistribution. This will not be aid, but ecological debt payments by the wealthy that could create, for example, the opportunity for massive investments in appropriate adaptation and renewable energy in poor countries. Sustainable development would also be supported by greater flexibility in the rules governing trade, migration finance and intellectual property.
- *The explicit recognition and protection in international law of environmental or 'climate' refugees,* displaced due to 'push' factors resulting from global warming. Measures to meet this large and growing challenge should operate along the lines of appropriate burden-sharing. Financial burdens should be met in proportion to both responsibility for the problem and ability to pay. More than that, there will need to be flexibility in immigration policy, protection of displaced people and compensation funds for those affected.
- *New and additional resources made available for adaptation.* In yet another climate change irony, in 2008 the rising price of oil was reported to have wiped out the value of aid to Africa.[30] While the costs of adapting to climate change in the majority world are large and unknown, new resources available to pay for adaptation are, conversely, known and small. Funds for this purpose under the

UNFCCC and the Kyoto Protocol need to increase in size by several orders of magnitude in order to match the costs of unavoidable adaptation and pay for clean energy substitution.

- *Technology transfer.* Free technology transfer is also important, especially energy technology, unconstrained by the restrictive regimes governing intellectual property in the global economy.

And an Oil (Fossil Fuel) Depletion Protocol

In parallel with the haggling over a climate agreement is the equally difficult task of managing a soft landing for the global economy as the support strings of once-cheap and abundant oil and gas are cut.

To this end, in 1996 petroleum geologist Dr Colin Campbell, founder of the Association for the Study of Peak Oil and Gas, proposed an *'Oil Depletion Protocol'*.[31] It works by agreeing annual reductions in the import and export of oil in producer and consumer countries with the aim of 'stabilizing prices, preserving the resource base, and reducing competition for remaining supplies', and has the target of reducing global consumption by 3 per cent a year.

Campbell's suggested protocol is designed with one eye clearly focused on current global economic imbalances. It is designed to 'avoid profiteering' by keeping oil prices 'in reasonable relationship with production cost'. The idea is to insulate against 'destabilizing financial flows arising from excessive oil' and excessive price rises on poor countries' imports, and to create new incentives for alternative energy and for consumers to avoid waste.

Many different formulas for capturing various of the points above are now in circulation. They can be pursued online by' the enthusiastic reader and include Kyoto 2,[32] 'cap and share',[33] and greenhouse development rights.[34]

But for all the talk of models, protocols and agreements, one thing has been missing. We have to believe that it will be possible to live, and for society to function, in a world where the use of fossil fuels is radically cut. We need pioneers prepared to explore this urgently-sought future land who can report back on what lies in store and how we will manage. Only then, perhaps, will it be possible to coax others along. Fortunately, there are a few spies to inform us – some accidental; some eager and deliberate. Chapter 16 contains a few of their reports.

16

How to Live on an Island

> What difference does it make how much is laid away in a man's safe or in his barns, how many head of stock he grazes or how much capital he puts out at interest, if he is always after what is another's and only counts what he has yet to get, never what he has already? You ask what is the proper limit to a person's wealth? First, having what is essential, and second, having what is enough.
>
> Lucius Annaeus Seneca, 4 BC–AD 65

Since I was a child, a book called *Memoirs of a Survivor* by Doris Lessing has quietly haunted me. In it, for some reason left vague, society had broken down. Everywhere people were on the move, displaced amid an increasingly brutal disorder, the lucky few leaving the city to stay with relatives in the country. The presiding government was useless, but just about able to 'adjust itself to events, while pretending probably even to itself, that it initiated them'.[1]

Nothing reveals the thin veneer of civilisation like a threat to its fuel or food supply, or the cracks in society like a major climate-related disaster. Just think of Hurrican Katrina hitting New Orleans in 2005. But, conversely, perhaps we should ask why some societies don't fall apart when under extreme pressure, and try to learn from them.

One country, very much maligned in the western media, has already lived through the economic and environmental shocks that climate change and peak oil hold in store for the rest of the world. Does it have any lessons for us? Cuba's sudden loss of access to oil imports and its economic isolation were so extreme in 1990, and its reaction to the shock so contrary to orthodox approaches and successful, that it was dubbed in Washington, DC, the 'anti-model'.

Following the collapse of the Soviet Union, Cuba lost its cheap supplies of oil. The country had become heavily dependent upon them for its transport, farming and wider economy, so the effect was disastrous.

At the same time it continued to endure one of the longest and most comprehensive economic embargoes imposed on any country. In that corner of the Caribbean, the United States refused to let the Cold War thaw. Cuba's location, too, means that it sits in the flight path of the annual hurricane season, and regularly has to contend with extreme weather events.

By all accounts, Cuba should be a complete basket case – battered equally by the weather and the neighbouring superpower. But it's not. Why isn't Cuba, in the face of all these problems, on a par with some of the worst failed states in the world, with shattered health and education systems, starvation and endemic malnutrition? The answer is planning, preparation and the fact that they dealt with the problem imaginatively, and head-on.

Before the Soviet collapse around 1990, Cuba imported most of its needs. It exported sugar and tobacco to the Soviet Union at agreed premium prices, and took oil in return, some of which was re-exported.

This set-up created a distorting incentive for large amounts of land to be given over to export crops grown in industrial monocultures, heavily dependent on oil-based inputs. Just before the collapse, in 1989 three times more land was dedicated to sugar rather than to food.

Then oil imports dropped by over half, crippling the economy and slashing foreign exchange earnings from the re-export trade. The use of chemical pesticides and fertilisers dropped by 80 per cent, sounding a death knell to its industrial approach to farming. The knock-on effect on people's daily lives was dramatic. The availability of basic food staples like wheat and other grains fell by half and, overall, the average Cuban's calorie intake fell by over one third in around five years, leading to an average weight loss of 20 lb per person.

But compared to the situation that most other majority world countries, and some rich nations too, find themselves in today, Cuba was in a position to respond. Serious and long-term investment in science, engineering, health and education meant the country had a strong social fabric and the capacity to act. Before its local 'oil shock', Cuba was already investigating forms of ecological farming far less dependent on fossil fuels. When the shock came, a system of 'regional research institutes, training centres and extension services' was in place to support farmers.[2]

But the foundations were laid much earlier. Successive reforms dating back to the early days of the revolution in 1959 reduced inequality and redistributed ownership of land. Though frequently and conveniently overlooked, in spite of the US economic boycott, in little more than a couple of decades Cuba achieved levels of literacy, health and nutrition that were the envy of the developing world. An educated and healthy population was the foundation of Cuba's miracle survival.

The threat of serious food shortages was overcome within five years. At the heart of the transition after 1990 was a rapid shift to the use of biofertilisers and biopesticides, crop rotation and intercropping, and the use of animal labour and manure (in other words, a largely organic system), and the success of small farms and urban farms and gardens.

Immediate crisis was averted by food programmes that targeted the most vulnerable people, the old, the young, pregnant women and young mothers, and a rationing programme that guaranteed a minimum amount of food to everyone.

Ironically, however, in spite of the planning, it was the large-scale state farms that found the change hardest. Small-scale farms responded quickly, raising their productivity above previous levels. Seeing the success of the peasant-run small farms, in 1993 state farms were turned into so-called Basic Units of Co-operative Production – owned and run by the workers themselves or as cooperatives. After that, land was made available to anyone who wanted to start an urban garden farm.

Shortages and rising food prices made urban farming very profitable. It also proved highly productive. Once the state backed the urban farming movement, it grew rapidly. Lots and backyards in Cuban cities became home to food crops and farm animals – grown and reared almost exclusively along organic lines. Half the food consumed in the capital, Havana, is grown in the city's own gardens and, overall, urban gardens provide 60 per cent of the vegetables eaten in Cuba.

The country's experience suggests huge, barely tapped global potential for urban farming. In Havana alone, there are more than 26,000 food gardens.[3]

In a comparison that might be generally unwelcome in the US, Cuba's recent experience both echoes and surpasses what America achieved in its push for 'Victory Gardening' during the Second World War. Back then, led by Eleanor Roosevelt, 30–40 per cent of vegetables for domestic consumption were produced by the Victory Gardening movement.

Cuba's eventual transition to a more self-sufficient food system wasn't smooth, but demonstrated that it is possible to feed a population under extreme economic stress with very little or even no fossil-fuel inputs. And, as with wartime Britain, there were unexpectedly positive outcomes.

Dramatic reductions in consumption, coupled with other dietary and lifestyle changes (people walked more), altered the health of the nation. As calorie intake fell by more than one third, the proportion of physically active adults more than doubled and obesity halved. Between 1997 and 2002, deaths attributed to diabetes fell by half, coronary heart disease by 35 per cent, stroke by a fifth, and all causes by just under.[4] These findings were published in 2007 in the *American Journal of Epidemiology* and carry a profound, broader message of the potential general benefits of reduced consumption.

The global food system is both fossil-fuel dependent and a major source of greenhouse gas emissions (and, of course, vulnerable to climate change). Reduced human consumption could improve health, ease the burden we place on the planet's ecosystems and introduce much-needed 'room to manoeuvre' in the face of external shocks. The article's authors comment:

'These results suggest that population-wide measures designed to reduce energy stores, without affecting nutritional sufficiency, may lead to declines in diabetes and cardiovascular disease prevalence and mortality.'[5]

But in spite of its successes (and partly unintentional positive consequences) the recent Cuban approach thoroughly contradicted the model of development normally sponsored by the international financial institutions. It was highly managed, focused on meeting domestic needs rather than being export-oriented, was largely organic and built on the success of small farms. Such a radical departure from orthodoxy explains why, with some startled respect, it was called the 'anti-model' by the World Bank. At least one analyst suggested that the Cuban experiment 'may hold many of the keys to the future survival of civilisation'.[6]

Certainly, in contrast to the tragic debacle in New Orleans following the impact of Hurricane Katrina, Cuba's ability to handle climate-related disasters appears exemplary and something from which many, including the United States, could learn.

Compared to the deaths in New Orleans, which totalled well over 1,000, and the lasting devastation left behind, when the 216 kmph winds of Hurricane Michelle hit Cuba in 2001, only five lives were lost, in spite of 20,000 homes being damaged (see Chapter 3). Proper planning in advance of the largely predictable hurricane season, and a collective approach managed by government but with strong local buy-in, saved lives and enabled communities to bounce back more quickly afterwards.

LEARN FROM SMALL ISLANDS

Britain is an island nation, and it seems there is more that we can learn from other islands, especially small ones.

The resilience of Tuvalu and other small island states in the face of economic isolation and an unpredictable and extreme climate may hold lessons now for how many millions more can withstand the upheaval of global warming on our small island planet.

Their first lesson for us is deceptively simple: to respect environmental limits, which admittedly are more obvious on small islands. Next, they evolved resilient local economies. These were, of necessity, based on reciprocity, sharing and co-operation, and not unlimited growth fed by individualistic, beggar-thy-neighbour competition. This may reverse an economic doctrine largely unquestioned for decades but, as economic historian Robert Heilbroner pointed out, for most of the last millennium, the 'notion that a general struggle for gain might actually bind together a community would have been held as little short of madness'.[7]

We are challenged at the global level to learn lessons in a few short years that such small communities often took millennia to arrive at. In Karl Polanyi's classic work *The Great Transformation*, he presents various types of social and economic organisation on islands as evidence against some of Adam Smith's more sweeping assumptions on the central role of markets.[8]

Complex forms of 'gift exchange', in which people partly meet their needs not through markets mediated with cash, but through the giving and receiving of gifts, operated over vast areas, revealing a system that not only met people's needs in a challenging environment but also bonded society together. In the face of our rising vulnerabilities, the degree to which different forms of economic organisation enhance or undermine social cohesion must become a basic test of their fitness for purpose.

From a sweeping historical and anthropological survey of societies across Europe, North Africa, the Middle East and Asia, Polanyi codified certain principles common to most up until the late Middle Ages: reciprocity, redistribution and 'householding', by which he meant a system that enables needs to be met in a largely self-reliant way. It's from the latter that we derive the root of the word 'economics' – *oikonomia*.

Conversely, of course, examples like Nauru and Easter Island demonstrate that it is equally possible to learn how to go wrong from looking at island life.

But many island nations are relative models of resilience, quality of life and ecological efficiency. The Happy Planet Index[9] assesses the efficiency with which natural resources are converted into meaningful human outcomes. It compares ecological footprint data with life expectancy and satisfaction. Across and within regions, island nations score particularly well.

There are many probable reasons why, and they are important enough to recap: contact with nature; an awareness of and adaptation to more obvious limits; sharing-based economies which have been seen to reduce inequality across a community and maintain supportive social relationships; crops bred for hardiness and grown in mixed, highly productive plots. Island diets, too, more typically follow the balance in most ecosystems which is the nine-word mantra of food and science writer Colin Tudge for a more sustainable food system: 'lots of plants, a little meat and maximum variety'.[10] To which you might add fish, of course, if you live on a small island.

Slightly more wordy, but equally worthy, were the findings of the recent report of the International Assessment of Agricultural Knowledge, Science and Technology. Its approach was parallel to the approach of the IPCC – gather together a large, diverse group of scientists and see what consensus emerges about the nature of a problem and its solutions. It found that a massive shift of support to small-scale farmers using a diverse range of agro-ecological methods would be one of the most efficient ways to build resilience, inoculate against food crises and insure against increasingly hostile weather patterns.

OPEN NEW PATHS TO POVERTY REDUCTION IN A CARBON-CONSTRAINED WORLD

If you had a toaster that could neither accept slices of bread nor heat them up, would it be a toaster or a 'un-toaster'? Similarly, if you have an expanding economy that is both anti-poor and damaging to the biosphere upon which it and we depend, do you have economic growth, or 'uneconomic' growth? The evidence of this and many other books points to the latter.

Two large, inherent weaknesses run like plate-tectonic cracks through the current export-oriented doctrine of development. First is its dependence on declining oil supplies, and second is its inability to direct sufficient benefits to the people who need them most, the poorest. Either flaw alone should be enough to arrange for the model's burial. Yet currently it defies gravity, floating aloft like the cartoon character who doesn't realise that the ground beneath him has been removed.

To organise a necessary soft landing, some other model needs to be in place. The development economist David Woodward helpfully suggests just such a plan.[11]

Its heart is the re-engineering of how the economies of poor countries hook up with the wider world. The problem to be solved, mentioned earlier, is the so-called 'fallacy of composition', the unfortunate facet that most of the products in which low- and lower-middle-income countries have a potential comparative advantage – things like tropical agricultural commodities, minerals and relatively labour-intensive manufactured goods such as textiles – have prices that go down as more of them enter the global market. So when producers try to earn more by increasing supply, the price goes down offsetting any raised income.

The aim, instead, is to make poverty reduction the central aim of policy, not the hoped-for outcome of a dozen other strategies. In practice, this means supporting the kind of models outlined above.

The point is, says Woodward, 'to make poverty reduction self-sustaining, by increasing demand for the goods and services on which poor households depend for their incomes'.[12] Supply and demand are raised in parallel, 'so that increases in the incomes of poor households feed through into stronger demand for the goods produced by other poor households'. Rather than running faster and falling further behind, the typical outcome for the poorest countries under economic globalisation, a 'local markets for local people first' approach, makes poverty reduction self-reinforcing rather than self-defeating.

The sorts of things this means in practice include: labour-intensive public works schemes using local contractors, to develop schools and health facilities, other infrastructure and environmental improvements; public procurement policies geared to encouraging procurement from small-scale local producers wherever possible; farming support programmes geared to small-scale farmers; land reform and redistribution; and social safety nets.

On the ground it will mean more production locally of high-value foodstuffs; basic household goods; building materials for housing and infrastructure; basic transport equipment, such as carts and bicycles; fuel and renewable energy; small-scale retailing; personal services; transport services; and communications services such as mobile phones. The strategy could be described as moving from export promotion to a virtuous circle or cycle of local economic regeneration – or 'home first, world second'.

ACCELERATE TRANSITION FOR RICH COUNTRIES (AND THE POOR PEOPLE WHO LIVE THERE)

Compared to the Cuban experience, what has been achieved in Britain looks rather tame in terms of adapting to the new realities of global warming and peak oil. But nature and society abhor a vacuum and attempts to reimagine fundamentally how communities are organised are not new.

In 1898, Ebenezer Howard published the book *Tomorrow: A Peaceful Path to Real Reform*, later republished more familiarly in 1902 as *Garden Cities of Tomorrow*.[13] Few experimental towns were actually built, but the influence of Garden Cities was great. In Japan it is now government policy to build on Garden City lines. These were planned communities that emphasised self-reliance, were surrounded by green belts of land, and contained a balance of residential, open green space and economically active areas.

The flowering of new social movements often has its seeds in the past. Almost exactly a century after the first Garden City was begun on land at Letchworth, the first of a new initiative called Transition Towns was set up in Kinsale, Co. Cork, Ireland. There are now dozens of Transition Towns in the UK and internationally, with hundreds more under consideration. The South West of England is trying to become a Transition region and Wales is considering being a Transition country. It is claimed to be the fastest-growing social movement in the country (although how this might be measured remains gently unclear).

The common aim is to reduce oil dependence, and lower the ecological impact of their economies by localising the way they meet their needs for food, energy, housing and other goods and services.

The first stage is to produce an Energy Descent Plan. By 2021, Kinsale Transition Initiative plans to source the majority of its energy from sources within a ten-mile radius. Its distributed energy system will include wind, biomass from short-rotation coppice, and anaerobic digesters for a combined heat and power plant, and solar.

Similar initiatives in Europe include the community of Vauban, near Freiburg in Germany. It claims to have achieved CO_2 emissions reductions of 80–90 per cent, due to good building design, renewable energy, car-sharing and good water management.[14]

The dramatic renaissance of urban gardening and horticulture in the UK is evidence of an unplanned cultural and economic self-medication. In the face of volatile food and fuel prices, and the alienation of spending six months of your life shopping in a supermarket, it's clearly meeting a need.[15]

Seed suppliers in the UK report 'astronomical' growth in the sale of vegetable seed varieties.[16] In the US, they are reported to be 'through the roof'.[17]

Anyone tempted to dismiss such grassroots flowering of alternatives as idle middle-class play should visit the Growing Communities project[18] pushing up through cracks in the concrete pavement in Hackney, East London, and situated just a quick sprint away from a road dubbed the 'murder mile'.

Growing Communities is urban agriculture at its best. They grow salad crops because of perishability and the fact that imported salad tends to be air-freighted to the UK. Their gardens are certified as organic. Their organic vegetable-box scheme supplies fresh, seasonal produce weekly to hundreds of local households. Everyone who participates can have a say in how the business is run. They also run a weekly farmers' market.

Growing Communities goes even further still. They encourage the local community to 'make, bake, grow or pick good food throughout the year', helping them to evolve from passive consumers into active producers in their own right. In the process, people relearn vanishing skills to do with growing and preparing food, and become more aware of the seasons and how to manage valuable resources. Each year in October, coinciding with the ageless celebration of the harvest, they hold the Good Food Swap. It's cash-free and allows people to exchange recipes and good food, and to get to know others in their community, enhancing general wellbeing.

RESPECT AND BUILD THE *CORE* ECONOMY

The success or failure of the core economy will determine whether or not humanity can enjoy high wellbeing while living within the budget of earth's biocapacity. That means, first of all, not undermining it, and, second, having policies to develop it. But what is the core economy?

While the biosphere can be seen as our natural resource 'operating system', the inventor of Time Banks, Edgar Cahn, writes of another fundamental system that has been called the 'core economy' by economist Neva Goodwin.[19]

Cahn writes of two economic systems, the money economy and the core economy. The core economy is the operating system that the money economy depends on, yet takes for granted and often cannibalises.

The core economy consists of family, neighbourhood, community and civil society. It is what you and I do when we provide care for children, families and the elderly. It produces safe neighbourhoods, enables democracy to happen and creates community and civil society. It comes to your rescue in times of need.

Back in 1998, household work done in the core economy in the US was valued at $1.9 trillion. In 2002, the informal care that keeps the elderly out of homes was given a replacement price of $253 billion.

Having for decades promoted the self-interest of finance above the wellbeing of the core economy, will it be strong enough now that we need it among the wreckage left behind by the chimera of triumphal capital?

The invisible hand of the market has been at odds with the invisible heart of the core economy, and it is the latter that we cannot do without and which must take precedence.

A healthy core economy will share the characteristics of those resilient island economies – strong in reciprocity, co-operation, sharing, and collaboration in the delivery of essential services, care provision and raising families. Think of Kropotkin's 'mutual aid'.[20]

To boost the core economy we need to imagine a significantly expanded and broadened role for public services – such as the so-called extended schools and health centres. In this way, people become involved in helping to 'produce' their own wellbeing. An elderly, frail person visiting the doctor complaining of symptoms linked to cold weather might, for example, be prescribed help from another patient to fit insulation or low-energy light bulbs to lower fuel bills. In return they might offer the practice to make supportive phone calls to check on people returning home from hospital. Their contribution is tailored to their ability to give.

It's called 'co-production', it's based on reciprocity, and it works. It builds more resilient and cohesive communities.[21] To grow, it will need a duty on public services to collaborate among themselves, and with the voluntary sector, and health and safety rules will need looking at again.

A shorter working week, freeing up time to contribute, and lower house prices so that we don't have to work so much would also help. But this alone is not enough.

IMPLEMENT A GREEN NEW DEAL

History shows that more co-operative forms of economic organisation can emerge in response to extreme hardship, dependence and exploitation.

For example, cultures and models of self-help were born under far harsher circumstances than now during the Industrial Revolution.

The great capitalist-turned-social-reformer (and deeply odd individual) Robert Owen formed the superbly named Grand National Moral Union of the Productive and Useful Classes, and the English labour movement stepped into the light.

He was hugely influential, but sometimes it took others to turn his ideas into practical realities. One group comprising 28 weavers became known as the Rochdale Society of Equitable Pioneers, and created the consumer co-operative movement.

Now, again, we need the co-ops, the credit unions and the mutuals like the original building societies which are in tune more with the needs of clients and local economies, and not, like City traders, distracted by playing international money markets or pursuing multimillion-pound Christmas bonuses. But we also need a Green New Deal to tackle the triple crunch and kickstart our environmental transformation.

The modernised Green New Deal, published by **nef** on behalf of the Green New Deal group on the 75th anniversary of Roosevelt's New Deal, is, like his plan, designed to happen in two waves.[22]

First, we outline a structural transformation of the regulation of the financial system, including major changes to taxation. Second, we call for a sustained programme to invest in, and deploy, energy conservation and renewable energies, coupled with effective demand management.

In place of Roosevelt's politically clever 100-day programme – in which all of his measures were passed – we find ourselves with the very real timeframe of less than 100 months from August 2008, imposed by the unthinkable prospect of runaway climate change.

The outcomes of our plan will create countless green-collar jobs, introduce greater economic stability, bring huge benefits to the real economy and establish prudent environmental policy.

Three interlocking elements make up the Green New Deal:

1. *Stabilising the financial system.* A financial system built on speculation and the reckless accumulation of debt needs saving from itself, with a thorough overhaul of regulation. This would include breaking up discredited financial institutions that have survived only through the injection of vast sums of public money.

   Instead of institutions that are 'too big to fail', we need institutions that are small enough to fail without creating problems for depositors and the wider public.

   We also need to minimise corporate tax evasion by clamping down on tax havens and obfuscatory corporate financial reporting.

2. *Raising the resources to invest in change.* The Green New Deal needs resourcing. As part of the financial reform described above, cheaper money is needed to invest in the environmental transformation of our energy, transport and building infrastructure.

   In parallel, to prevent inflation, we want to see much tighter regulation of the wider financial environment. There are plenty of other ways of urgently freeing-up necessary finance.

   As just one part of a wide-ranging package of financial innovations, the Deal calls for the establishment of an Oil Legacy Fund, similar to a highly successful Norwegian government initiative paid for by a windfall tax on the profits of oil and gas companies.

   More realistic fossil fuel prices, raised to include their cost to the environment, will generate further revenue and create economic incentives that drive efficiency and bring alternative fuels to market. Importantly, this multiple approach will help to pay for the safety nets needed for those vulnerable to higher food and fuel prices, and help to keep chaos from the door.

3. *Environmental transformation.* The end-game of the Green New Deal is to bring about a low-carbon, high-wellbeing economy.

   There are numerous benefits in shifting to a more efficient, decentralised energy system that uses a wide range of renewable energy technologies applied at different scales, and in which demand is actively managed.

Centralised energy infrastructures can be extremely inefficient.[23] In the UK, Greenpeace estimates that up to two thirds of potential energy is lost between generator and consumer.[24] Far more efficient models developed by the World Alliance for Decentralised Energy have been used by the UK Foreign Office to project China's energy future; by the Federal Government of Canada to look at the country's energy system; and by the European Commission to investigate the options for the EU.

But, once again, some small islands are showing the way. The tiny island of Niue in the South Pacific plans to become the first nation on earth to meet all its energy requirements from renewable sources. Sagar Island in the Sunderbans Delta, off the mainland in West Bengal, home to just under 200,000 people living in 43 villages, has the same objective.[25]

With the right economic incentives, the foundations of a new energy system could be laid tomorrow.

Increasing our energy security and independence by making every building a power station and efficiency centre will create a 'carbon army' of countless green-collar workers.

BUILD A NEW FOOD CULTURE

Ecological debt puts the way we produce our food in a unique bind. Farming is both a major source of greenhouse gases (some types of farming much more than others, particularly livestock), and especially vulnerable to global warming and rising oil prices. Of all the monumental challenges we face, developing a food system that will reduce its own impact on the biosphere while simultaneously increasing its resilience to climate change is possibly the biggest.

In the spring of 2008, food riots driven by shortages and rising prices were reported in 33 countries ranging from Bolivia to Senegal, and Uzbekistan to Egypt and Indonesia. The prices, in turn, are being pushed by the high cost of oil and, in some places, competition between the use of crops for food and biofuels. In response, major countries like China and India, who together account for over one third of humanity, are de-prioritising their international food trade and restricting the export of staples like rice in order to prioritise the feeding of their own people. The lessons of the Cuban miracle, too, are taking on ever wider significance.

For example, according to figures from the Department for Environment, Food and Rural Affairs (Defra), organic farming uses in general over a quarter less energy compared to non-organic farming to produce the same amount of food.[26]

But why is the world food system not currently designed to feed people? asks Colin Tudge, the food writer and former contributing editor at *New Scientist* magazine, and he calls for something he refers to as 'enlightened agriculture'. Asked what that means, he said: 'agriculture that is designed to feed people'. But surely all farming is designed to feed people, isn't it?, comes the perplexed response. No, and that's the point. If the existing and future world population is to eat adequately, even well, in the face of mounting ecological debts and declining oil supplies, a substantial redesign of the global food chain is unavoidable.[27]

This enigma wrapped inside a paradox comes down to the law of primary purpose. That is to say, a system's primary purpose shapes, to a great extent, how it operates, whatever its hoped-for secondary benefits might be. In recent decades, ever more of the world food system, from seed companies, to manufacturers of pesticides and fertilisers, the farms themselves, grain and shipping firms, wholesalers, distribution networks and retailers, have slipped into the control of ever fewer and ever larger global companies.

These companies, locked into and in the act of expanding a particular market system, have to generate financial returns to institutional investors at a certain rate, or face serious consequences. This primary purpose shapes all their decisions. The result is a system designed to meet the needs of a certain group of global consumers – those who can pay, the middle classes with money. Some others might benefit at the margins, but the resulting food system is increasingly geared against meeting the needs of all the world's people, especially the poorest.

Typical anomalies are not hard to spot, from the redirection of scarce water resources that bypass the local community to feed thirsty export crops of luxury horticulture in South America or West Africa, like flowers and sugarsnap peas, to supermarkets squeezing the livelihoods of small farmers and producers, to the environmental and economic carpet-bombing of large parts of Asia with palm oil plantations (palm oil is the discreet ingredient in countless products lining supermarket shelves).

Then, most strikingly, there is the use of good arable land, not to produce food for direct human consumption, but for cereals and other crops, grown in vast monocultures, and destined increasingly to produce biofuels to fill the tanks of European and American motorists, or fodder for calorie-hungry and methane-making cattle, who are themselves headed to decorate the plates of the world's wealthier consumers whose diets are increasingly meat-based and are, as a result, terribly inefficient in energy terms.

According to another branch of the UN, the Food and Agriculture Organization (FAO), livestock production in particular accounts for nearly one fifth of all emissions.[28] One study estimated that producing just 1 kg of beef emits the equivalent in CO_2 emissions of an average European car driving 250 km.[29]

Globally, one third of arable land is set aside for growing animal feed, and over 90 per cent of soya beans and around 60 per cent of maize and barley are destined for cattle, pigs and poultry.[30]

The 'push' factor of massively rising biofuel demand is also having striking effects. The International Monetary Fund (IMF) estimated that 70 per cent of the rise in corn prices and 40 per cent of soya bean price rises were for this reason.[31]

In summer 2008, the president of the FAO lamented how, in 2006, $11–12 billion a year in subsidies and protective tariff policies had 'the effect of diverting 100 million tonnes of cereals from human consumption, mostly to satisfy the thirst for fuel for vehicles'.[32]

Such characteristics thrown up by an increasingly centralised and commercialised global agriculture are unfortunately, according to Tudge, the very antithesis of enlightened agriculture, whose essence can be spelt out in just these nine words, 'lots of plants, a little meat and maximum variety'.[33] Of course, there is more to it than that.[34] But his case is that a food system actually designed to feed everyone must be based on two overriding considerations: sound biology and social justice. The above formula, emulating the efficiency and balance of natural systems, represents the 'sound biology'.

Now, in a world much more aware of climate change and the need to reduce fossil fuel use, we can add the urgent need for an orientation toward greater seasonality in what we eat, the uptake of organic techniques and, where practicable, local production for local consumption.

Food Sovereignty

For the second half of the food system equation, 'social justice', a growing international movement for 'food sovereignty' has sought to spell out the meaning of social justice in the food chain, boiling it down to four key elements.[35]

First is the right to food, meaning that people need physical access to land, water and the seeds to grow the food that's right for them. And, that they must also be able to afford to buy what they need or cannot grow. This, in turn, means tackling the power of those who set prices and control land, water and seeds.

Second is getting access to resources. A programme of reform is required that gives smallholder farmers, pastoralists and fisherfolk the means to exercise their right to food. It's here that clashes with powerful vested interests occur. The Cuban example above gives one successful illustration of radically widening access to productive land, motivated by the need to ensure a whole nation can feed itself. This element also means a major relaxation in favour of the poorest people and countries of restrictive rules at the international level that currently control the intellectual property on seeds, breeds of livestock and other types of biodiversity.

Third is to take positive, ecological approaches to farming. Environmentally friendly approaches to farming that grow a wider range of crops are, over time and a wide range of conditions and climates, more friendly to small-scale farmers, less vulnerable to external shocks, and more resilient and productive. Such 'agroecology' works. A study published by the FAO in 2002 showed that the approach produced increases in crop yields that averaged 94 per cent. In the best cases, yields went up by an astonishing 600 per cent.[36]

Fourth and finally is escaping the trade trap. Instead of just assuming that any increase in international trade will benefit people in need, this suggests that new policies are needed that prioritise enabling 'communities and countries vulnerable to hunger and malnutrition to produce sufficient quantities of safe and secure food supplies'. At the same time, rules are needed to stop 'the negative effects of subsidized exports, food dumping [and] artificially low prices' that mark the current model of agricultural trade.[37]

GROW AN ECONOMY WITH THE SAME SHOE SIZE (OR A BIT SMALLER) THAN THE PLANET

The Stationary State

With a typically modern approach to encircling ideas, some have sought to own by trademark the phrase 'one planet living'. But like all big ideas its lineage escapes such temporal capture. At a minimum, we can travel back to the early nineteenth-century philosopher and political economist John Stuart Mill. He was shaped by the human and environmental havoc of the voracious Industrial Revolution.

In reaction to that, he argued that, once certain conditions had been met, the economy should aspire to exist in a 'stationary state'.[38] It was a hugely radical notion and nothing to do with a world run by paper clips, staplers and cheap biros. Mill thought that an intelligent application of technology, family planning, equal rights, and a dynamic combination of a progressive workers' movement with the growth of consumer co-operatives could tame the worst excesses of capitalism and liberate society from the motivation of conspicuous consumption.

He prefigured Kropotkin's analysis that economics could learn from the success of cooperation, or *mutual aid*,[39] as he coined it, in ecological systems (itself a riposte to the fashionable misappropriation of Darwinism to social and economic problems). Mill also prefigured Keynes' hope, and similar faith in technology, that once the 'economic problem' was solved, we would all be able to turn to more satisfying pursuits and put our feet up more. He also prepared the ground for the emergence of ecological economics.

The Steady State

In a fairly direct line of intellectual descent, economist Herman Daly has done more than anyone to popularise the notion of what he calls 'steady state' economics. His comprehensive critique, worked up over decades, decries the absence of any notion of optimal scale in macro-economics, and the persistent, more general refusal of the economics profession to accept that it, too, like the rest of life on the planet, is bound by the laws of physics.

As Daly wrote in *Beyond Growth*,

> Since the earth itself is developing without growing, it follows that a subsystem of the earth (the economy) must eventually conform to the same behavioural mode of development without growth.[40]

Of course, the big question concerns when, precisely, the 'eventually' moment comes. Daly borrows a public safety analogy from the shipping industry to demonstrate what is needed ecologically at the planetary level.

The introduction of the 'Plimsoll line' was, so to speak, a watershed to do with a watermark. When a boat is too full, rather obviously it is more likely to sink. The problem used to be that, without any clear warning that a safe maximum carrying capacity had been reached, there was always an economic incentive to err on the incautious side by overfilling. The Plimsoll line solved the problem with elegant simplicity: a mark painted on the outside of the hull that indicates a maximum load once level with the water. But, Samuel Plimsoll, the man who devised and campaigned for its introduction, was once damned as the most dangerous man in Britain. Why? Because, improved safety measures for shipping, just like the abolition of slavery and almost every other attempt to better the human condition and protect the environment, are routinely and vigorously resisted on the grounds of cost to the economy. Like fish with little memory, it is a lesson that we seem incapable of learning from. Stuck, we are condemned to expend our precious life's energies fighting the same battles repeatedly. And now do so again with climate change.

Daly's challenge to economics is to adopt or design an equivalent, 'To keep the weight, the absolute scale, of the economy from sinking our biospheric ark.'[41] Lest anyone conclude Daly to be a crude environmental determinist, for any model to work he insists that alongside optimal scale, equally important is a mechanism for optimal distribution based on equity and sufficiency.

To date, the nearest – in fact, only – leading contender to provide the environmental Plimsoll line is the ecological footprint. Before the contraction and convergence model, which is designed to manage greenhouse gas emissions safely, was ever thought of (see above), Daly identified its basic mechanism as the way to manage the global environmental commons. First, he said, you need to identify the limit of whichever aspect of our natural resources and biocapacity concerns you, then within that, allocate equitable entitlements and, in order to allow flexibility, make them tradable. Such an approach could be applied to the management of the world's forests and oceans as much as carbon dioxide. Daly credits the innovative American architect and polymath Richard Buckminster Fuller for first suggesting the approach.[42] At a fundamental level, this is the primary mechanism to avoid the 'tragedy of the commons'.[43]

In addition, I believe that an indicator such as the Happy Planet Index which incorporates the ecological footprint helps to reveal the degree of efficiency with which precious natural resources are converted into the meaningful human outcomes of long and happy lives.

So back to that 'eventually' moment, at which these other ways of organising and measuring the economy become vital. In one sense it has already passed. According to the ecological footprint, the world has been overburdening its biocapacity – consuming too many natural resources and producing more waste than can be safely absorbed – since the mid 1980s. To repeat, we've been living beyond our ecological means. But at what point does damage become irreversible? This will be different for different ecosystems. But in this new edition of the book, where climate change is concerned, a line in the sand has been drawn. If we are lucky, I've said we have until the end of 2016 to prevent the risk of runaway global warming becoming unacceptably high.

Dynamic Equilibrium

'Stationary', 'steady' – surely we get the message that, logically, a subset of a system (the economy) cannot outgrow the system itself (the planet). Why suggest yet another term for an essential characteristic of true sustainability? And why engage in the uncomfortable audacity of correcting your elders and very-much-betters?

First, the terms 'stationary' and 'steady' are unattractive for our purposes. They seem covered in dust, static and susceptible to mildew. Second, they do not capture sufficiently the dynamism of the challenge ahead and its many solutions. They appear to suggest for economics what was once famously and with epic error announced for history – namely, its end.[44]

Somehow, by identifying the limits to growth prescribed by inescapable physical laws, you appear to be announcing the redundancy of the entire profession of economics (though this is as much a comment on the profession's growth mania as anything else). But, on the contrary, writes Daly, it is just that a very different economics is needed, one that is:

a subtle and complex economics of maintenance, qualitative improvements, sharing frugality, and adaptation to natural limits, It is an economics of better, not bigger.[45]

'Dynamic equilibrium' is both a more accurate description of the condition we have to find and manage, and a more attractive term. Found typically in discussions of population biology and forest ecology, it captures better a mirror of nature for society in which, within ecosystem limits, there is constant change, shifting balances, and evolution. 'Dynamic' in the sense that little is steady or stationary, but 'equilibrium' in that the vibrant, chaotic kerfuffle of life, economics and society must organise its affairs within the parent-company boundaries of available biocapacity. As Daly advocates, for general use it is possibly sufficient to replace the word 'growth' with 'development'.[46]

As said, for an international climate agreement to work it must globally cap greenhouse gases at a safe level and share out allowable emissions. From these inescapable dynamics it is possible to imagine the shape of other deals to manage finite resources and ecosystems that have limits. Whether fossil fuels, forest timber or fish taken from the oceans of the world, to work within nature's budget – its biocapacity – and prevent an ecological solvency crisis, we must, as best we can, identify the safe limits of use and extraction, cap them at that level and have a formula for allocation. At a fundamental level, this is the primary mechanism to avoid the tragedy of the commons and move toward one-planet living, or dynamic equilibrium.

CONCLUSION

For much of human history, change happened slowly. Generations passed in which, for many, almost no change would have been noticeable. Whole communities would have been born, lived and died, with most rarely leaving the boundaries of their town or village. But in the modern age, change is the rule, not the exception. Change is built into a consumer-based, hi-tech economy.

But rapid change outside of any meaningful human control is something different again. Responding to such unchosen demands for rapid transition is an art in itself. This is what we now face: a multiple crunch driven by energy shock, credit crunch and climate change. We can now include a linked, growing, global food and water crisis. A renewed interest in Britain's wartime experiences might even be a form of cultural self-medication. It is almost as if we are preparing to adapt by reminding ourselves that we have done so before.

In our national living memory, the scale of economic re-engineering needed to prevent catastrophic climate change has only been witnessed during wartime. No other current approach looks remotely capable of delivering the necessary volume of emissions reductions in the time needed. In that light we can learn from those experiences, positive and negative. The best of those lessons can then be translated into our contemporary circumstance. One difference is that we need to work out how to maintain acceptance of lifestyle changes over a long period, unlike during wartime when there was a general assumption that, sooner or later, hostilities would end.

In November 2008, Barack Obama was elected President of the United States. To many, that event signalled the end of an era in which the US seemed to be aggressively at war with the world. History will judge, however, whether even that undeniable cultural revolution is enough to hold together international fault lines under pressure from epochal environmental and economic shifts. For now I will enjoy the apparent political ceasefire.

About 30 miles off the coast of south-west Cornwall, England, the tiny Scilly Isles speckle in the Gulf Stream, like Britain's own accidental Pacific atoll (except, of course, that they are made of granite, not coral). A little bit further south, a little warmer – plants grow there that wouldn't survive outdoors anywhere else in the country. I go there for my holidays.

One large island was formed separate to the mainland after the last Ice Age around 10,000 years ago. Since the Bronze

Age, when the land was settled and farmed, the islands have been losing a gradual battle with rising seas. Unfortunately for the inhabitants, they are also at the opposite end of the tilting underlying land mass that still gently lifts the West Coast of Scotland.

As you sit on a hill, looking across the channels between the rocky bumps of land, it's easy to imagine the old patchwork of fields lost beneath the waves. At low tides you can still walk

13. Tresco viewed from Bryher in the Scilly Isles.

between some islands. Just as France can be seen from the Kent and Essex coasts, in clear weather you can see Cornwall from the Scillies. Yet they are quite another place.

Overhead, high tracers from aircraft make patterns in the sky like spokes in an immense bicycle wheel as they head out to the rim of North America.

Sat among the quiet heather on the top of Tresco, or the grassed-over granite cliffs of Bryher, the mournful beauty of the oystercatchers' echoing cries drifts into hearing. Sudden sea fogs come and go, leaving behind over the years a collection of disembodied figureheads from wrecked ships. Today they perch in Tresco's botanic gardens, still staring in frozen anticipation for the shore of some difficult colonial territory, like bomb victims in shock unaware yet that they have lost their legs.

Without the light pollution of the mainland, on clear nights the Milky Way spills across the sky more like a swirl of thick, astronomical cream. Stand patiently, and every few minutes you'll be rewarded with a shooting star or, perhaps, a falling angel.

On the farm where I stayed, they grow flower bulbs and asparagus, sweetcorn, potatoes, cucumber, onions, peppers and tomatoes. Raspberries and tayberries for jam. A few chicken and cattle also roam, flutter and peck around.

You could walk around the island quicker than small, fragile Funafuti in Tuvalu in the South Pacific. Yet it manages to embrace woods and heathland, blasted headlands and mirage-like beaches.

Together the islands are beautiful, diverse, isolated but inter-connected and interdependent. They have an uncertain future. But in adversity, with ingenuity, and like many other small islands, they have supported human society for thousands of years. We all live on an island.

Notes

PREFACE TO SECOND EDITION

1. Winston Churchill speaking in the House of Commons, 12 November 1936, <http://hansard.millbanksystems.com/commons/1936/nov/12/debate-on-the-address#S5CV0317P0-03560>.
2. International Rescue Committee (2008) *Mortality in the Democratic Republic of Congo: An Ongoing Crisis*, January.
3. Shaohua Chen and Martin Ravallion (2004) *How Have the World's Poorest Fared since the Early 1980s?*, Development Research Group, World Bank, Washington DC.
4. E. Beinhocker (2007) *The Origin of Wealth: Evolution Complexity, and the Radical Remaking of Economics*, Random House, London. Figure derived from P. Ormerod (1994) *The Death of Economics*, Faber & Faber, London, p. 10, who cites a 1982 study by Angus Maddison showing a related statistic, that western economies grew as much in percentage terms between 1950 and 1970 as they did between 500 and 1500.
5. See, for example, Kenneth Pomeranz (1998) *The Great Divergence*, Princeton University Press, Princeton; Eric S. Reinert (2007) *How Rich Countries Got Rich ... and Why Poor Countries Stay Poor*, Constable, London; Mike Davis (2001) *Late Victorian Holocausts – El Nino Famines and the Making of the Third World*, Verso, London; Jared Diamond (1997) *Guns, Germs and Steel*, Vintage, London.

CHAPTER I

1. Robert Heilbroner (1953) *The Worldly Philosophers: The Lives, Times, and Ideas of the Great Economic Thinkers*, seventh edition, Penguin, London, 2000.
2. James Hall (1994) *Illustrated Dictionary of Symbols in Eastern and Western Art*, John Murray, London.
3. Bjorn Lomborg (2001) *The Skeptical Environmentalist: Measuring the Real State of the World*, Cambridge University Press, Cambridge.

4. *Larousse Encyclopedia of Mythology*, Paul Hamlyn, London, 1951.

5. Andrew Simms, Nick Robins and Ritu Kumar (2000) *Collision Course: Free Trade's Free Ride on the Global Climate*, **nef** (New Economics Foundation) and TERI, London.

6. Jose Lutzenberger, 'Gaia's fever', *The Ecologist*, Vol. 29 No. 2.

7. Andrew Simms and Matthew Lockwood (1997) *One Every Second: Cutting Unpayable Poor Country Debt*, Christian Aid & World Development Movement, London; Andrew Simms and Jenny Reindorp (1997) *The New Abolitionists: Slavery in History and the Modern Slavery of Poor Country Debt*, Christian Aid, London.

8. *Human Development Report 1997*, United Nations Development Programme, Geneva/New York.

9. Aubrey Meyer (2000) *Contraction & Convergence: The Global Solution to Climate Change*, Schumacher Briefing number 5, Green Books, Dartington, Devon.

10. Hugh Barty-King (1997 edition) *The Worst Poverty – A History of Debt and Debtors*, Budding Books, Stroud, Gloucestershire.

11. *World Disasters Report 2001*, International Federation of Red Cross and Red Crescent Societies, Geneva.

CHAPTER 2

1. Myles Allen (2003), 'Liability for climate change', *Nature*, 27 February.

2. There is limited biographical material for Svante Arrhenius available in English. The information about him in this chapter is drawn from a range of sources including: NASA <http://earthobservatory. nasa.gov>; The Woodrow Wilson Leadership Programme in Chemistry <www.woodrow.org>; Isaac Asimov (1985) *New Guide to Science*, Viking, London; <http://scienceworld.wolfram.com>; The Institute of Chemistry at The Hebrew University of Jerusalem Faculty of Science; The Northwest Council on Climate Change <www.nwclimate.org>; The Anderson Research Group at Harvard University <www.arp.harvard.edu>; and The Nobel e-Museum <www.nobel.se>.

3. The Tyndall Centre for Climate Change Research at the University of East Anglia, <www.tyndall.ac.uk>, based on J.A. Burchfield (1981) *John Tyndall – A Biographical Sketch in John Tyndall, Essays on a Natural Philosopher*, Royal Dublin Society, Dublin.

4. Barbara Freese (2003) *Coal: A Human History*, Perseus Books, Cambridge, Mass.

5. Svante Arrhenius (1895) 'On the Influence of Carbonic Acid in the Air Upon the Temperature of the Ground', paper presented to the Stockholm Physical Society.

6. Spencer Weart, *The Public and Climate Change*, August 2003, at <www.aip.org>.

7. Herman E. Daly (ed.) (1973) *Toward a Steady-state Economy*, Freeman, San Francisco.

8. Spencer Weart, *The Discovery of Global Warming*, August 2003, <www.aip.org/history>.

9. Susan J. Buck (1998) *The Global Commons – an Introduction*, Island Press, Washington DC.

10. *Predictions of Accelerated Climate Change*, Met Office, available at: <www.metoffice.gov.uk/research/hadleycentre/pubs/brochures/B2000/climate.html>.

11. *Climate Change Observations and Predictions: Recent Research on Climate Change Science from the Hadley Centre*, Met Office Hadley Centre, December 2003.

12. Shaoni Bhattacharya (2004) 'Arctic warming at twice global rate', *New Scientist*, 2 November.

13. Shaoni Bhattacharya (2004) 'Greenhouse gas level hits record high', *New Scientist*, 22 March; Paul Brown (2004) 'Climate fear as carbon levels soar', *Guardian*, 11 October.

14. *Key World Energy Statistics 2003*, International Energy Agency, Paris.

15. ASPO newsletter (Association for the Study of Peak Oil), November 2003; Global Dynamics Institute briefing for Conference of the Parties (COP) 9, December 2003; David Fleming, *Prospect* magazine, November 2000.

16. 'Still holding customers over a barrel', *The Economist*, 25 October 2003.

17. Colin Campbell (2003) 'When will the world's oil and gas production peak?' in Richard Douthwaite (ed.) *Before the Wells Run Dry*, Feasta, Green Books, Dartington, Devon; also Global Dynamics Institute briefing for COP 9, December 2003.

18. Fleming, *Prospect* magazine.

19. Measured as World Industrial Product, a generalised measure of GDP, cleaned of inflation and inclusive of real goods and materials rather than merely monetary indicators.

20. Alberto di Fazio (2000), quoted in a paper distributed at COP 6, The Hague.

21. *World Disasters Report 2002*, International Federation of Red Cross and Red Crescent Societies, Geneva.

CHAPTER 3

1. Some of the quoted material in this chapter is taken from personal interviews held during my stay in Tuvalu.

2. *Natural Disaster Mitigation in Pacific Island Countries*, SOPAC, Suva, Fiji, undated.

3. Jon Barnett and Neil Adger (2001) 'Climate dangers and atoll countries', October, University of Canterbury (New Zealand) and University of East Anglia (UK).

4. Michael Fields (2001) Agence France Presse, 13 December.

5. R.J. Nicholls, 'An analysis of the flood implications of the IPCC Second Assessment global sea level rise scenarios' in J.D. Parker (ed.), *Floods*, Routledge, London, forthcoming.

6. World Meteorological Organisation, 'Statement on the status of the global climate in 2001', <www.wmo.ch>.

7. Ben Wisner (2001) 'Socialism and storms', *Guardian*, 14 November.

8. 'Planning for the 21st century – responding to climate variability and change in the Pacific Islands' in *Pacific Island Regional Assessment of the Consequences of Climate Change and Variability (The Pacific Assessment)*, East West Centre, Hawaii, 2001.

9. Keith and Ann Chambers (2001) *Unity of Heart: Culture and Change in a Polynesian Atoll Society*, Waveland Press, Long Grove, Ill.

10. Laumua Kofe (1981) 'Palagi and pastors' in Hugh Laracy (ed.), *Tuvalu: A History*.

11. E. Maude (1981) 'Slavers in paradise' in Laracy, *Tuvalu*.

12. *Pacific Human Development Report 1999*, UNDP, Suva, Fiji.

13. Geneva Convention on the Status of Refugees and Stateless Persons convened under General Assembly resolution 429 (V) of 14 December 1950, entry into force 22 April 1954.

14. Interviewed on British television Channel 4 News, 27 January 2002.

CHAPTER 4

1. William Morris (1888) *A Dream of John Ball and a King's Lesson*, Longmans, London.

2. In 1998 while working for the British development agency Christian Aid I went to Jamaica to do field research for the report *Forever in Your Debt? Millennium Debt Relief for Eliminating Poverty*, Christian Aid, London, 1998. Some material in this chapter is taken from personal interviews held during my stay.

3. Joseph Stiglitz (2000) 'The insider – what I learned at the world economic crisis', *The New Republic*, 4 April.

4. HIPC (2001) *Flogging a Dead Process*, Jubilee Research, London.

5. Joseph Hanlon (1998) *We've Been Here Before*, Jubilee 2000, London.

6. J.K. Galbraith (1975) *Money: Whence it Came, Where it Went*, Andre Deutsch, London.

7. Quoted in Andrew Simms and Jenny Reindorp (1997) *The New Abolitionists: Slavery in History and the Modern Slavery of Poor Country Debt*, Christian Aid, London.

8. *Real World Economic Outlook No 1: The Legacy of Globalisation – Debt and Deflation*, ed. Ann Pettifor (2003) **nef** & Palgrave Macmillan, London.

9. Michael Lewis (1990) *Liar's Poker: Rising Through the Wreckage on Wall Street*, Penguin, London.

10. Catherine Caulfield (1996) *Masters of Illusion: The World Bank and the Poverty of Nations*, Macmillan, London.

11. <www.un.org/millenniumgoals/> or <www.developmentgoals. org>.

12. Address to the Millennium Forum, New York, 22 May 2000.

13. This section is substantially based on a project I did jointly with Jonathan Walter, the editor of the World Disasters Report, and published as *The End of Development?* by **nef**, London, 2002. Source material for this section can be found in that briefing which is available at <www.neweconomics.org>. The order of the goals is slightly simplified here without changing anything about the goals themselves.

14. Trygve Berg, Fernando Dava and Judite Muchanga (March 2001) *Post-disaster Rehabilitation and Seed Restoration in Flood Affected Areas of Xai-Xai District, Mozambique. Gender, Biodiversity and Local Knowledge Systems (LinKS) to Strengthen Agricultural and Rural Development: Summary of Findings from Visits to Affected Villages and Suggestions for Action Research 2–10 December 2000,*

Sustainable Development Department, UN Food and Agriculture Organisation, Rome.

15. Intergovernmental Panel on Climate Change (2001) *Third Assessment Report*, Chapter 10, 'Africa'.

16. Presentation at the Sixth Conference of Parties to the United Nations Framework Convention on Climate Change, 13 November 2000.

17. Andrew Dobson (2002) 'Climate warming and disease risks for terrestrial and marine biota', *Science*, 21 June.

18. *Climate Change and Human Health: Risks and Responses*, World Health Organisation, UN Environment Programme, World Meteorological Organisation, Geneva, 2003.

CHAPTER 5

1. *Chambers English Dictionary* (1989) Cambridge University Press, Cambridge.

2. J.M. Keynes (1930) 'The economic possibilities for our grandchildren', in *Essays in Persuasion*, Norton, New York, 1963.

3. That original £40,000 appreciating at 3.25 per cent would today be worth around £40,000,000,000.

4. Guaicaipuro Cuautemoc (1997) 'The real foreign debt', *Resurgence Magazine*, September/October.

5. 'US battle for $2 billion undersea treasure', *Guardian*, 7 January 2003.

6. J.K. Galbraith, *Money: Whence it Came, Where it Went*, Andre Deutsch, London.

7. Quoted in Galbraith, *Money*.

8. Mike Davis (2001) *Late Victorian Holocausts: El Niño Famines and the Making of the Third World*, Verso, London.

9. R. Baldwin, P. Martin and G.I.P. Ottaviano (1999) *Global Income Divergence, Trade and Industrialisation: The Geography of Growth Take-offs*, CEPR, London.

10. Quoted in Davis, *Late Victorian Holocausts*.

11. Angus Maddison (1998) *Chinese Economic Performance in the Long Run*, quoted in Davis, *Late Victorian Holocausts*.

12. Quoted in Andrew Simms and Jenny Reindorp, *The New Abolitionists: Slavery in History and the Modern Slavery of Poor Country Debt*, Christian Aid, London.

13. Simms and Reindorp, *The New Abolitionists*.
14. Thomas Pakenham (1992) *The Scramble for Africa*, Abacus, London.
15. Quoted in Pakenham, *The Scramble for Africa*.
16. Quoted in Pakenham, *The Scramble for Africa*.
17. Quoted in Pakenham, *The Scramble for Africa*.
18. Quoted in Pakenham, *The Scramble for Africa*.
19. 'UN "should" act on Congo plunder', BBC Online, 28 October 2003.
20. See <www.unctad.org>.
21. Sven Lindqvist (1998) *Exterminate All the Brutes*, Granta, London.
22. Alfred W. Crosby (1986) *Ecological Imperialism: The Biological Expansion of Europe, 900–1900*, Canto, Cambridge.
23. Jared Diamond (1998) *Guns, Germs and Steel*, Vintage, London.
24. Crosby, *Ecological Imperialism*.
25. 'Feeling the heat: climate change and biodiversity loss', *Nature*, Vol. 427, January 2004.
26. World Bank (1995) *World Development Report*, World Bank, New York.
27. Paul Ormerod (1994) *The Death of Economics*, Faber & Faber, London.
28. *Real World Economic Outlook* (2003).
29. Galbraith, *Money* (2003).
30. *Real World Economic Outlook* (2003).
31. Statement made by Shri Murasoli Maran, Minister of Commerce and Industry, India, Plenary at UNCTAD X, Bangkok, Thailand, 13 February 2000.
32. For further references see Nick Robins (1993) *Citizen's Action to Lighten Britain's Footprints*, IIED, London.
33. Robert Southey (1807) *Letters from England*, quoted in Robins, *Citizen's Action*.
34. George Orwell (1937) *The Road to Wigan Pier*, quoted in Robins, *Citizen's Action*.
35. Ivan Illich (1974) *Energy and Equity* (Open Forum Series), Marion Boyars Publishers, London.
36. Anil Agarwal and Sunita Narain (1990) *Global Warming in an Unequal World – A Case for Environmental Colonialism*, Centre for Science and Environment, New Delhi.

37. *Our Common Agenda*, The Latin American and Caribbean Commission on Development and Environment, report to UNCED.

38. Accion Ecologica is based in Quito, Ecuador.

39. Andrew Simms (1999) *Who Owes Who? Climate Change, Debt, Equity and Survival*, Christian Aid, London, in collaboration with Nick Robins of the International Institute for Environment and Development and Aubrey Meyer of the Global Commons Institute.

40. 'Central American leaders urge debt relief', BBC News, 10 November 1998.

41. 'Cyclone slams into Pacific island', BBC News, 7 January 2004.

42. For example, Simms, *Who Owes Who?*, and Joan Martinez-Alier (1999) *Ecological Debt vs. External Debt – A Latin American Perspective*, Universitat Autonoma de Barcelona, Barcelona.

CHAPTER 6

1. David S. Landes (1972) *The Unbound Prometheus: Technological Change and the Industrial Development in Western Europe from 1750 to the Present*, Cambridge University Press, Cambridge.

2. This section is taken from a collaborative performance between James Marriott of Platform and the author, Andrew Simms, at the UK's first conference on ecological debt held at the Institute of Contemporary Arts, London, in the summer of 2001.

3. *Key World Energy Statistics 2003*, International Energy Agency (IEA), Paris.

4. L. Beer and T. Boswell (2002) 'The resilience of dependency effects in explaining income inequality in the global economy: a cross national analysis, 1975–1995', *Journal of World Systems Research*, Vol. III, Winter.

5. E.J. Hobsbawm (1968) *Industry and Empire*, Pelican, London.

6. Wilfred Owen (1921), 'Miners' in *An Anthology of Modern Verse*, ed. A. Methuen, Methuen & Co., London.

7. Landes, *The Unbound Prometheus*.

8. Hobsbawm, *Industry and Empire*.

9. Quoted in Barbara Freese, *Coal: A Human History*, Perseus Books, Cambridge, Mass.

10. Freese, *Coal*.

11. Alberto Di Fazio, *The Fallacy of Pure Efficiency Gain Measures to Control Future Climate Change*, Astronomical Observatory of Rome and Global Dynamics Institute, Rome, undated.

12. Extrapolated from IEA, *Key World Energy Statistics 2003*, the share of coal, oil and gas from total primary energy supply was up from 3542.8 mtoe (million tons of oil equivalent) to 4420.2 mtoe for the OECD. Globally the rise was from 5195.3 mtoe to 7973 mtoe.

13. Andrew Simms, Nick Robins and Ritu Kumar (2000) *Collision Course: Free Trade's Free Ride on the Global Climate*, **nef** (New Economics Foundation) and TERI, London.

14. Bruce Podobnik (2002) 'Global energy inequalities: exploring the long-term implications', *Journal of World Systems Research*, Vol. III, Winter.

15. A. Sampson (1975) *The Seven Sisters: The Great Oil Companies and the World They Made*, Hodder and Stoughton, London.

16. Sven Lindqvist (2001) *A History of Bombing*, Granta, London.

17. Quoted in Lindqvist, *A History of Bombing*.

18. Quoted in Lindqvist, *A History of Bombing*.

19. Kwesi Owusu (2001) *Drops of Oil in a Sea of Poverty: The Case for a New Debt Deal for Nigeria*, **nef** & Jubilee Plus, London.

20. *The Warri Crisis: Fuelling Violence*, Human Rights Watch, December 2003.

21. Simms, Robins and Kumar, *Collision Course*.

22. 'Development and poverty reduction: a multilateral approach', address by Michel Camdessus, Managing Director of the International Monetary Fund, at the Tenth United Nations Conference on Trade and Development, Bangkok, Thailand, 13 February 2000.

23. Robert Engleman (1998) *Profiles in Carbon: An Update on Population, Consumption and Carbon Dioxide Emissions*, Population Action International, Washington DC; Andrew Simms in *Real World Economic Outlook* (2003).

24. *Energy White Paper: Our Energy Future – Creating a Low Carbon Economy*, DTI, London, 2003.

25. Andrew Simms (1999) *Who Owes Who? Climate Change, Debt, Equity and Survival*, Christian Aid, London, in collaboration with Nick Robins of the International Institute for Environment and Development and Aubrey Meyer of the Global Commons Institute.

26. *World Disasters Report 2002*, International Federation of Red Cross and Red Crescent Societies, Geneva.
27. Taken from the author's contribution to *Chasing Shadows: Reimagining Finance for Development*, **nef**, London, 2002.
28. 'US climate change plan does not alter UK's commitment to Kyoto', statement by Rt Hon Margaret Beckett MP, Defra, London, 19 February 2002.

CHAPTER 7

1. Sigmund Freud (1920) *Beyond the Pleasure Principle*, W.W. Norton & Company, New York and London.
2. Peter Ackroyd (1986) *Hawksmoor*, HarperCollins, London.
3. T.S. Eliot (1969) *The Complete Poems and Plays of T.S. Eliot*, Faber & Faber, London and Boston.
4. Wilfred Owen (1921), 'Miners' in *An Anthology of Modern Verse*, ed. A. Methuen, Methuen & Co., London.
5. This anecdote is apparently the most common one used by corporate consultants lecturing on the management of growth and change in business, and is equally apparently, entirely bogus.
6. Consultant Debunking Unit (1995) *Fast Company*, Issue 1, November.
7. Daniel Pick (1993) *War Machine: The Rationalisation of Slaughter in the Modern Age*, Yale University Press, Yale.
8. Quoted from Virginia Woolf (1938) *Three Guineas*, quoted in Pick, *War Machine*.
9. Charles Ryecroft (1968) *A Critical Dictionary of Psychoanalysis*, Penguin, London.
10. Stanley Cohen (2001) *States of Denial: Knowing About Atrocities and Suffering*, Polity, Cambridge.
11. W.G. Sebald (2003) *On the Natural History of Destruction*, Hamish Hamilton, London.
12. Sven Lindqvist (2001) *A History of Bombing*, Granta, London.
13. Lindqvist, *A History of Bombing*.
14. Sebald, *On the Natural History of Destruction*.
15. Thanatos was the Greek god of death, depicted on vase painting from the 5th century BC as a winged deity. See *Hall's Illustrated Dictionary of Symbols in Eastern and Western Art*.
16. Marshall Berman (1983) *All That Is Solid Melts into Air – The Experience of Modernity*, Verso, London and New York.

17. George Marshall and Mark Lynas (2003) 'Who's who among the climate change deniers', *New Statesman*, 1 December; 'Toxic sceptics' (2003) *New Internationalist*, No. 357, June.

18. Martin Wolf (2000) *Financial Times*, November 29.

19. 'The science of climate change', statement by national science academies initiated by The Royal Society (UK), published in *Science*, 18 May 2001.

20. This is based largely on a review of Bjorn Lomborg's book, *The Skeptical Environmentalist*, which I wrote for the *Financial Times*.

21. J.M. Finger (Head of Trade Policy, World Bank) and P. Schuler (1999) *Implementation of Uruguay Round Commitments: The Development Challenge*, World Bank, Washington DC.

22. *Guardian*, 10 January 2004.

23. 'Cars', *Guardian*, 13 November 2004.

CHAPTER 8

1. *World Disasters Report 1998*, International Federation of Red Cross and Red Crescent Societies, Geneva.

2. Owen Bowcott (2004) '10,000 killed [in South Africa] a year on perilous roads', *Guardian*, 2 January.

3. Bradford Snell (1995) 'The StreetCar Conspiracy: How General Motors Destroyed Public Transit', first published in *The New Electric Railway Journal*, Autumn. Also *Taken for a Ride*, a documentary film shown on US station PBS, August 1996.

4. Union of Concerned Scientists (2000) *Pollution Lineup: An Environmental Ranking of Automakers*, Cambridge, Mass.

5. 'Automakers rev up U.S. advertising spending', Reuters, 12 May 2003. Analysis by Merrill Lynch showed spending up from $8.5 billion in 2002, to $9.9 billion in 2003, and predicted to reach $10.7 billion in 2004.

6. World Resources Institute quoting: American Automobile Manufacturers Association (AAMA) World Motor Vehicle Data 1993, and AAMA Motor Vehicle Facts and Figures 1996.

7. Roy Foster (2003) 'Beep beep yeah', *Financial Times*, 8 November.

8. Alfa Romeo's strapline in English is 'Stir Your Soul'.

9. BBC Radio 5 interview with spokeswoman for the RAC (Royal Automobile Club), 2 January 2004.

10. Working Group on Public Health and Fossil Fuel Combustion (1997) 'Short-term improvements in public health from global-climate policies on fossil-fuel combustion: an interim report', *The Lancet*, November.

11. Robert Heilbroner (1953) *The Worldly Philosophers: The Lives, Times, and Ideas of the Great Economic Thinkers*, seventh edition, Penguin, London, 2000.

CHAPTER 9

1. Elazar Barkan (2000) *The Guilt of Nations*, Norton, New York & London.

2. Robert Heilbroner (1953) *The Worldly Philosophers: The Lives, Times, and Ideas of the Great Economic Thinkers*, seventh edition, Penguin, London, 2000.

3. Barkan, *The Guilt of Nations*.

4. Carl Mortished (2002) 'Banks named in apartheid victims' lawsuit', *The Times*, 12 November.

5. David Fickling (2003) 'Child asylum seeker sues Australian government for mental trauma', *Guardian*, 28 October.

6. Tim Cocks (2003) '100 years on the consul of Uganda is accused of war crimes', *Guardian*, 23 October.

7. Andrew Simms (2001) 'The ecology of disaster recovery', *World Disasters Report 2001: Focus on Recovery*, International Federation of Red Cross and Red Crescent Societies, Geneva.

8. Andrew Simms and Molly Conisbee (2003) *Environmental Refugees: The Case for Recognition*, **nef**, London.

9. According to British Development charity Christian Aid. Policy Position Paper: 'Global warming, unnatural disasters and the world's poor', Christian Aid, London, November 2000.

10. Jean-François Dhainaut, Yann-Erick Claessens, Christine Ginsburg and Bruno Riou (2003) 'Unprecedented heat-related deaths during the 2003 heat wave in Paris: consequences on emergency departments', *Critical Care*, <www.pubmedcentral.nih.gov>, 4 December.

11. Myles Allen (2003) 'Liability for climate change', *Nature*, 27 February.

12. Andrew Simms (2003) *Free Riding on the Climate*, **nef**, London.

13. Simms, *Free Riding on the Climate*.

14. Personal correspondence between Dr Caroline Lucas MEP and EU Trade Commissioner Pascal Lamy.
15. *Business Guide to the World Trading System*, WTO, Geneva, undated; also, Jerry Taylor, 'Salting the earth: the case for repealing superfund', in *Regulation: The Cato Review of Business and Government*, Cato Institute, <www.cato.org>.

CHAPTER 10

1. Vassily Kliuchesky, Russian medievalist, quoted in Robert Heilbroner (1993) *21st Century Capitalism*, Norton, New York and London.
2. John Maynard Keynes (1940) *How to Pay for the War*, Macmillan & Co, London.
3. Kevin Pilley (1999) 'Deadly harvest of an unending war', *Financial Times*, 6/7 November.
4. Norman Longmate (1971) *How We Lived Then*, Hutchinson, London.
5. All consumer goods and services percentage changes in per capita purchases by groups in the UK, in *The Impact of the War on Civilian Consumption in the United Kingdom, the United States and Canada*, a Report to the Combined Production and Resources Board from a Special Combined Committee on Nonfood Consumption Levels, US Government Printing Office, Washington DC, 1945.
6. W.K. Hancock and M.M. Gowing (1949) *The British War Economy*, HMSO, London.
7. *On the State of Public Health During Six Years of War – Report of the Chief Medical Officer of the Ministry of Health, 1939–1945*, HMSO, London 1946.
8. United States Code, Title 15: Commerce and Trade, Chapter 16B – Federal Energy Administration, Subchapter I, Section 761. Congressional Declaration of Purpose.
9. R.S. Sayers (1956) *Financial Policy 1939–45 – History of the Second World War*, HMSO & Longmans, London.
10. Quoted in Sayers, *Financial Policy 1939–45*.
11. Quoted in Sayers, *Financial Policy 1939–45*.
12. Thorstein Veblen (1899) *The Theory of the Leisure Classes*, The Macmillan Company, New York.

CHAPTER 11

1. This description of Dennis Hope's planetary speculation is taken from my introduction to a report I produced with colleagues from the New Economics Foundation, *Limits to Property*, 2003, see <www.neweconomics.org>.

2. See <www.MoonEstates.com>.

3. Garrett Hardin (1968) 'The tragedy of the commons', *Bioscience*, No. 162.

4. *Climate Change and Human Health – Risks and Responses*, report published by WHO in collaboration with UNEP and WMO, Geneva, 2003. The report estimated that there was now an additional 150,000 deaths annually due to global warming.

5. *Caring for the Future: Report of the Independent Commission on Population and Quality of Life*, UNESCO, Paris, 1996.

6. See the Global Commons Institute at <www.gci.org.uk>.

7. Before the time of industrial revolution the concentration of carbon dioxide in the atmosphere was measured at around 280 ppmv (parts per million by volume), today it is between 370 and 380 ppmv.

8. Andrew Simms and Romilly Greenhill (2002) *Balancing the Other Budget: Proposals for Solving the Greater Debt Crisis*, **nef**, London.

9. 'The scientific case for setting a long-term emission reduction target', internal government paper, Defra, London, undated.

10. A2 is defined by Working Group 1 of the IPCC as follows: the A2 storyline and scenario family describes a very heterogeneous world. The underlying theme is self-reliance and preservation of local identities. Fertility patterns across regions converge very slowly, which results in continuously increasing population. Economic development is primarily regionally oriented and per capita economic growth and technological change more fragmented and slower than other storylines.

11. Greenpeace briefing, The Hague, November 2000.

12. Andrew Simms (2001) *An Environmental War Economy: The Lessons of Ecological Debt and Climate Change*, **nef**, London.

13. *Financial Times*, 16 June 2000.

14. James Tobin (1998) 'Flawed fund – the IMF's misguided policies', *The New Republic*, 3 September.

15. R. Douthwaite (1999) *The Ecology of Money*, Green Books, Dartington, Devon.

16. For a comparative assessment of competing international frameworks to manage climate change see: A. Evans (2002) *Fresh Air? Options for the Future Architecture of International Climate Change Policy*, **nef**, London.

CHAPTER 12

1. Tracy Chevalier (2001) *Falling Angels*, HarperCollins, London.
2. Jay Reeves (2002) 'Storms kill 10 in state', Associated Press in *The Decatur Daily News*, 11 November.
3. 'BP lowers growth target again', CNN (Reuters), 29 October 2002.
4. Research by Prof. Harvey Weiss, Yale University and Prof. Raymond Bradley, University of Massachusetts, *Daily Telegraph*, 26 January 2002.
5. Stuart Clark (2002) 'Acidic clouds of Venus could harbour life', *New Scientist*, 26 September.
6. UNDP CSD, *Critical Trends: Global Change and Sustainable Development*, New York, 1997.
7. J.M. Keynes (1930) 'The economic possibilities for our grandchildren', in *Essays in Persuasion*, Norton, New York, 1963.
8. Robert Heilbroner, *21ˢᵗ Century Capitalism*, Norton, New York and London.
9. Richard Reeves (2003) *The Politics of Happiness*, **nef**, London.
10. C.N. McDaniel and J.M. Gowdy (2000) *Paradise for Sale: A Parable of Nature*, University of California Press, Berkeley.
11. McDaniel and Gowdy, *Paradise for Sale*.
12. Robert Heilbroner (1953) *The Worldly Philosophers: The Lives, Times, and Ideas of the Great Economic Thinkers*, seventh edition, Penguin, London, 2000.
13. Keynes, 'The economic possibilities for our grandchildren'.
14. Keynes, 'The economic possibilities for our grandchildren'.
15. *The Big Question* with Richard Dawkins, Channel Five, 7.30pm, 7 January 2004.

CHAPTER 13

1. 'World Bank faces questions over Congo mining contracts', *Financial Times*, 17 November 2006.

2. Greenpeace International (2007) *Carving up the Congo*, Greenpeace International, Amsterdam.

3. A. Simms and V. Johnson (2007) *Chinadependence: The Second UK Interdependence Report*, **nef**, London.

4. *The United Kingdom's Imports of Illegal Timber – An Overview*, prepared for <www.globaltimber.org.uk>.

5. Javier Blas (2008) 'UN warns of food "neo-colonialism"', *Financial Times*, 19 August.

6. Christian Aid (2001) *The Scorched Earth: Oil and War in Sudan*, Christian Aid, London.

7. Mary Turner (2007) 'Scramble for Africa', *Guardian*, 2 May.

8. See evidence gathered by research group Platform. For example, the Baker-Hamilton Iraq Study Group report, 'Section II.B.5 of the Iraq Study Group Report' (pp. 83–5) recommends that the US government advises on writing an oil law for the country and encourages foreign oil companies to take advantage of commercial opportunities in Iraq. Also comments by Secretary of State Condoleezza Rice, <www.state.gov/secretary/rm/2006/75418. htm>.

9. Friends of the Earth International (2007) 'Shell fails to obey court order to stop Nigeria flaring, again', 2 May, <www.climatelaw. org/media/gas.flaring/report>.

10. Reuters (2007) 'Peru communities sue Occidental for oil operations', 10 May, <www.reuters.com>.

11. See <www.bp.com/sectiongenericarticle.do?categoryId=14&con tentId=2002063>.

12. 'Colombia holds out for a big oil find', *Financial Times*, 1 February 2002.

13. Reuters (2006), 'BP shuts giant Alaska oil field on pipe damage', 7 August, <www.reuters.com>.

14. According to *Meeting the Climate Challenge* (2005) by The International Climate Change Taskforce, published by the Institute for Public Policy Research, the Center for American Progress and the Australia Institute, 'achieving a high probability of limiting global average temperature rise to 2 °C will require that the increase in greenhouse-gas concentrations as well as all the other warming and cooling influences on global climate in the year 2100, as compared with 1750, should add up to a net warming no greater than what would be associated with a CO_2 concentration

of about 400 parts per million (ppm)'. But according to BP Chief Executive Lord Browne (2003), 'We've come to the judgment that to avoid serious impact upon societies or the environment it is necessary to stabilise atmospheric concentrations of greenhouse gases at around 500–550 parts per million.' Lord Browne, speech at the Institutional Investors Group, Gibson Hall, Bishopsgate, London, 26 November.

15. Quoted in 'Can planting trees really give you a clear carbon conscience?' *Guardian*, 7 October 2006.

16. See case notes at <www.climatelaw.org>.

17. Petition to the Inter-American Commission on Human Rights Seeking Relief from Violations Resulting from Global Warming Caused by Acts and Omissions of the United States: Submitted by Sheila Watt-Cloutier, with the Support of the Inuit Circumpolar Conference, on Behalf of All Inuit of the Arctic Regions of the United States and Canada, <www.ciel.org/Publications/ICC_Petition_7Dec05.pdf>.

18. A continuation of the older coalition of the same name that concluded its campaign in the year 2000.

19. Jubilee Debt Campaign (2007) *Debt and Climate Change*. See <www.jubileedebtcampaign.org.uk/download.php?id=498> (accessed 25 March 2008).

20. In terms of Net Present Value.

21. T. Srinivasan, S. Carey, E. Hallstein, P. Higgins, A. Kerr, L. Koteen, A. Smith, R. Watson, J. Harte and R. Norgaard (2008) 'The debt of nations and the distribution of ecological impacts from human activities', *Proceedings of the National Academy of Sciences*, Vol. 105 No. 5, 1768–73.

22. See 'The Economics of Ecosystems and Biodiversity' (TEEB) at <http://ec.europa.eu/environment/nature/biodiversity/economics/index_en.htm>, reported at <http://news.bbc.co.uk/1/hi/sci/tech/7662565.stm>.

23. Global Footprint Network (2007) *Overshoot Clarified: Key Definitions, Concepts, Days*, July, <www.footprintnetwork.org>.

24. Reuters (2008) 'GM's third-quarter global sales fall 11.4 percent', 29 October, <www.reuters.com/article/ousiv/idUSTRE49S5GH20081029>.

25. Graham M. Turner (2008) 'A comparison of *The Limits to Growth* with 30 years of reality', Global Environmental Change Vol. 18, 397–411.

26. D. Meadows, R. Randers and D. Meadows (2004) *Limits to Growth: The 30-Year Update*, Chelsea Green Publishing, Vermont.

CHAPTER 14

1. James Hansen (2008) 'Global Warming: The Perfect Storm', presentation to the Health Implications of Climate Change Conference at the Royal College of Physicians, London, 29 January 2008, later published as J. Hansen et al. (2008) 'Target atmospheric CO_2: where should humanity aim?' *Open Atmospheric Science Journal*, Vol. 2, 217–31.

2. For example, P. Huybrechts et al. (1991) 'The Greenland Ice-Sheet and greenhouse warming', *Global and Planetary Change*, Vol. 89, pp. 399–412, and J. Gregory et al. (2004) 'Climatology: threatened loss of the Greenland ice-sheet', *Nature*, Vol. 428, 616.

3. See the work of Prof. Tim Lenton of the University of East Anglia, reported in 'Scientists warn on climate tipping points', *Guardian*, 16 August 2007.

4. IPCC (2007) *Fourth Assessment Report: Climate Change*, IPCC, Geneva.

5. Eleanor J. Burke, Simon J. Brown and Nikolaos Christidis (2006) 'Modelling the recent evolution of global drought and projections for the twenty-first century with the Hadley Centre Climate Model', Hadley Centre for Climate Prediction and Research. In *Journal of Hydrometeorology*, Vol. 7 No. 5, 1113–25.

6. Christian Aid (2006) *Life on the Edge of Climate Change: The Plight of Pastoralists in Northern Kenya*, Christian Aid, London.

7. Reuters Alertnet, 'Floods in Africa kill dozens and wipe out crops', 14 September 2007; BBC News, 'Flood misery hits arc of Africa', 15 September 2007.

8. Burke et al., 'Modelling the recent evolution of global drought and projections for the twenty-first century'.

9. Michael J. Behrenfeld et al. (2006) 'Climate-driven trends in contemporary ocean productivity', *Nature*, Vol. 444, 752–5, 7 December.

10. Richard B. Alley (2004) 'Abrupt climate changes: oceans, ice and us', *Oceanography*, Vol. 17 No 4, December; Richard B. Alley and Anna Maria Agustsdottir (2004) 'The 8k event: cause and

consequences of a major Holocene abrupt climate change', Quaternary Science Reviews, Vol. 24 (2005), 1123–49.

11. Richard B. Alley (2003) 'Statement of Chairman, Committee on Abrupt Climate Change, The National Academies, and Professor, Pennsylvania State University on *Abrupt Climate Change: Inevitable Surprises*, before the Committee on Commerce, Science and Transportation U.S. Senate', 7 May; <www7.nationalacademies. org/ocga/testimony/Abrupt_Climate_Change.asp>.

12. Nicholas Stern (2006) *Stern Review of the Economics of Climate Change*, available at <www.hm-treasury.gov.uk/stern_review_ report.htm>.

13. C.D. Keeling et al. (2008) 'Exchanges of atmospheric CO_2 and $^{13}CO_2$ with the terrestrial biosphere and oceans from 1978 to 2000', in *I. Global Aspects*, Scripps Institution of Oceanography (SIO) Reference Series, No. 01-06, SIO, San Diego, 2001, with updates provided by Stephen Piper, SIO, San Diego, e-mail to Janet Sawin, Worldwatch Institute, 8 February 2008.

14. J. Hansen et al. (2008) 'Global land-ocean temperature index in .01C, base period 1951–1980 (January–December)', Goddard Institute for Space Studies (GISS), <http://data.giss.nasa.gov/ gistemp/tabledata/GLB.Ts+dSST.txt>.

15. Hansen et al., 'Target atmospheric CO_2'.

16. Hansen et al., 'Target atmospheric CO_2'.

17. Global Carbon Project (2008) 'Carbon budget and trends 2007', <www.globalcarbonproject.org, 26 September 2008>.

18. **nef** (2008) '100 Months Technical note', **nef**, London, August, <www.neweconomics.org/gen/uploads/sbfxot55p5k3kd454n14 zvyy01082008141045.pdf>.

19. As defined by rising gross domestic product and gross national product (collectively, gross world product).

20. A. Simms, V. Johnson and P. Chowla (2009) *Growth Isn't Possible: The Carbon Limits to Orthodox Global Economic Growth*, **nef**, London, forthcoming.

21. M.R. Raupach, G. Marland, P. Cias, C. Le Quéré, J. Canadell, G. Klepper and C. Field (2007) 'Global and regional drivers of accelerating CO_2 emissions', *Proceedings of the National Academy of Sciences of the USA*, Vol. 104 No. 24, 10288–93.

22. Prof. Roderick Smith FREng (2007) The 2007 Lloyd's Register Educational Trust Lecture, 29 May, 'Carpe diem: the dangers of

risk aversion', Royal Academy of Engineering, Imperial College, London.

23. Smith, 'Carpe diem'.

24. Smith, 'Carpe diem'.

25. Seth Lloyd (2004) 'Going into reverse', *Nature*, Vol. 430, 26 August, 971.

26. Herman E. Daly, *Beyond Growth: The Economics of Sustainable Development*, Beacon Press, Boston, 1996.

27. Daly, *Beyond Growth*.

28. B. Worm et al. (2007) 'Impacts of biodiversity loss on ocean ecosystem services', *Science*, Vol. 314 No. 3, 787–9.

29. In 2006, the threshold for entering ecological 'overshoot' occurred on 9 October. Because there is always a data lag of a few years, the new date has been arrived at by projecting forward to 2007 the five-year average from the latest available national footprint accounts. In 2007 the date advanced to 6 October. The big jump forward in date in 2008 was due to both an improved methodology and rising consumption. See <www.neweconomics.org/gen/23september.aspx>.

30. David Woodward and Andrew Simms (2006) *Growth Isn't Working: The Uneven Distribution of Benefits and Costs from Economic Growth*, **nef**, London.

31. Shaohua Chen and Martin Ravallion (2004) *How Have the World's Poorest Fared since the Early 1980s?*, Development Research Group, World Bank, Washington DC.

32. Woodward and Simms, *Growth Isn't Working*.

33. Robert F. Kennedy (1968) *Recapturing America's Moral Vision in RFK: Collected Speeches*, Viking Penguin, New York.

34. N. Marks, A. Simms, S. Thompson and S. Abdallah (2006) *The Happy Planet Index: An Index of Human Well-being and Environmental Impact*, **nef**, London.

35. Without a word of complaint, my colleague Dr Victoria Johnson, trained for much higher things as an atmospheric physicist, made this calculation at my request while gripped by an unshakeable fit of hilarity. It was prepared for inclusion in a report we were working on together: Andrew Simms and Victoria Johnson (2009) *Growth Isn't Possible*, **nef**, London.

36. Ann Pettifor (2006) *The Coming First World Debt Crisis*, Palgrave Macmillan, Basingstoke.

37. Pettifor, *The Coming First World Debt Crisis*.

38. Prof. Stephen Hawking interviewed on ITV News, 17 January 2007.

39. Foreign Secretary the Rt. Hon. Margaret Beckett MP (2007) Annual Winston Churchill Memorial Lecture, 'Climate Change: "The Gathering Storm"', British American Business Inc., New York, 16 April.

40. Beckett, 'Climate Change: "The Gathering Storm"'.

41. Stavros Dimas, European Commissioner for the Environment (2007) 'Climate change: why a global response needs European leadership', speech at the launch event of the European Commission and the All Party Parliamentary Group on Climate Change Co-operation, London, 11 January, <http://europa. eu/rapid/pressReleasesAction.do?reference=SPEECH/07/ 8&format=HTML&aged=0&language=EN&guiLanguage=en>; EurActiv, 11 January 2007.

42. Lecture by the Foreign Secretary the Rt. Hon. Margaret Beckett MP (2007) 'The case for climate security', Royal United Services Institute, London, 10 May.

43. 'Move to identify climate change security hotspots', *Guardian*, 11 September 2007.

44. Aeschylus, *Agamemnon*, translated by Herbert Weir Smyth (1926), Loeb Classical Library, Volumes 145 and 146, Harvard University Press, Cambridge, MA.

45. International Energy Agency (2008) *Medium-Term Oil Market Report*, 'Despite slowing oil demand, IEA sees continued market tightness over the medium term', IEA, Madrid, July; see <www. iea.org/Textbase/press/pressdetail.asp?PRESS_REL_ID=267>.

46. International Energy Agency, 'Despite slowing oil demand'.

47. Andrew Simms and Molly Conisbee (2003) *Environmental Refugees: The Case for Recognition*, **nef**, London. (After publication, I engaged in public and written debate with officials from UNHCR who opposed the concept.)

48. 'UN agencies highlight climate change's impact on human security, health', 5 June 2007, <www.un.org/apps/news/story. asp?NewsID=22793&Cr=environment&Cr1>.

49. Ann Pettifor (ed.) (2003) *Real World Economic Outlook*, **nef**/Palgrave Macmillan, London, pp. xxv–xxvii.

50. Andrew Clark and Jill Treanor (2008) 'Greenspan – I was wrong about the economy', *Guardian*, 24 October.

CHAPTER 15

1. Chris Stringer (2006) *Homo Britannicus – The Incredible Story of Human Life in Britain*, Penguin, London.
2. Mark Campanale, in interview with the author.
3. UNFCCC (2007) 'Emissions of industrialized countries rose to all time high in 2005', UNFCCC, Bonn, 20 November.
4. Bibb Latané and John M. Darley (1970) *The Unresponsive Bystander: Why Doesn't He Help?* Appleton-Century Crofts, New York.
5. Camilla Cavendish (2007), 'Wake up and smell the smoke of disaster', *The Times*, 8 November.
6. A. Hooijer, M. Silvius, H. Wösten and S. Page (2006) *PEAT-CO$_2$, Assessment of CO$_2$ Emissions from Drained Peatlands in SE Asia*, Delft Hydraulics Report Q3943.
7. Kevin Anderson, cited in Andrew Simms and Victoria Johnson (2009) *Growth Isn't Possible*, nef, London.
8. Anderson, cited in Simms and Johnson, *Growth Isn't Possible*.
9. Target atmospheric CO$_2$: where should humanity aim?' *Open Atmospheric Science Journal*, Vol. 2, 217–31.
10. David Fleming (2007) *The Lean Guide to Nuclear Energy: A Life-Cycle in Trouble*, The Lean Economy Connection, London; Andrew Simms, David Woodward and Petra Kjell (2005) *Mirage and Oasis: Energy Choices in an Age of Global Warming*, nef, London.
11. Simms et al., *Mirage and Oasis*.
12. Vaclav Klaus (2008) *Blue Planet in Green Shackles*, Competitive Enterprise Institute, Washington, DC.
13. Karl Popper (2002), *The Open Society and its Enemies*, Routledge, New York; first published in two volumes, 1945.
14. Quoted in Andrew Simms and Joe Smith (eds) (2008) *Do Good Lives Have to Cost the Earth?*, Constable, London.
15. Barry Schwartz (2004), *The Paradox of Choice: Why More is Less*, HarperCollins, New York.
16. nef (2007), *The European Happy Planet Index*, nef, London.
17. nef, *European Happy Planet Index*.
18. Foresight Mental Capital and Wellbeing Project – Final Project Report (2008), Government Office for Science, Department for Innovation, Universities and Skills, October.

19. See Andrew Simms (2007) *Tescopoly: How One Shop Came Out on Top and Why it Matters*, Constable, London.
20. See <www.wrap.org.uk>.
21. Stuart Hylton (2001) *Their Darkest Hour: The Hidden History of The Home Front 1939–1945*, Sutton Publishing, Stroud.
22. Fifteen of these broadcasts were published recently: Dr. Charles Hill (2007) *Wise Eating in Wartime*, Imperial War Museum, London.
23. Monica Felton (1945) *Civilian Supplies in Wartime Britain*, in the series 'British Achievements of the War Years', Ministry of Information. Facsimile reproduction by the Imperial War Museum, London, 2003.
24. J.M. Keynes (1940) *How to Pay for the War*, Macmillan, London.
25. Felton, *Civilian Supplies in Wartime Britain*.
26. Felton, *Civilian Supplies in Wartime Britain*.
27. Mark Roodhouse (2007) 'Rationing returns: a solution to global warming?' *History and Policy*, March, <www.historyandpolicy.org/papers/policy-paper-54.html#summ>.
28. Roodhouse, 'Rationing returns'.
29. J. Hansen et al. (2008) 'Target atmospheric CO_2: where should humanity aim?' *Open Atmospheric Science Journal*, Vol. 2, 217–31.
30. Ed Crooks and William Wallis (2007) 'Africa aid wiped out by rising cost of oil', *Financial Times*, 28 December.
31. See <www.oildepletionprotocal.org>.
32. Kyoto 2 is fully explained at <www.kyoto2.org>.
33. 'Cap and share' is fully explained at <www.capandshare.org>.
34. Greenhouse development rights are fully explained at <www.ecoequity.org/GDRs>.

CHAPTER 16

1. Doris Lessing (1974) *Memoirs of a Survivor*, Octagon Press, London.
2. Dale Allen Pfeiffer (2006) *Eating Fossil Fuels – Oil, Food and the Coming Crisis in Agriculture*, New Society Publishers, Gabriola Island, BC, Canada.
3. M.G. Novo and C. Murphy (2001) 'Urban agriculture in the city of Havana: a popular response to a crisis', *Growing Cities Growing Food: Urban Agriculture on the Policy Agenda. A Reader on Urban*

Agriculture, Resource Centres on Urban Agriculture and Food Security. See <www.ruaf.org/node/82>, accessed 11 March 2008.

4. M. Franco et al. (2007) 'Impact of energy intake, physical activity, and population-wide weight loss on cardiovascular disease and diabetes mortality in Cuba, 1980–2005, *American Journal of Epidemiology*, Vol. 166 No. 12, 1374–80.

5. Franco et al., 'Impact of energy intake'.

6. Pfeiffer, *Eating Fossil Fuels*.

7. R. Heilbroner (1999) *The Worldly Philosophers*, revised edn, Penguin, London.

8. K. Polanyi (1944) *The Great Transformation: The Political and Economic Origins of Our Time*, Beacon Press, Boston.

9. N. Marks, A. Simms, S. Thompson and S. Abdallah (2006) *The Happy Planet Index: An Index of Human Well-being and Environmental Impact*, **nef**, London.

10. Colin Tudge (2007) *Feeding People is Easy*, Pari Publishing, Pari, Italy.

11. David Woodward (2009) *MORE with Less: Towards a New Economics Paradigm*, **nef**, London, forthcoming.

12. Woodward, *MORE with Less*.

13. Ebenezer Howard (1898), *Tomorrow: A Peaceful Path to Real Reform*, republished as *Garden Cities of Tomorrow*; 1965 edition MIT Press.

14. Habitat International Coalition (HIC) (2005) *Sustainable Urban District Freiburg-Vauban*, HIC, Freiburg.

15. A. Simms (2007) *Tescopoly: How One Shop Came Out on Top and Why it Matters*, Constable, London.

16. 'Boom in home-grown veg', *Western Morning News*, 22 September 2008, <www.thisiswesternmorningnews.co.uk/news/Boom-home-grown-veg/article-343265-detail/article.html>.

17. 'Home grown in the fall', *The State*, 29 September 2008, available at <https://www.istockanalyst.com/article/viewiStockNews/articleid/2656236>.

18. See the Growing Communities homepage at <www.btinternet.com/~grow.communities/index.htm>.

19. See <http://coreeconomy.com>.

20. Peter Kropotkin (1902) *Mutual Aid: A Factor of Evolution*, Heinemann, London.

21. L. Stephens, R. Ryan-Collins and D. Boyle (2008) *Co-production: A Manifesto for Growing the Core Economy*, **nef**, London.

22. A. Simms, A. Pettifor, C. Lucas, C. Secrett, C. Hines, J. Leggett, L. Elliott, R. Murphy and T. Juniper (2008) *A Green New Deal: Joined-up Policies to Solve the Triple Crunch of the Credit Crisis, Climate Change and High Oil Prices*, nef, London, on behalf of the Green New Deal.

23. T. Casten and R. Ayers (2006) 'Energy Myth Eight – Worldwide power systems are economically and environmentally optimal', in *Energy and American Society – Thirteen Myths*, ed. B.K. Sovacool and M.A. Brown, Springer, Netherlands.

24. Greenpeace (2005) *Decentralising Power: An Energy Revolution for the 21st Century*, Greenpeace UK, London.

25. A. Simms, H. Reid and V. Johnson (2007) *Up in Smoke? Asia and Pacific: The Threat from Climate Change to Human Development and the Environment*, **nef**, London.

26. Dr W.F. Cormack (2000) Energy use in organic farming systems (OF0182), ADAS Consulting Ltd, Terrington, for Defra, <http://orgprints.org/8169/>.

27. Colin Tudge, in interview with the author.

28. H. Steinfeld, P. Gerber, T. Wassenaar, V. Castel, M. Rosales and C. de Haan (2006) *Livestock's Long Shadow: Environmental Issues and Options*, FAO, Rome. NB: the figure is around 18 per cent, measured in CO_2e, including transportation of livestock and production of feed. Increasingly meat-based diets stand to worsen this problem.

29. Daniele Fanelli (2007) 'Meat is murder on the environment', *New Scientist*, 18 July.

30. Compassion in World Farming (CIWF) (2008) *Global Warning: Climate Change and Farm Animal Welfare*, Summary Report, CIWF, Godalming, Surrey.

31. John Lipsky, First Deputy Managing Director, IMF, speaking at the Council on Foreign Relations, 8 May 2008, <www.imf.org>.

32. FAO Director-General Jacques Diouf, speaking at the Rome summit, 3 June 2008, <www.fao.org/foodclimate>.

33. Colin Tudge (forthcoming; draft December 2007) 'An introduction to enlightened agriculture and all that it implies', Mimeo.

34. See also Tudge, *Feeding People is Easy*, and Colin Tudge (2004) *So Shall We Reap: What's Gone Wrong with the World's Food – And How to Fix It*, London, Penguin.

35. Michael Windfuhr and Jennie Jonsen (2005) *Food Sovereignty: Towards Democracy in Localized Food Systems*, ITDG Publishing, Rugby, for FIAN-International.

36. Jules Pretty and Parviz Koohafkan (2002) *Land and Agriculture: From UNCED, Rio de Janeiro 1992 to WSSD, Johannesburg 2002: A Compendium of Recent Sustainable Development Initiatives in the Field of Agriculture and Land Management*, FAO, Rome.

37. Windfuhr and Jonsen, *Food Sovereignty*.

38. J.S. Mill (2008) *Principles of Political Economy*, ed. and introduced by Jonathan Riley, Oxford University Press, New York.

39. Kropotkin, *Mutual Aid*.

40. Herman Daly (1996) *Beyond Growth: The Economics of Sustainable Development*, Beacon Press, Boston.

41. Daly, *Beyond Growth*.

42. Daly, *Beyond Growth*.

43. G. Hardin (1968) 'The tragedy of the commons', *Science*, Vol. 162, 1243–8.

44. See Francis Fukuyama (1992) *The End of History and the Last Man*, Hamish Hamilton, London.

45. Daly, *Beyond Growth*.

46. Daly, *Beyond Growth*.

Index

Compiled by Sue Carlton